A*List VOCA

중학필수

A*List

How to Use 이 책의 구성과 특징

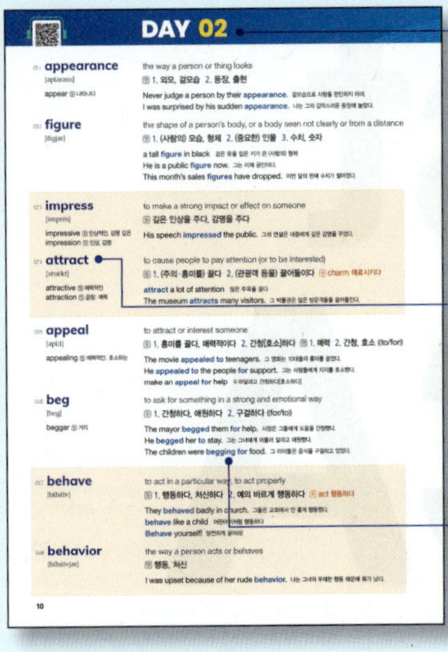

DAY 02

appearance [əpíərəns]
appear
the way a person or thing looks
명 1. 외모, 겉모습 2. 등장, 출현
Never judge a person by their appearance.
I was surprised by his sudden appearance.

figure [fígjər]
the shape of a person's body, or a body seen not clearly or from a distance
명 1. (사람의) 모습, 형체 2. (중요한) 인물 3. 수치, 숫자
a tall figure in black
He is a public figure now.
This month's sales figures have dropped.

impress [imprés]
impressive
impression
to make a strong impact or effect on someone
동 깊은 인상을 주다, 감명을 주다
His speech impressed the public.

attract [ətrǽkt]
attractive
attraction
to cause people to pay attention (or to be interested)
동 1. (주의·흥미를) 끌다 2. (관광객 등을) 끌어들이다 charm
attract a lot of attention
The museum attracts many visitors.

appeal [əpíːl]
appealing
to attract or interest someone
동 1. 흥미를 끌다, 매력적이다 2. 간청[호소]하다 명 1. 매력 2. 간청, 호소 (to/for)
The movie appealed to teenagers.
He appealed to the people for support.
make an appeal for help

beg [beg]
beggar
to ask for something in a strong and emotional way
동 1. 간청하다, 애원하다 2. 구걸하다 (for/to)
The mayor begged them for help.
He begged her to stay.
The children were begging for food.

behave [bihéiv]
to act in a particular way, to act properly
동 1. 행동하다, 처신하다 2. 예의 바르게 행동하다 act 행동하다
They behaved badly in church.
behave like a child
Behave yourself!

behavior [bihéivjər]
the way a person acts or behaves
명 행동, 처신
I was upset because of her rude behavior.

10

1 **새 교육과정 중학 교과서 필수 어휘를 완벽 반영한 640개의 표제어**

DAY별로 18개의 단어와 2개의 숙어를 쉽고 빠르게 익힐 수 있는 8주 완성 학습 플랜을 제시합니다.

2 **연관성 높은 단어들을 2개씩 짝지어 외우는 주제별 구성**

주제별로 연관된 어휘끼리 짝지어 학습하면 더 쉽고 빠르게 단어를 암기할 수 있습니다.

3 **암기 효과를 극대화하는 교과서 빈출 숙어 및 구문 표현 컬러 표기**

단어의 의미와 용법을 즉각적으로 파악할 수 있어 영어 문장 이해의 든든한 밑바탕이 됩니다.

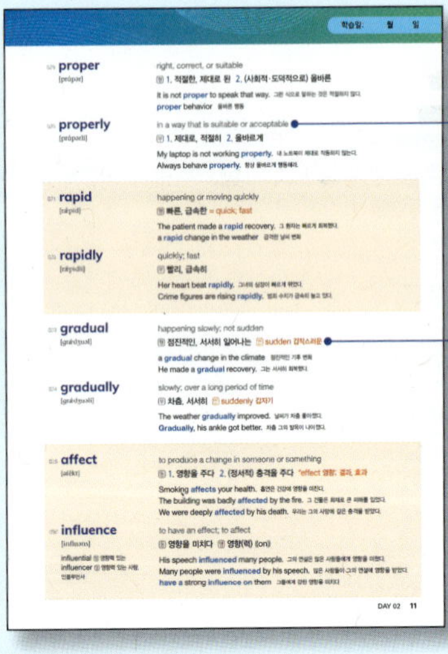

학습일: 월 일

proper [prάpər]
right, correct, or suitable
형 1. 적절한, 제대로 된 2. (사회적·도덕적으로) 올바른
It is not proper to speak that way.
proper behavior

properly [prάpərli]
in a way that is suitable or acceptable
부 1. 제대로, 적절히 2. 올바르게
My laptop is not working properly.
Always behave properly.

rapid [rǽpid]
happening or moving quickly
형 빠른, 급속한 = quick; fast
The patient made a rapid recovery.
a rapid change in the weather

rapidly [rǽpidli]
quickly; fast
부 빨리, 급속히
Her heart beat rapidly.
Crime figures are rising rapidly.

gradual [grǽdʒuəl]
happening slowly; not sudden
형 점진적인, 서서히 일어나는 반 sudden 갑작스러운
a gradual change in the climate
He made a gradual recovery.

gradually [grǽdʒuəli]
slowly; over a long period of time
부 차츰, 서서히 반 suddenly 갑자기
The weather gradually improved.
Gradually, his ankle got better.

affect [əfékt]
to produce a change in someone or something
동 1. 영향을 주다 2. (정서적) 충격을 주다 *effect 영향, 결과, 효과
Smoking affects your health.
The building was badly affected by the fire.
We were deeply affected by his death.

influence [ínfluəns]
influential
influencer
to have an effect; to affect
동 영향을 미치다 명 영향(력) (on)
His speech influenced many people.
Many people were influenced by his speech.
have a strong influence on them

DAY 02 11

4 **실력 Up 영영풀이**

영어로만 단어의 뜻을 설명해 보는 영영풀이로 자연스럽게 영어식 표현에 익숙해집니다.

5 **누적 반복되는 연관 단어/숙어와 풍부한 추가 어휘**

자연스러운 반복 학습과 함께 유의어, 반의어, 파생어, 참고 어휘 등 관련된 어휘를 함께 익힐 수 있어 단어에 대한 이해와 활용 능력을 더욱 넓힐 수 있습니다.

QR코드로 바로 듣는 MP3

각 DAY별 어휘의 발음과 예문을 바로 듣고 따라 읽으며 소리로도 익힐 수 있는 QR코드 삽입

QR코드로 바로 연결되는 어휘 학습앱

표지의 QR코드를 통해 어휘 학습이 가능한 앱으로 바로 연결

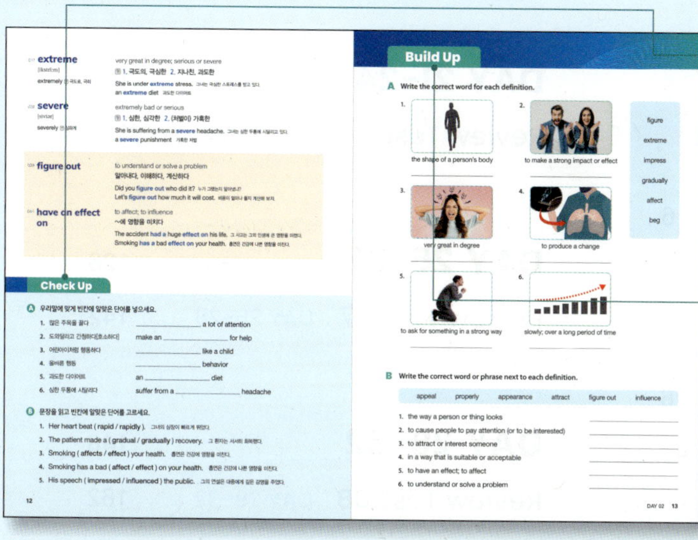

6 각 DAY별로 학습한 어휘를 점검할 수 있는 Check Up

오늘 배운 단어를 문제를 통해 확인하며 얼마나 외웠는지 스스로 점검할 수 있습니다.

7 영영풀이 테스트로 심화 학습이 가능한 Build Up

시각효과를 통한 연상작용의 극대화와 심화 테스트를 통해 단어를 더 오래 기억할 수 있습니다.

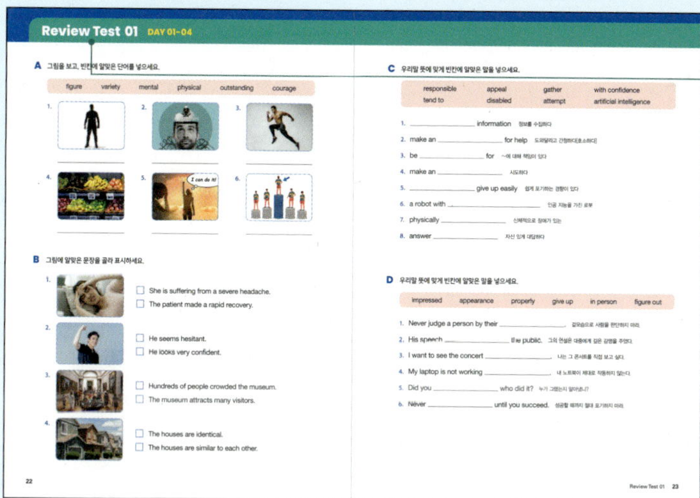

8 누적된 어휘를 반복 확인할 수 있는 Review Test

4일차를 학습한 후 유의어, 반의어, 숙어 등 다양한 문제를 풀어 보며 누적된 어휘를 반복 확인할 수 있습니다.

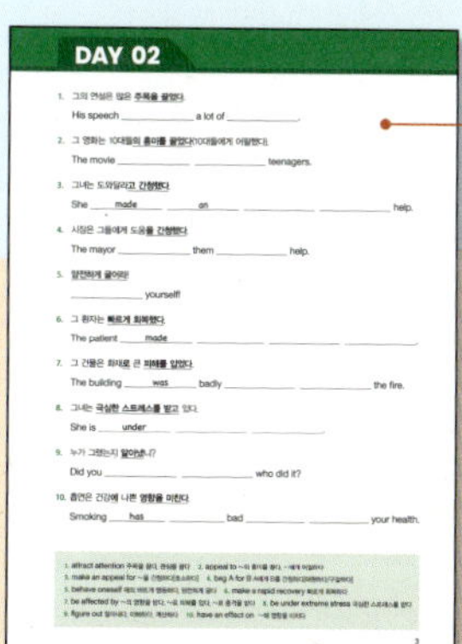

9 실력 Up 숙어·구문 표현 연습장

10 휴대하며 외우는 어휘 암기장

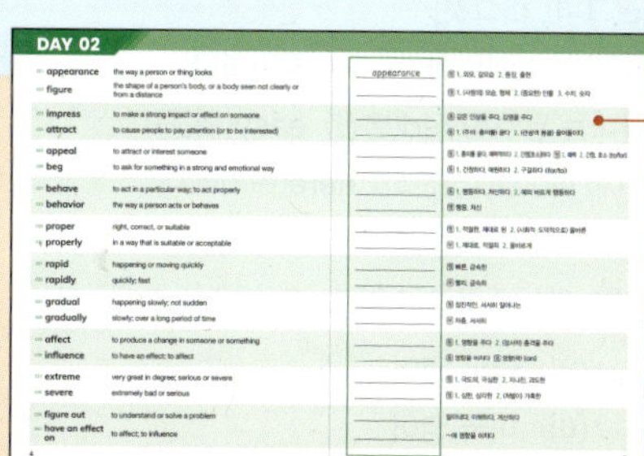

〈숙어·구문 표현 연습장〉과 간편히 휴대하며 암기할 수 있는 〈어휘 암기장〉으로 단어를 더 오래 기억할 수 있습니다.

Contents 차례

이 책에 나오는 품사와 약어

1 **명사** 명 사람, 사물, 동물 등의 이름을 나타내는 말 예) friend(친구), cat(고양이)
2 **대명사** 대 명사를 대신하는 말 예) you(너), she(그녀), it(그것)
3 **동사** 동 동작이나 상태를 나타내는 말 예) go(가다), tell(말하다), like(좋아하다)
4 **형용사** 형 상태, 성질, 모양, 크기, 수량 등을 나타내는 말 예) red(빨간), easy(쉬운)
5 **부사** 부 동사, 형용사, 부사 등을 꾸며주는 말 예) slowly(천천히), here(여기에)
6 **전치사** 전 명사, 대명사 앞에서 다른 단어와의 관계를 나타내는 말 예) on(~ 위에), in(~ 안에)
7 **접속사** 접 단어와 단어, 문장과 문장을 이어주는 말 예) and(그리고), but(그러나), or(또는)

*유의어 유 비슷한 의미를 갖는 말 *(영) 영국 영어
*반의어 반 반대의 의미를 갖는 말 *(미) 미국 영어

Study Planner 학습 계획표

하루에 1 DAY씩 8주 완성

각 DAY별로 학습한 날짜를 써 나가며 단어 실력을 키워 봅시다.

Week 1	DAY 01	DAY 02	DAY 03	DAY 04	Review Test 01
1차 학습일					
2차 학습일					

Week 2	DAY 05	DAY 06	DAY 07	DAY 08	Review Test 02
1차 학습일					
2차 학습일					

Week 3	DAY 09	DAY 10	DAY 11	DAY 12	Review Test 03
1차 학습일					
2차 학습일					

Week 4	DAY 13	DAY 14	DAY 15	DAY 16	Review Test 04
1차 학습일					
2차 학습일					

Week 5	DAY 17	DAY 18	DAY 19	DAY 20	Review Test 05
1차 학습일					
2차 학습일					

Week 6	DAY 21	DAY 22	DAY 23	DAY 24	Review Test 06
1차 학습일					
2차 학습일					

Week 7	DAY 25	DAY 26	DAY 27	DAY 28	Review Test 07
1차 학습일					
2차 학습일					

Week 8	DAY 29	DAY 30	DAY 31	DAY 32	Review Test 08
1차 학습일					
2차 학습일					

001 **personal**
[pə́rsənl]

person 명 사람
personally 부 개인적으로

belonging or relating to one particular person
형 1. 개인의 2. 개인적인, 사적인 = private

It is based on my **personal** experience. 그것은 내 개인적인 경험을 바탕으로 한 것이다.
May I ask you a **personal** question? 사적인 질문을 드려도 될까요?

002 **personality**
[pə̀ːrsənǽləti]

the way you are as a person; someone's character
명 1. 성격, 인격 2. 특성, 개성 유 character 성격, 기질

She has a very lovely **personality**. 그녀는 아주 사랑스러운 성격을 가졌다.
He's handsome, but he has little **personality**. 그는 잘생겼지만 개성이 별로 없다.

003 **mental**
[méntl]

mentally 부 정신적으로

relating to the mind
형 1. 정신의, 마음의 2. (건강상의) 정신적인

how to build **mental** strength 정신력을 기르는 법
Exercise is good for **mental** health. 운동은 정신 건강에 좋다.

004 **physical**
[fízikəl]

physically 부 신체적으로
physics 명 물리학

relating to the body
형 1. 신체의, 육체의 2. 물질의, 물질[물리]적인

The player has great **physical** strength. 그 선수는 강한 체력을 가지고 있다.
the **physical** environment 물리적인 환경

005 **super**
[súːpər]

very good; excellent
형 대단한, 굉장한 부 특별히, 대단히 = very

He is a **super** nice guy. 그는 아주 멋진 친구이다.
The party was **super** fun. 그 파티는 정말 재미있었다.

006 **potential**
[pəténʃəl]

potentially 부 잠재적으로

likely to develop into something
형 가능성이 있는, 잠재적인 = possible 명 가능성, 잠재력

They are our **potential** customers. 그들은 우리의 잠재적 고객들이다.
He has great **potential** as a writer. 그는 작가로서 큰 잠재력을 가지고 있다.

007 **mature**
[mətjúər]

behaving like an adult; fully grown or developed
형 1. 어른스러운, 성숙한 2. 성인이 된, 다 자란 반 immature 미숙한

She is very **mature** for her age. 그녀는 나이에 비해 아주 어른스럽다.
a **mature** elephant 다 자란 코끼리

008 **mate**
[meit]

a friend or partner; someone you work with or share with
명 1. (영) 친구 = (미) buddy 2. [합성어에서] 짝 3. (한 쌍의) 짝 동 짝짓기를 하다

We have been best **mates** since childhood. 우리는 어린 시절부터 가장 친한 친구였다.
my room**mate** 내 룸메이트
A male bird sings to attract a **mate**. 수컷 새는 짝을 유혹하기 위해 노래한다.
Birds **mate** in spring. 새들은 봄에 짝짓기를 한다.

009 **actual**
[ǽktʃuəl]

real; true
형 실제의, 사실의

I don't know her **actual** age. 나는 그녀의 실제 나이를 모른다.
It's a true story based on **actual** events. 그것은 실제 사건들을 기반으로 한 실화이다.

010 **actually**
[ǽktʃuəli]

really; in fact
부 1. 실제로, 정말로 2. 사실은, 실은

She looks 30, but she is **actually** 40. 그녀는 30살로 보이지만, 실제로는 40살이다.
Actually, she didn't say anything. 사실 그녀는 아무 말도 하지 않았다.

011 **private**
[práivət]
privately 부 사적으로, 은밀히

personal; not open to or shared with the public
형 1. 사적인, 개인의 2. 사립의, 개인 소유의 반 public 공공의

She didn't want to talk about her **private** life.
그녀는 자신의 사생활에 대해 말하고 싶어 하지 않았다.
She owns a **private** jet. 그녀는 개인 제트기(전용기)를 소유하고 있다.

012 **privacy**
[práivəsi]

the state of being alone and not seen or heard by others
명 사생활(을 누리는 상태), 프라이버시

It's important to protect people's **privacy**. 사람들의 사생활을 보호하는 것은 중요하다.
the right to **privacy** 사생활권(사생활에 대한 권리)

013 **crowd**
[kraud]
crowded 형 붐비는, 복잡한

a large group of people
명 군중, 사람들 동 가득 메우다; 붐비다

There was a large **crowd** on the street. 거리에는 많은 사람들이 있었다.
Hundreds of people **crowded** the streets. 수백 명의 사람들이 거리를 가득 메웠다.

014 **gather**
[gǽðər]

to come together
동 1. (사람들이) 모이다; 모으다 2. (정보 등을) 모으다, 수집하다 = collect

A crowd **gathered** to watch the event. 그 행사를 보기 위해 군중이 모여들었다.
gather information 정보를 수집하다

015 **probably**
[prɑ́bəbli]

very likely; maybe
부 아마(도)

The show will **probably** be fun. 그 쇼는 아마 재미있을 것이다.

016 **perhaps**
[pərhǽps]

maybe
부 아마, 어쩌면

Perhaps Jack will come. 아마도 잭이 올 것이다.
Hundreds, **perhaps** thousands, of people will gather together.
수백, 어쩌면 수천 명의 사람들이 모여들 것이다.

017 **frankly**

[frǽŋkli]

frank 형 솔직한

honestly; to be honest

부 1. 솔직히 2. 솔직히 말하면

He spoke **frankly** about the matter. 그는 그 일에 대해 솔직히 털어놓았다.

Frankly speaking, I don't like him. 솔직히 말해서, 나는 그가 맘에 들지 않는다.

018 **responsible**

[rispánsəbl]

responsibility 명 책임, 책임감

having caused something to happen, especially something bad

형 1. (~에 대해) 책임이 있는 2. (~을) 책임지고 있는 ((for))

Frankly, he is **responsible for** the accident. 솔직히, 그가 그 사고에 대해 책임이 있다.

He was **responsible for** the entire project. 그는 전체 프로젝트를 책임지고 있었다.

019 **in person**

personally; face to face

본인이 직접, 몸소, 실물로

I want to see the concert **in person**. 나는 그 콘서트를 직접 보고 싶다.

Have you ever met him **in person**? 너는 그 사람을 직접 만난 적이 있니?

020 **as a matter of fact**

in fact; actually; to tell the truth

사실, 사실은

As a matter of fact, I met him yesterday. 사실 나는 어제 그를 만났다.

As a matter of fact, he was my classmate in middle school.
사실 그는 중학교 때 반 친구였다.

Check Up

A 우리말에 맞게 빈칸에 알맞은 말을 넣으세요.

1. 잠재적 고객 — a ________ customer
2. 나이에 비해 성숙하다 — be ________ for one's age
3. 실제 사건들을 기반으로 한 실화 — a true story based on ________ events
4. 그녀의 사생활 — her ________ life
5. 사생활에 대한 권리 — the right to ________
6. ~에 대해 책임이 있다 — be ________ for

B 우리말에 알맞은 말을 골라 문장을 완성하세요.

1. He's handsome, but he has little (personal / personality). 그는 잘생겼지만 개성이 별로 없다.
2. He looks 30, but he is (actual / actually) 40. 그는 30살로 보이지만, 실제로는 40살이다.
3. He spoke (frankly / probably) about the matter. 그는 그 일에 대해 솔직히 털어놓았다.
4. Have you ever met him (person / in person)? 너는 그 사람을 직접 만난 적이 있니?
5. It is based on my (personal / personality) experience. 그것은 내 개인적인 경험을 바탕으로 한 것이다.

Build Up

A Write the correct word for each definition.

1. 
relating to the body
____

2. 
relating to the mind
____

3. 
fully grown or developed
____

4. 
a friend or partner
____

5. 
a large group of people
____

6. 
to come together
____

mental
physical
crowd
gather
mature
mate

B Write the correct word or phrase next to each definition.

potential personality actually responsible private as a matter of fact

1. the way you are as a person; someone's character __________
2. likely to develop into something __________
3. really; in fact __________
4. personal; not open to or shared with the public __________
5. having caused something to happen, especially something bad __________
6. in fact; actually; to tell the truth __________

DAY 02

021 **appearance**
[əpíərəns]
appear 동 나타나다

the way a person or thing looks
명 1. 외모, 겉모습 2. 등장, 출현

Never judge a person by their **appearance**. 겉모습으로 사람을 판단하지 마라.
I was surprised by his sudden **appearance**. 나는 그의 갑작스러운 등장에 놀랐다.

022 **figure**
[fígjər]

the shape of a person's body, or a body seen not clearly or from a distance
명 1. (사람의) 모습, 형체 2. (중요한) 인물 3. 수치, 숫자

a tall **figure** in black 검은 옷을 입은 키가 큰 (사람의) 형체
He is a public **figure** now. 그는 이제 공인이다.
This month's sales **figures** have dropped. 이번 달의 판매 수치가 떨어졌다.

023 **impress**
[imprés]
impressive 형 인상적인, 감명 깊은
impression 명 인상, 감명

to make a strong impact or effect on someone
동 깊은 인상을 주다, 감명을 주다

His speech **impressed** the public. 그의 연설은 대중에게 깊은 감명을 주었다.

024 **attract**
[ətrǽkt]
attractive 형 매력적인
attraction 명 끌림; 매력

to cause people to pay attention (or to be interested)
동 1. (주의·흥미를) 끌다 2. (관광객 등을) 끌어들이다 유 charm 매료시키다

attract a lot of attention 많은 주목을 끌다
The museum **attracts** many visitors. 그 박물관은 많은 방문객들을 끌어들인다.

025 **appeal**
[əpí:l]
appealing 형 매력적인; 호소하는

to attract or interest someone
동 1. 흥미를 끌다, 매력적이다 2. 간청[호소]하다 명 1. 매력 2. 간청, 호소 ((to/for))

The movie **appealed to** teenagers. 그 영화는 10대들의 흥미를 끌었다.
He **appealed to** the people **for** support. 그는 사람들에게 지지를 호소했다.
make an **appeal for** help 도와달라고 간청하다[호소하다]

026 **beg**
[beg]
beggar 명 거지

to ask for something in a strong and emotional way
동 1. 간청하다, 애원하다 2. 구걸하다 ((for/to))

The mayor **begged** them **for** help. 시장은 그들에게 도움을 간청했다.
He **begged** her **to** stay. 그는 그녀에게 머물러 달라고 애원했다.
The children were **begging for** food. 그 아이들은 음식을 구걸하고 있었다.

027 **behave**
[bihéiv]

to act in a particular way; to act properly
동 1. 행동하다, 처신하다 2. 예의 바르게 행동하다 유 act 행동하다

They **behaved** badly in church. 그들은 교회에서 안 좋게 행동했다.
behave like a child 어린아이처럼 행동하다
Behave yourself! 얌전하게 굴어라!

028 **behavior**
[bihéivjər]

the way a person acts or behaves
명 행동, 처신

I was upset because of her rude **behavior**. 나는 그녀의 무례한 행동 때문에 화가 났다.

029 **proper**
[prάpər]

right, correct, or suitable
형 1. 적절한, 제대로 된 2. (사회적·도덕적으로) 올바른

It is not **proper** to speak that way. 그런 식으로 말하는 것은 적절하지 않다.
proper behavior 올바른 행동

030 **properly**
[prάpərli]

in a way that is suitable or acceptable
부 1. 제대로, 적절히 2. 올바르게

My laptop is not working **properly**. 내 노트북이 제대로 작동하지 않는다.
Always behave **properly**. 항상 올바르게 행동해라.

031 **rapid**
[rǽpid]

happening or moving quickly
형 빠른, 급속한 = quick; fast

The patient made a **rapid** recovery. 그 환자는 빠르게 회복했다.
a **rapid** change in the weather 급격한 날씨 변화

032 **rapidly**
[rǽpidli]

quickly; fast
부 빨리, 급속히

Her heart beat **rapidly**. 그녀의 심장이 빠르게 뛰었다.
Crime figures are rising **rapidly**. 범죄 수치가 급속히 늘고 있다.

033 **gradual**
[grǽdʒuəl]

happening slowly; not sudden
형 점진적인, 서서히 일어나는 반 sudden 갑작스러운

a **gradual** change in the climate 점진적인 기후 변화
He made a **gradual** recovery. 그는 서서히 회복했다.

034 **gradually**
[grǽdʒuəli]

slowly; over a long period of time
부 차츰, 서서히 반 suddenly 갑자기

The weather **gradually** improved. 날씨가 차츰 좋아졌다.
Gradually, his ankle got better. 차츰 그의 발목이 나아졌다.

035 **affect**
[əfékt]

to produce a change in someone or something
동 1. 영향을 주다 2. (정서적) 충격을 주다 *effect 영향; 결과, 효과

Smoking **affects** your health. 흡연은 건강에 영향을 미친다.
The building was badly **affected** by the fire. 그 건물은 화재로 큰 피해를 입었다.
We were deeply **affected** by his death. 우리는 그의 사망에 깊은 충격을 받았다.

036 **influence**
[ínfluəns]

influential 형 영향력 있는
influencer 명 영향력 있는 사람, 인플루언서

to have an effect; to affect
동 영향을 미치다 명 영향(력) ((on))

His speech **influenced** many people. 그의 연설은 많은 사람들에게 영향을 미쳤다.
Many people were **influenced** by his speech. 많은 사람들이 그의 연설에 영향을 받았다.
have a strong **influence on** them 그들에게 강한 영향을 미치다

037 **extreme**
[ikstríːm]
extremely 부 극도로, 극히

very great in degree; serious or severe
형 1. 극도의, 극심한 2. 지나친, 과도한
She is under **extreme** stress. 그녀는 극심한 스트레스를 받고 있다.
an **extreme** diet 과도한 다이어트

038 **severe**
[sivíər]
severely 부 심하게

extremely bad or serious
형 1. 심한, 심각한 2. (처벌이) 가혹한
She is suffering from a **severe** headache. 그녀는 심한 두통에 시달리고 있다.
a **severe** punishment 가혹한 처벌

039 **figure out**

to understand or solve a problem
알아내다, 이해하다, 계산하다
Did you **figure out** who did it? 누가 그랬는지 알아냈니?
Let's **figure out** how much it will cost. 비용이 얼마나 들지 계산해 보자.

040 **have an effect on**

to affect; to influence
~에 영향을 미치다
The accident **had a** huge **effect on** his life. 그 사고는 그의 인생에 큰 영향을 미쳤다.
Smoking **has a** bad **effect on** your health. 흡연은 건강에 나쁜 영향을 미친다.

Check Up

A 우리말에 맞게 빈칸에 알맞은 말을 넣으세요.

1. 많은 주목을 끌다 ________________ a lot of attention
2. 도와달라고 간청하다[호소하다] make an ________________ for help
3. 어린아이처럼 행동하다 ________________ like a child
4. 올바른 행동 ________________ behavior
5. 과도한 다이어트 an ________________ diet
6. 심한 두통에 시달리다 suffer from a ________________ headache

B 우리말에 알맞은 말을 골라 문장을 완성하세요.

1. Her heart beat (**rapid** / **rapidly**). 그녀의 심장이 빠르게 뛰었다.
2. The patient made a (**gradual** / **gradually**) recovery. 그 환자는 서서히 회복했다.
3. Smoking (**affects** / **effect**) your health. 흡연은 건강에 영향을 미친다.
4. Smoking has a bad (**affect** / **effect**) on your health. 흡연은 건강에 나쁜 영향을 미친다.
5. His speech (**impressed** / **influenced**) the public. 그의 연설은 대중에게 깊은 감명을 주었다.

Build Up

A Write the correct word for each definition.

figure	extreme	impress	gradually	affect	beg

1. 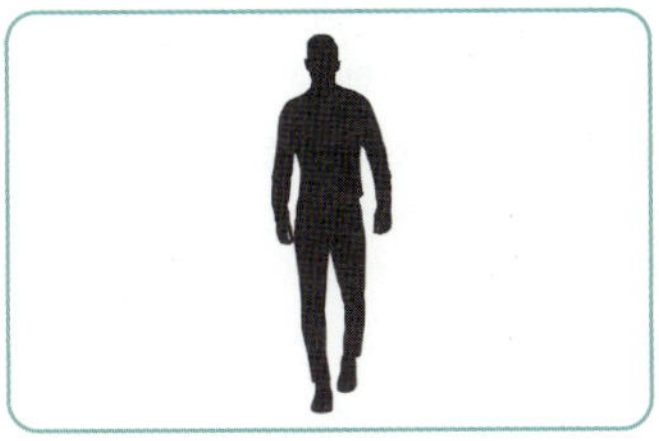

the shape of a person's body

____

2. 

to make a strong impact or effect

____

3. 

very great in degree

____

4. 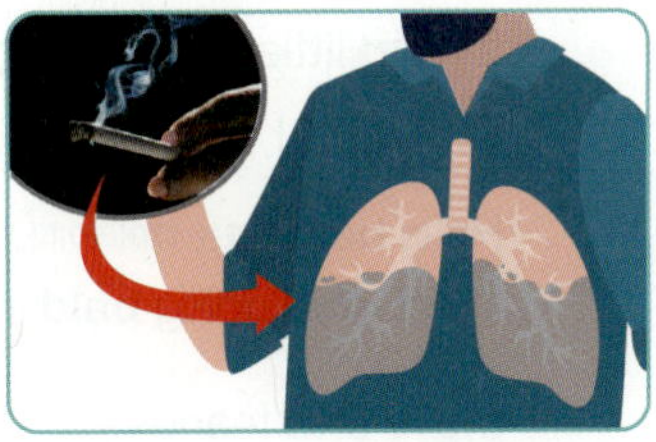

to produce a change

____

5. 

to ask for something in a strong way

____

6. 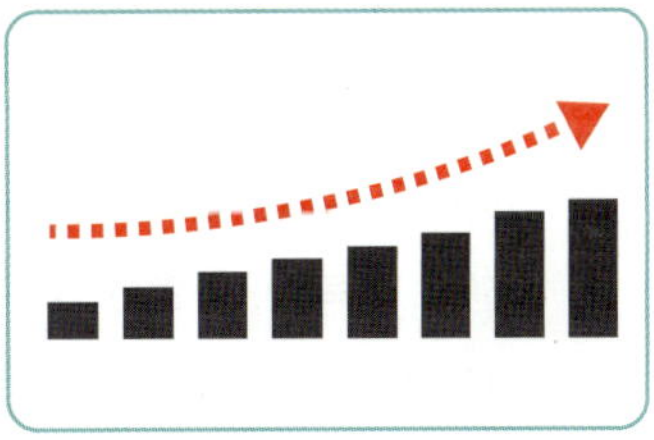

slowly; over a long period of time

____

B Write the correct word or phrase next to each definition.

appeal	properly	appearance	attract	figure out	influence

1. the way a person or thing looks ____________________
2. to cause people to pay attention (or to be interested) ____________________
3. to attract or interest someone ____________________
4. in a way that is suitable or acceptable ____________________
5. to have an effect; to affect ____________________
6. to understand or solve a problem ____________________

DAY 03

041 **feature** [fíːtʃər]

a special or important part of something

명 특징, 특색, 기능 동 ~을 특징으로 하다, ~을 특색으로 삼다

the main **feature** of the new smartphone 그 새 스마트폰의 주요 특징[기능]
It **features** an AI system. 그것은 인공 지능 시스템을 특징으로 한다.
an exhibition **featuring** paintings by Picasso 피카소의 그림을 전시하는 전시회

042 **characteristic** [kæriktərístik]

character 명 성격, 기질; 캐릭터

a quality or feature of something or someone

명 (특유의) 특징, 특성 형 특유의, 독특한

Loyalty is a **characteristic** of dogs. 충성심은 개들의 한 특성이다.
the **characteristic** style of the artist 그 예술가 특유의 스타일

043 **bald** [bɔːld]

having little or no hair on the head

형 대머리의, 머리가 벗겨진

He is **bald**. 그는 대머리이다.
He started going **bald** in his thirties. 그는 30대에 머리가 벗겨지기 시작했다.

044 **bold** [bould]

brave and fearless

형 1. 대담한, 용감한 2. 굵은, 선명한

It was a **bold** decision. 그것은 대담한 결정이었다.
His paintings feature **bold** lines and colors. 그의 그림은 굵은 선과 선명한 색을 특징으로 한다.

045 **unique** [juːníːk]

very special or unusual; being the only one of its kind

형 1. 독특한, 특별한 2. 유일한, 고유의 *rare 드문, 희귀한

The building has a **unique** design. 그 건물은 독특한 디자인을 가지고 있다.
Everyone has a **unique** fingerprint. 누구나 고유한 지문을 가지고 있다.

046 **typical** [típikəl]

typically 부 보통, 전형적으로

having the usual features

형 전형적인, 일반적인 *usual 보통의, 흔히 있는 *normal 보통의, 정상적인

typical British weather 전형적인 영국 날씨
It was a **typical** day at school. 학교에서의 평범한 하루였다.

047 **capable** [kéipəbl]

capability 명 능력

able to do something

형 ~을 할 수 있는, 능력 있는 ((of)) = able

He is **capable of** speaking three languages. 그는 세 가지 언어를 구사할 수 있다.
He is a very **capable** teacher. 그는 아주 유능한 교사이다.

048 **disabled** [diséibld]

disability 명 장애

having a disability

형 장애를 가진 반 abled 능력 있는, 장애가 없는

physically **disabled** 신체적으로 장애가 있는
They volunteered to help **disabled** children. 그들은 장애아들을 돕기 위해 자원봉사를 했다.

049 **truth**
[truːθ]
true ⓗ 진실인, 사실인

the real facts about something
ⓜ 진실, 사실 ⓤ fact 사실

tell the **truth** 진실[사실]을 말하다
Nobody knows what the **truth** is. 진실이 무엇인지는 아무도 모른다.

050 **dare**
[dɛər]

to be brave enough to do something
ⓓ 감히 ~하다, ~할 용기가 있다

How **dare** you talk to me like that? 네가 어떻게 감히 나한테 그런 말을 해?
I wanted to ask her, but I didn't **dare**. 나는 그녀에게 물어보고 싶었지만 용기가 없었다.

051 **hesitate**
[hézətèit]

to be slow to speak or act (because you feel uncertain)
ⓓ 주저하다, 망설이다 ((to))

Don't **hesitate to** ask any questions. 주저하지 말고 무엇이든 질문하세요.
She **hesitated** for a moment. 그녀는 잠시 망설였다.

052 **hesitant**
[hézətənt]
hesitantly ⓑ 머뭇거리며

slow to speak or act (because you feel uncertain)
ⓗ 주저하는, 망설이는

She seemed **hesitant**. 그녀는 주저하는 것처럼 보였다.
She gave me a **hesitant** smile. 그녀는 내게 망설이는 듯한 미소를 지어 보였다.

053 **confident**
[kánfədənt]
confidently ⓑ 자신 있게

feeling sure about your own ability
ⓗ 1. 자신감 있는 2. 확신하는 ((of)) ↔modest 겸손한

He looked very **confident**. 그는 아주 자신감 있어 보였다.
He was **confident of** winning. 그는 우승을 확신하고 있었다.

054 **confidence**
[kánfədəns]

a feeling or belief that you can do something well
ⓜ 1. 자신감 2. 신뢰, 신임 ((in))

He answered **with confidence**. 그는 자신 있게 대답했다.
The coach **has confidence in** his players. 그 코치는 자신의 선수들을 신뢰하고 있다.

055 **courage**
[kə́ːridʒ]
courageous ⓗ 용감한

the quality of being brave when you are facing a difficult or dangerous situation
ⓜ 용기, 담력 ((to)) = bravery

I didn't **have the courage to** tell him the truth. 나는 그에게 사실을 말할 용기가 없었다.

056 **encourage**
[inkə́ːridʒ]
encouragement ⓜ 격려, 장려

to give someone support or courage
ⓓ 1. 격려하다, 용기를 북돋우다 2. 장려하다 ((to)) ⓑ discourage 의욕을 꺾다

My parents always **encourage** me. 우리 부모님은 항상 나를 격려해 주신다.
She **encouraged** the students **to** read more. 그녀는 학생들에게 더 많이 읽기를 장려했다.

057 **attempt**
[ətémpt]

to try to do something
동 시도하다 명 시도 ((to))

I'll **attempt to** climb Mt. Everest someday. 나는 언젠가 에베레스트 산 등반을 시도할 것이다.
make an **attempt** 시도하다

058 **tend**
[tend]

tendency 명 경향

to be likely to do something
동 ~하는 경향이 있다, ~하기 쉽다 ((to))

tend to give up easily 쉽게 포기하는 경향이 있다
Women **tend to** live longer than men. 여성이 남성보다 더 오래 사는 경향이 있다.
I **tend to** gain weight easily. 나는 쉽게 살이 찐다.

059 **give up**

to stop doing something
포기하다, 그만두다

Never **give up** until you succeed. 성공할 때까지 절대 포기하지 마라.
I won't **give up**. 나는 포기하지 않을 것이다.

060 **succeed in V-ing**

to achieve a goal successfully
~에 성공하다 반 fail in ~에 실패하다

I **succeeded in** climb**ing** the mountain. 나는 그 산을 오르는 데 성공했다.
She **succeeded in** solv**ing** the problem. 그녀는 그 문제를 푸는 데 성공했다.

Check Up

A 우리말에 맞게 빈칸에 알맞은 말을 넣으세요.

1. 그 새 스마트폰의 주요 특징[기능] the main __________ of the new smartphone
2. 전형적인 영국 날씨 __________ British weather
3. 신체적으로 장애가 있는 physically __________
4. 진실[사실]을 말하다 tell the __________
5. 시도하다 make an __________
6. 쉽게 포기하는 경향이 있다 __________ give up easily

B 우리말에 알맞은 말을 골라 문장을 완성하세요.

1. Loyalty is a (character / characteristic) of dogs. 충성심은 개들의 한 특성이다.
2. Don't (hesitant / hesitate) to ask any questions. 주저하지 말고 무엇이든 질문하세요.
3. He is (confident / confidence) of winning. 그는 우승을 확신하고 있다.
4. My parents always (courage / encourage) me. 우리 부모님은 항상 나를 격려해 주신다.
5. I succeeded in (climb / climbing) the mountain. 나는 그 산을 오르는 데 성공했다.

Build Up

A Write the correct word for each definition.

hesitant
feature
unique
bald
courage
confident

1.

a special or important part of something

____

2.
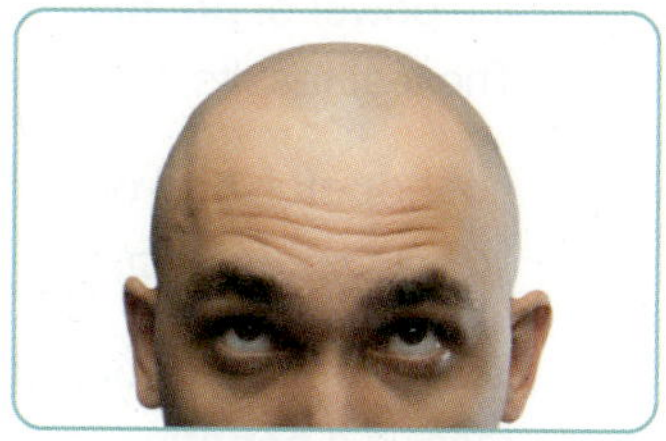

having little or no hair on the head

____

3.

very special or unusual

____

4.

slow to speak or act

____

5.

feeling sure about your own ability

____

6.

the quality of being brave

____

B Write the correct word or phrase next to each definition.

capable   bold   encourage   characteristic   give up   tend to

1. a quality or feature of something or someone __________________
2. brave and fearless __________________
3. able to do something __________________
4. to give someone support or courage __________________
5. to be likely to do something __________________
6. to stop doing something __________________

DAY 04

061 **positive**
[pázətiv]
positively 부 긍정적으로

hopeful and confident (about life or a situation)
형 1. 긍정적인, 낙관적인 = optimistic 2. (검사 결과가) 양성의
the power of **positive** thinking 긍정적 사고의 힘
The test results were **positive**. 검사 결과는 양성이었다.

062 **negative**
[négətiv]
negatively 부 부정적으로

not hopeful; bad or harmful
형 1. 부정적인, 비관적인; 나쁜 2. (검사 결과가) 음성의
Don't be so **negative** about everything. 매사에 그렇게 부정적이지 마라.
receive a **negative** reply 부정적인(거절하는) 답을 받다
The book had a **negative** effect on children. 그 책은 아이들에게 나쁜 영향을 미쳤다.

063 **generous**
[dʒénərəs]
generosity 명 후함; 관대함

often giving people money or presents
형 1. 후한 ((with)) 반 stingy 인색한 2. 관대한, 너그러운 ((to))
He is **generous with** his money. 그는 돈을 잘 쓴다(아끼지 않는다).
My grandma was always **generous to** me. 우리 할머니는 항상 내게 너그러우셨다.

064 **strict**
[strikt]
strictly 부 엄하게, 엄격히

not loose; following the rules
형 엄한, 엄격한
My parents were very **strict** with us. 우리 부모님은 우리에게 아주 엄하셨다.
strict rules 엄격한 규칙들
a **strict** vegetarian 엄격한(철저한) 채식주의자

065 **diligent**
[dílidʒənt]
diligently 부 부지런히, 열심히
diligence 명 근면

working hard with care and effort
형 부지런한, 성실한 반 lazy; idle 게으른
Tom is a very **diligent** student. 톰은 아주 성실한 학생이다.

066 **sincere**
[sinsíər]
sincerely 부 진심으로

honest and true; having or showing true feelings
형 진실된, 진심 어린
She gave him **sincere** advice. 그녀는 그에게 진심 어린 충고를 해 주었다.
Please accept our **sincere** apology. 부디 저희의 진심 어린 사과를 받아 주십시오.

067 **violent**
[váiələnt]
violently 부 격렬하게, 맹렬히
violence 명 폭력

using physical force
형 1. 폭력적인, 난폭한 2. 격렬한, 맹렬한 *cruel 잔인한
He was a **violent** man. 그는 폭력적인 사람이었다.
The movie contains some **violent** scenes. 그 영화에는 폭력적인 장면들이 들어 있다.
a **violent** argument 격렬한 논쟁

068 **panic**
[pǽnik]

a sudden strong feeling of fear (that cannot be controlled)
명 극심한 공포, 공황 동 겁을 먹다, 공황 상태에 빠지다
She was in a **panic**. 그녀는 겁에 질려 있었다.
a state of **panic** 공황 상태
Don't **panic**; everything will be okay. 당황하지 마. 모든 게 다 괜찮아질 거야.

069 **differ**
[dífər]

to be different from someone or something
동 1. 다르다 ((from)) 2. 의견이 다르다 ((with))

He **differs from** his brother in many ways. 그는 그의 형과는 많은 점에서 다르다.
I **differ with** you on that. 나는 그 점에 대해서 당신과 의견을 달리한다.

070 **difference**
[dífərəns]

different 형 다른, 차이가 있는
differently 부 다르게

the quality or state of being different
명 차이(점), 다름 반 similarity 유사성

Can you tell me the **difference**? 차이점을 말해 줄 수 있나요?
What is the **difference** between cats and dogs? 고양이와 개의 차이점은 무엇인가요?

071 **vary**
[vέəri]

various 형 다양한

to be different from each other
동 1. (서로) 다르다 = differ 2. (상황에 따라) 달라지다, 변하다 = change

Prices **vary** from store to store. 가격은 가게마다 다르다.
The menu **varies** with the seasons. 메뉴는 계절에 따라 달라진다.

072 **variety**
[vəráiəti]

many different types of things or people
명 1. 여러 가지, 갖가지 2. 다양성 = diversity

There is a wide **variety** of fruits in the market. 시장에는 다양한 과일이 있다.
Add **variety** to your diet. 당신의 식단에 다양성을 더하세요.

073 **equal**
[íːkwəl]

equally 부 동일하게
equality 명 평등

the same in amount, number, or size
형 1. 동일한, 같은 2. 동등한, 평등한 동 같다, ~이다

The two rooms are **equal** in size. 그 두 방은 크기가 같다.
All people are **equal**. 모든 사람은 평등하다.
Two plus three **equals** five. 2 더하기 3은 5이다. (2+3=5)

074 **identical**
[aidéntikəl]

exactly the same or very similar
형 동일한, 똑같은 ((to))

The houses on the street are **identical**. 이 거리의 집들은 동일하다.
Her dress is almost **identical to** mine. 그녀의 드레스는 내 것과 거의 같다.
identical twins 일란성 쌍둥이

075 **outstanding**
[autstǽndiŋ]

extremely good or excellent
형 뛰어난, 걸출한, 두드러진

He is an **outstanding** player. 그는 뛰어난 선수이다.
an **outstanding** example of teamwork 팀워크의 두드러진 예

076 **indeed**
[indíːd]

really; truly
부 정말, 참으로, 실로

His performance was outstanding **indeed**. 그의 활약[공연]은 정말 뛰어났다.
Do you agree? – Yes, **indeed**. 동의하세요? – 네, 정말로(그럼요).

077 **intelligent**
[intéləʤənt]

able to learn and understand things easily

형 1. 총명한, 똑똑한 2. 지능이 있는[높은]

She was a highly **intelligent** child. 그녀는 대단히 총명한 아이였다.
Is there **intelligent** life on other planets? 다른 행성에 지적 생명체가 있을까?

078 **intelligence**
[intéləʤəns]

the ability to learn or understand things

명 지능, 이해력

Dolphins have a high level of **intelligence**. 돌고래는 높은 수준의 지능을 가지고 있다.
a robot with artificial **intelligence** 인공 지능(AI)을 가진 로봇

079 **be different from**

to differ from

~와 다르다

His opinion **is different from** mine. 그의 의견은 내 의견과 다르다.
Cats **are** very **different from** dogs. 고양이는 개와 아주 다르다.

080 **be similar to**

to be alike; to look alike

~와 비슷하다

Their houses **are similar to** each other. 그들의 집은 서로 비슷하다.
This painting **is** very **similar to** his. 이 그림은 그의 그림과 아주 비슷하다.

Check Up

A 우리말에 맞게 빈칸에 알맞은 말을 넣으세요.

1. 긍정적 사고의 힘 — the power of ________________ thinking
2. 엄격한 규칙들 — ________________ rules
3. 아주 성실한 학생 — a very ________________ student
4. 진심 어린 사과 — a ________________ apology
5. 대단히 총명한 아이 — a highly ________________ child
6. 인공 지능을 가진 로봇 — a robot with artificial ________________

B 우리말에 알맞은 말을 골라 문장을 완성하세요.

1. He is (**generous** / **strict**) with his money. 그는 돈을 아끼지 않는다.
2. He (**differs** / **different**) from his brother in many ways. 그는 그의 형과는 많은 점에서 다르다.
3. Can you tell me the (**similarity** / **difference**)? 차이점을 말해 줄 수 있나요?
4. Prices (**vary** / **variety**) from store to store. 가격은 가게마다 다르다.
5. Two plus three (**equal** / **equals**) five. 2 더하기 3은 5이다.

Build Up

A Write the correct word for each definition.

panic	identical	generous	violent	intelligence	outstanding

1. 

often giving people money or presents

____

2. 

using physical force

____

3. 

a sudden strong feeling of fear

____

4. 

exactly the same or very similar

____

5. 

extremely good or excellent

____

6. 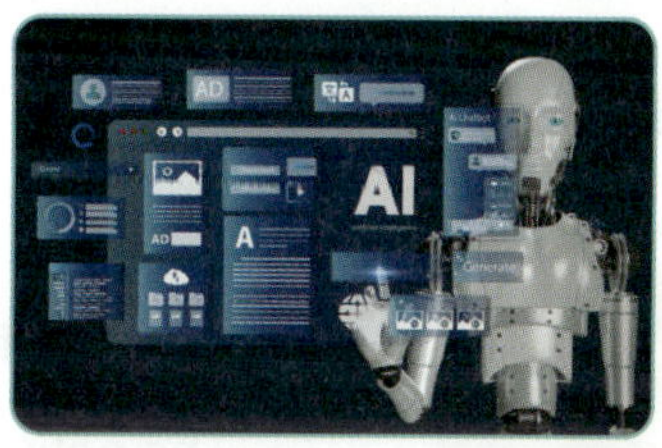

the ability to learn or understand things

____

B Write the correct word or phrase next to each definition.

be different from	be similar to	negative	strict	equal	indeed

1. not hopeful; bad or harmful ______________________
2. not loose; following the rules ______________________
3. really; truly ______________________
4. the same in amount, number, or size ______________________
5. to differ from ______________________
6. to be alike; to look alike ______________________

Review Test 01 DAY 01-04

A 그림을 보고, 빈칸에 알맞은 단어를 넣으세요.

figure variety mental physical outstanding courage

1. 
______

2. 
______

3. 
______

4. 
______

5. 

______

6. 
______

B 그림에 알맞은 문장을 골라 표시하세요.

1. 

☐ She is suffering from a severe headache.

☐ The patient made a rapid recovery.

2. 

☐ He seems hesitant.

☐ He looks very confident.

3. 

☐ Hundreds of people crowded the museum.

☐ The museum attracts many visitors.

4. 

☐ The houses are identical.

☐ The houses are similar to each other.

C 우리말 뜻에 맞게 빈칸에 알맞은 말을 넣으세요.

responsible	appeal	gather	with confidence
tend to	disabled	attempt	artificial intelligence

1. ____________________ information 정보를 수집하다
2. make an ____________________ for help 도와달라고 간청하다[호소하다]
3. be ____________________ for ~에 대해 책임이 있다
4. make an ____________________ 시도하다
5. ____________________ give up easily 쉽게 포기하는 경향이 있다
6. a robot with ____________________ 인공 지능을 가진 로봇
7. physically ____________________ 신체적으로 장애가 있는
8. answer ____________________ 자신 있게 대답하다

D 우리말 뜻에 맞게 빈칸에 알맞은 말을 넣으세요.

impressed	appearance	properly	give up	in person	figure out

1. Never judge a person by their ____________________. 겉모습으로 사람을 판단하지 마라.
2. His speech ____________________ the public. 그의 연설은 대중에게 깊은 감명을 주었다.
3. I want to see the concert ____________________. 나는 그 콘서트를 직접 보고 싶다.
4. My laptop is not working ____________________. 내 노트북이 제대로 작동하지 않는다.
5. Did you ____________________ who did it? 누가 그랬는지 알아냈니?
6. Never ____________________ until you succeed. 성공할 때까지 절대 포기하지 마라.

E 밑줄 친 단어와 비슷한 뜻을 가진 단어를 고르세요.

1. The movie appeals to teenagers.
   a. impresses b. attracts c. begs

2. She is under extreme stress.
   a. proper b. severe c. sudden

3. Smoking affects your health.
   a. effects b. impresses c. influences

4. I don't want to talk about my private life.
   a. privacy b. personal c. personality

F 밑줄 친 단어와 반대의 뜻을 가진 단어를 고르세요.

1. Gradually, his ankle got better.
   a. Suddenly b. Frankly c. Slowly

2. The building has a unique design.
   a. rare b. unusual c. typical

3. The test results were negative.
   a. gradual b. capable c. positive

4. My parents were very strict with us.
   a. hesitant b. generous c. similar

G 주어진 영영풀이에 알맞은 단어를 고르세요.

1. to act in a particular way; to act properly

   a. behave　　b. gather　　c. impress

2. a special or important part of something

   a. figure　　b. feature　　c. personality

3. likely to develop into something

   a. capable　　b. potential　　c. mature

4. to try to do something

   a. succeed　　b. appeal　　c. attempt

5. behaving like an adult; fully grown or developed

   a. proper　　b. mature　　c. confident

6. to give someone support or courage

   a. vary　　b. discourage　　c. encourage

H 빈칸에 알맞은 동사 형태를 넣어 문장을 완성하세요.

1. The building was badly ____________________ by the fire. (affect)
2. Many people were ____________________ by his speech. (influence)
3. She succeeded in ____________________ the problem. (solve)
4. He ____________________ from his brother in many ways. (differ)

081 **detect**
[ditékt]
detective 명 형사, 탐정

to notice or discover something (that is hidden or not clear)
동 감지하다, 탐지하다, 발견하다 유 sense 감지하다; 감각

detect a gas leak 가스 누수를 감지하다
Hidden cameras are difficult to **detect**. 숨겨진 카메라들은 발견하기 어렵다.

082 **detector**
[ditéktər]

a device that detects something
명 탐지기, 감지기

a smoke **detector** (화재 경보용의) 연기 탐지기
The **detector** goes off as soon as smoke is detected. 연기가 감지되면 즉시 감지기가 울린다.

083 **visible**
[vízəbl]
visibility 명 눈에 보임, 가시성

able to be seen
형 1. (눈에) 보이는 2. 뚜렷한, 가시적인

The fire was **visible** from 5 kilometers away. 그 화재는 5킬로미터 떨어진 곳에서도 보였다.
some **visible** advantages of the new system 새 시스템의 몇 가지 뚜렷한 장점들

084 **invisible**
[invízəbl]
invisibility 명 눈에 보이지 않음, 불가시성

not visible; impossible to see
형 보이지 않는, 볼 수 없는

*The **Invisible** Man* is a novel by H. G. Wells. 〈투명 인간〉은 H. G. 웰스의 소설이다.

085 **emergency**
[imə́:rdʒənsi]

a serious or dangerous situation (that needs immediate action)
명 비상사태, 응급 상황

In an **emergency**, call this number. 비상시에는 이 번호로 전화하세요.
an **emergency** exit 비상구

086 **escape**
[iskéip]

to get away from a dangerous or bad situation
동 1. 탈출하다 ((from)) 2. 피하다, 모면하다 명 탈출, 도망

escape from an emergency 비상 상황에서 탈출하다
I was lucky to **escape** injury. 나는 다행히 부상을 면했다.
make an **escape** plan 탈출 계획을 세우다

087 **remain**
[riméin]

to continue to exist; to be left
동 1. 남다 2. 계속[여전히] ~이다 명 (-s) 남은 것, 유물

Nothing **remained** after the fire. 화재 후에 아무것도 남지 않았다.
He **remained** silent. 그는 계속 침묵을 지켰다(잠자코 있었다).
the **remains** of the house 그 집의 잔해

088 **maintain**
[meintéin]
maintenance 명 지속, 유지

to make something continue in the same way
동 지속하다, 계속하다, 유지하다

Try to **maintain** a positive mind. 긍정적인 마음을 유지하려고 노력해라.
A large house is expensive to **maintain**. 큰 집은 유지 관리하는 데 비용이 많이 든다.

089 **arrange**
[əréindʒ]
arrangement 명 준비; 배치

to plan something in advance
동 1. (미리) 계획하다, 준비하다 2. 정리하다, 배열하다

arrange a surprise party 깜짝 파티를 준비하다
I **arranged** the chairs for the party. 나는 파티를 위해 의자들을 정리했다.

090 **organize**
[ɔ́ːrgənàiz]
organization 명 조직, 단체

to arrange and plan something
동 1. (어떤 일을) 준비하다, 조직하다 2. 정리하다, 체계화하다

The event was **organized** by a party planner. 그 행사는 파티 기획자에 의해 준비되었다.
organize the details by category 세부 사항을 카테고리별로 정리하다

091 **dirt**
[dəːrt]
dirty 형 더러운

mud or dust that makes things unclean
명 1. 먼지, 때 2. 흙 유 dust (흙)먼지

There's a lot of **dirt** on the floor. 바닥에 먼지가 많다.
The children are playing in the **dirt**. 아이들은 흙에서 놀고 있다.

092 **stain**
[stein]
stained 형 얼룩진

a dirty mark that is difficult to remove
명 얼룩 동 더럽히다, 얼룩을 남기다

a **stain** on the carpet 카펫의 얼룩
I hope it doesn't **stain** the carpet. 카펫에 얼룩이 지지 않기를 바란다.

093 **stare**
[stɛər]

to look at someone or something for a long time
동 응시하다, 빤히 쳐다보다 ((at)) 유 gaze 응시하다, 비리보다

She **stared** out the window. 그녀는 창밖을 응시했다.
What are you **staring at**? 뭘 쳐다보고 있니?

094 **glance**
[glæns]

to look at someone or something quickly
동 1. 흘끗 보다 2. 대충 훑어보다 명 흘끗 봄 ((at))

She **glanced at** her watch. 그녀는 그녀의 시계를 흘끗 보았다.
At first **glance**, it looked like a bug. 처음 얼핏 봤을 때, 그것은 벌레처럼 보였다.

095 **disgust**
[disgʌ́st]

a strong feeling of dislike for something
명 역겨움, 넌더리 동 역겹게 하다

She covered her nose **in disgust**. 그녀는 역겨움에 코를 막았다.
The smell of garbage **disgusted** her. 쓰레기 냄새가 그녀를 역겹게 했다.

096 **disgusting**
[disgʌ́stiŋ]

extremely unpleasant
형 역겨운, 구역질 나는

What a **disgusting** smell! 정말 역겨운 냄새야!
The food was so **disgusting**. 그 음식은 너무 역겨웠다(형편없었다).

097 **realize**

[rí:əlàiz]

realization 명 깨달음; 실현

to begin to understand something

동 1. 깨닫다, 인식하다 2. (목표 등을) 실현하다

I **realized** something was wrong. 나는 뭔가 잘못되었다는 것을 깨달았다.

He **realized** his dream of becoming a doctor. 그는 의사가 되는 꿈을 이뤘다.

098 **recognize**

[rékəgnàiz]

recognition 명 알아봄; 인식

to know who someone is (or what something is)

동 1. 알아보다 2. 인정하다, 인식하다

I didn't **recognize** her at first. 나는 처음에는 그녀를 알아보지 못했다.

He finally **recognized** his mistake. 그는 결국 자신의 실수를 인정했다.

099 **stare at**

to gaze at

~을 응시하다, ~을 빤히 쳐다보다

We sat and **stared at** each other. 우리는 앉아서 서로를 응시했다.

Why are you **staring at** me like that? 왜 나를 그렇게 빤히 쳐다보니?

Don't **stare at** people; it's rude. 사람들을 빤히 쳐다보지 마라, 무례한 짓이야.

100 **keep an eye on**

to watch over

~을 지켜보다, ~을 주시하다, ~을 눈여겨보다

Can you **keep an eye on** my bag? 제 가방 좀 지켜봐 주실래요?

Keep an eye on the soup so it doesn't boil over. 수프가 끓어 넘치지 않게 지켜봐 줘.

Check Up

A 우리말에 맞게 빈칸에 알맞은 말을 넣으세요.

1. 가스 누수를 감지하다 ________________ a gas leak
2. 비상구 an ________________ exit
3. 비상 상황에서 탈출하다 ________________ from an emergency
4. 깜짝 파티를 준비하다 ________________ a surprise party
5. 세부 사항을 카테고리별로 정리하다 ________________ the details by category
6. 서로를 응시하다[빤히 쳐다보다] ________________ at each other

B 우리말에 알맞은 말을 골라 문장을 완성하세요.

1. It goes off as soon as smoke is (**detect** / **detected**). 그것은 연기가 감지되면 즉시 울린다.
2. Most gases are (**visible** / **invisible**). 대부분의 가스는 보이지 않는다.
3. The event was (**organize** / **organized**) by a party planner. 그 행사는 파티 기획자에 의해 준비되었다.
4. The smell of garbage (**disgusted** / **disgusting**) her. 쓰레기 냄새가 그녀를 역겹게 했다.
5. I (**realized** / **recognized**) something was wrong. 나는 뭔가 잘못되었다는 것을 깨달았다.

Build Up

A Write the correct word for each definition.

emergency	detector	disgusting	recognize	stain	glance

1. 

a device that detects something

____

2. 

a serious or dangerous situation

____

3. 

a dirty mark

____

4. 

to look at something quickly

____

5. 

extremely unpleasant

____

6. 

to know who someone is

____

B Write the correct word or phrase next to each definition.

escape	invisible	keep an eye on	realize	remain	maintain

1. not visible; impossible to see __________________
2. to get away from a dangerous or bad situation __________________
3. to continue to exist; to be left __________________
4. to make something continue in the same way __________________
5. to begin to understand something __________________
6. to watch over __________________

DAY 06

101 **simple**
[símpl]
simplicity 명 간단함; 소박함

not difficult or complicated
형 1. 간단한, 쉬운 = easy 2. 단순한, 소박한 반 fancy 화려한

It's very **simple** to use. 그것은 사용하기 매우 간단하다[쉽다].
a **simple** black dress 단순한 검정 드레스
have a **simple** meal 소박한 식사를 하다

102 **routine**
[ru:tí:n]

a regular way of doing things in a particular order
명 (매일 똑같이 하는) 일, 일상, 루틴 *habit 습관

What's your morning **routine**? 너의 아침 루틴은 무엇이니?
My daily **routine** starts at 7:00 AM. 나의 하루 일과는 오전 7시에 시작된다.

103 **asleep**
[əslí:p]
sleep 동 자다

sleeping
형 잠이 든, 잠자고 있는

He usually falls **asleep** around 11:00 PM. 그는 보통 오후 11시쯤 잠이 든다.
Shh! The baby is **asleep**. 쉬(조용)! 아기가 자고 있어.

104 **awake**
[əwéik]
wake 동 깨다; 깨우다

not sleeping; not asleep (awoke–awoken)
형 잠들지 않은, 깨어 있는 동 (잠에서) 깨다; 깨우다 = wake up

stay **awake** all night 밤새 깨어 있다
He always **awakes** early in the morning. 그는 항상 아침에 일찍 깬다.
I **awake** from sleep at 6:00 AM. 나는 오전 6시에 잠에서 깬다.

105 **shave**
[ʃeiv]

to cut hair from the skin, especially the face
동 면도하다 명 면도

Have you **shaved** today? 너는 오늘 면도했니?
He showered and had a **shave**. 그는 샤워를 하고 면도를 했다.

106 **carefully**
[kέərfəli]
careful 형 조심하는, 주의 깊은
care 명 조심, 주의; 돌봄

in a careful way
부 조심스럽게, 주의 깊게 반 carelessly 부주의하게

He **carefully** shaved his beard. 그는 조심스럽게 (턱)수염을 면도했다.
Please listen **carefully**. 주의 깊게 잘 들어 주세요.

107 **skip**
[skip]

to not do something that you usually do
동 1. (일을) 거르다, 빼먹다 2. (어떤 부분을) 건너뛰다, 생략하다

He often **skips** breakfast. 그는 종종 아침을 거른다.
You can **skip** the next chapter if you like. 원하면 다음 장은 건너뛰어도 된다.

108 **rush**
[rʌʃ]

to move very quickly
동 급히 움직이다, 서두르다 = hurry 명 1. 돌진 2. 혼잡

He had to **rush** to catch the bus. 그는 버스를 타기 위해 서둘러야 했다.
Shoppers made a **rush** for the exits. 쇼핑객들이 출구로 몰려들었다.
rush hour 혼잡 시간대

109 **lack**
[læk]

not having (enough of) something
명 결핍, 부족 ((of)) = shortage 동 ~이 없다, ~이 부족하다

I'm tired from a **lack of** sleep. 나는 수면 부족으로 피곤하다.
I think he **lacks** confidence. 내 생각에 그는 자신감이 부족하다.

110 **plenty**
[plénti]
plentiful 형 풍부한

a large amount of something
대 충분한 양(의 ~), 풍부한 양(의 ~) ((of)) *enough 충분한

Try to get **plenty of** sleep. 충분한 수면을 취하도록 해라.
You have **plenty of** time to finish the project. 너는 그 프로젝트를 끝낼 충분한 시간이 있다.

111 **extra**
[ékstrə]

more, or more than usual
형 추가의, 여분의 = additional 부 추가로

He often works **extra** hours. 그는 종종 추가 시간을 근무한다.
save some **extra** money 약간의 여분의 돈을 저축하다
pay **extra** for a better room 더 좋은 방을 위해 추가로 요금을 내다

112 **extraordinary**
[ikstrɔ́ːrdənèri]

not ordinary; very special or unusual
형 보통이 아닌, 비범한, 특별한 반 ordinary 보통의, 평범한

You have an **extraordinary** talent for music. 너는 음악에 비범한 재능이 있다.
This is an **extraordinary** opportunity for you. 이것은 너에게 특별한 기회이다.

113 **instance**
[ínstəns]

a particular example or case of something
명 사례, 경우 ((of)) 유 example 예, 사례

For **instance**, you can be a musician. 예를 들면, 너는 음악가가 될 수 있다.
in the **instance of** a fire in the building 건물에 화재가 발생할 경우
In this **instance**, you should ask for help. 이런 경우에는 도움을 요청해야 한다.

114 **case**
[keis]

a particular situation or example of something
명 1. (특정한 상황의) 경우 ((of)) 2. 사건 3. 용기, 통

In **case of** fire, break the glass. 화재 발생 시 유리(창)를 깨시오.
a murder **case** 살인 사건
a pencil **case** 필통

115 **exhausted**
[igzɔ́ːstid]
exhaust 동 기진맥진하게 만들다
exhaustion 명 탈진, 기진맥진

very tired
형 지쳐 버린, 기진맥진한

He was **exhausted** after the long hike. 긴 하이킹 후에 그는 지쳐 버렸다.

116 **drag**
[dræg]

to pull something along the ground, usually with difficulty
동 1. (힘들여) 끌다 2. (몸을) 힘들게 움직이다

He **dragged** the heavy box to the door. 그는 그 무거운 상자를 문 쪽으로 질질 끌었다.
He **dragged** his feet on the way home. 그는 집으로 가면서 발을 질질 끌었다(힘들게 움직였다).

117 **odd**
[ɑːd]
oddly ⓟ 이상하게, 이상하게도

strange or unusual
㉠ 1. 이상한, 묘한 2. 홀수의 *the odds (어떤 일이 있을) 가능성, 확률

His behavior was **odd** yesterday. 어제 그의 행동이 이상했다.
1, 3, and 5 are **odd** numbers. 1, 3, 5는 홀수이다.

118 **even**
[íːvən]
evenly ⓟ 고르게, 균등하게

flat, level, or smooth
㉠ 1. 평평한 2. 고른, 일정한 3. 짝수의 ⓟ (심지어) ~조차도

We set up the tent on **even** ground. 우리는 평평한 땅에 텐트를 쳤다.
the **even** beat of the drum 일정한 드럼의 비트
4 is an **even** number. 4는 짝수이다.
Even a child can understand it. 심지어 어린아이도 그것을 이해할 수 있다.

119 **stay up (late)**

to stay awake (until a late hour)
(늦게까지) 깨어 있다, 잠을 안 자다

I **stayed up late** to finish my homework. 나는 숙제를 끝내기 위해 늦게까지 깨어 있었다.
They **stayed up** all night talking. 그들은 밤새도록 자지 않고 이야기를 나누었다.

120 **just in case**

as a way of being safe
~할 경우에 대비하여, 혹시 모르니까

Take an umbrella **just in case** it rains. 비가 올 경우를 대비해 우산을 가지고 가라.
I'll bring some extra cash **just in case**. 혹시 모르니까 여분의 현금을 가져갈게.

Check Up

A 우리말에 맞게 빈칸에 알맞은 말을 넣으세요.

1. 나의 하루 일과 — my daily ______
2. 아침을 거르다 — ______ breakfast
3. 수면 부족 — a ______ of sleep
4. 충분한 수면을 취하다 — get ______ of sleep
5. 화재가 발생할 경우 — in the ______ of a fire
6. ~할 경우에 대비하여, 혹시 모르니까 — just ______

B 우리말에 알맞은 말을 골라 문장을 완성하세요.

1. He usually falls (awake / asleep) around 11:00 PM. 그는 보통 오후 11시쯤 잠이 든다.
2. In (case / instance) of fire, break the glass. 화재 발생 시 유리(창)를 깨시오.
3. He (exhausted / was exhausted) after the long hike. 긴 하이킹 후에 그는 지쳐 버렸다.
4. His behavior was (odd / even) yesterday. 어제 그의 행동이 이상했다.
5. 4 is an (odd / even) number. 4는 짝수이다.

Build Up

A Write the correct word for each definition.

asleep	awake	rush	extraordinary	shave	exhausted

1. 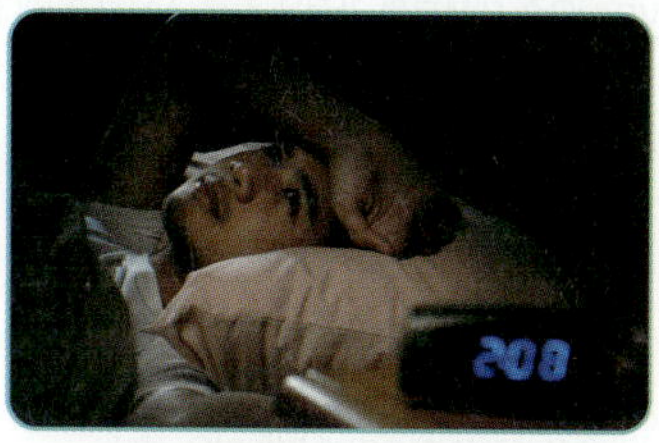

   not sleeping; not asleep

   ____

2. 

   sleeping

   ____

3. 

   to cut hair from the skin

   ____

4. 

   to move very quickly

   ____

5. 

   not ordinary

   ____

6. 

   very tired

   ____

B Write the correct word or phrase next to each definition.

drag	odd	simple	lack	stay up late	routine

1. not difficult or complicated ______________________
2. a regular way of doing things in a particular order ______________________
3. not having (enough of) something ______________________
4. strange or unusual ______________________
5. to pull something along the ground, usually with difficulty ______________________
6. to stay awake until a late hour ______________________

DAY 07

121 **household**
[háushòuld]

all the people living together in a house
명 가정, 가구 형 가정의, 가사의

Most **households** own a car nowadays. 요즘 대부분의 가정은 차를 소유하고 있다.
household goods 가정용품, 가사용품

122 **chore**
[tʃɔːr]

a small job that you do regularly
명 (일상에서 하는) 허드렛일, 집안일 유 housework 가사, 집안일

do the household **chores** 집안일을 하다
She always does **chores** on Sundays. 그녀는 항상 일요일에 집안일을 한다.

123 **task**
[tæsk]

a piece of work (that someone has to do)
명 (해야 하는) 일, 과제, 과업

Doing chores can be a boring **task**. 집안일을 하는 것은 지루한 일이 될 수 있다.
a difficult **task** 어려운 과제

124 **lawn**
[lɔːn]

an area of grass in a garden or park
명 잔디밭 *grass 잔디, 풀

water the **lawn** 잔디(밭)에 물을 주다
We mow the **lawn** twice a week. 우리는 일주일에 두 번 (잔디밭의) 잔디를 깎는다.

125 **tap**
[tæp]

a device that controls the flow of water from a pipe
명 수도꼭지 = (미) faucet 동 (가볍게) 톡톡 치다 ((on/at))

turn off the **tap** 수도꼭지를 잠그다
tap water 수돗물
Someone **tapped on** the door. 누군가 문을 톡톡 두드렸다.

126 **knock**
[nɑk]

to hit a door or window repeatedly
동 (문 등을) 두드리다, 노크하다 명 노크 소리 ((on/at))

She **knocked on** the door and waited. 그녀는 문을 노크하고 기다렸다.
There was a **knock at** the door. 문에서 노크 소리가 났다.

127 **leak**
[liːk]

leaky 형 새는, 새기 쉬운

to allow liquid or gas to pass through a small hole
동 (액체·기체가) 새다; 새게 하다

The tap was **leaking**. 수도꼭지가 새고 있었다.
a **leaking** pipe 물이 새는 파이프

128 **fasten**
[fǽsn]

to close or fix something together
동 1. (꽉) 잠그다, 고정시키다 = tighten 2. 채우다, 매다 반 unfasten 풀다

Fasten the tap tightly. 수도꼭지를 단단히 잠가라.
Fasten your seatbelts, please. 안전벨트를 매 주세요.

129 **shut**
[ʃʌt]

to close something; to become closed (shut–shut)
동 (문 등을) 닫다; 닫히다 = close 형 닫힌 반 open 열다; 열린

Shut the door. 문을 닫아라.
Keep the window **shut**. 창문을 닫아 두어라.

130 **firmly**
[fə́:rmli]
firm 형 단단한

strongly and tightly
부 1. 단단히 2. 단호히, 확고히

I shut the window **firmly**. 나는 창문을 단단히 잠갔다.
"I can do it," he said **firmly**. "제가 할 수 있어요." 그가 단호하게 말했다.

131 **lift**
[lift]

to raise something to a higher position
동 (위로) 들다, 들어 올리다

This box is too heavy to **lift**. 이 상자는 들기에는 너무 무겁다.
He **lifted** the heavy box carefully. 그는 그 무거운 상자를 조심스레 들어 올렸다.

132 **break**
[breik]
broken 형 깨진, 고장 난

to separate or become separated into pieces (broke–broken)
동 1. 깨다; 깨어지다 2. 고장 내다; 고장 나다 명 (짧은) 휴식

Be careful not to **break** the glass. 유리를 깨뜨리지 않도록 조심해.
My watch has **broken**. 내 시계가 고장 났어.
Let's take a **break**. 좀 쉬었다 합시다.

133 **ladder**
[lǽdər]

a device that is used to reach high places
명 사다리

He climbed up the **ladder** to fix the roof. 그는 지붕을 고치기 위해 사다리를 올라갔다.

134 **repair**
[ripέər]

to fix something that is damaged or broken
동 수리하다, 보수하다 = fix, mend 명 수리, 보수

The roof is being **repaired**. 지붕은 수리(되고 있는) 중이다.
It is under **repair**. 그것은 수리 중이다.
The building was shut for **repairs**. 그 건물은 보수를 위해 폐쇄되었다.

135 **pause**
[pɔ:z]

to stop talking or doing something for a short time
동 1. 잠시 멈추다 2. (정지 버튼을 눌러) 정지시키다 명 멈춤

She **paused** for a moment and then spoke. 그녀는 잠시 (말을) 멈추었다가 말했다.
Pause the video, please. 비디오를 잠시 멈춰 주세요.
The rain fell **without pause**. 비가 쉬지 않고 내렸다.

136 **briefly**
[brí:fli]
brief 형 간결한, 짧은

for a short time
부 1. 잠시 2. 간단히, 짧게

At the doorway, she paused **briefly**. 문 앞에서 그녀는 잠시 멈췄다.
Let me tell you **briefly** what happened. 무슨 일이 있었는지 간단히 말할게.

137 **complete**
[kəmplí:t]
completion 명 완료, 완성

to the greatest degree possible; having all parts
형 완전한, 완벽한 = total 동 1. 완료하다 = finish 2. (빠짐없이) 기입하다 = fill out

a **complete** change 완전한 변화
She **completed** the whole course. 그녀는 전 과정을 완료했다.
Please **complete** the form below. 아래 양식을 작성해 주세요.

138 **completely**
[kəmplí:tli]

in every way possible
부 완전히, 전적으로 = totally

The house was **completely** changed. 그 집은 완전히 달라졌다.
At night, it looked **completely** different. 밤에 그것은 완전히 달라 보였다.

139 **break down**

to stop working properly
1. (기계 등이) 고장 나다 2. 분해하다, 나누다

My car **broke down** on the highway. 내 차가 고속도로에서 고장이 났다.
Food is **broken down** in the stomach. 음식은 위에서 분해된다.

140 **be busy V-ing**

to fill your time doing an activity or task
~하느라 바쁘다

I **am busy** clean**ing** the house. 나는 집을 청소하느라 바쁘다.
They **were busy** fix**ing** the broken fence. 그들은 부서진 울타리를 수리하느라 바빴다.

Check Up

A 우리말에 맞게 빈칸에 알맞은 말을 넣으세요.

1. 집안일을 하다 — do the household ____________
2. 어려운 과제 — a difficult ____________
3. 수도꼭지를 잠그다 — turn off the ____________
4. 문을 노크하다 — ____________ on the door
5. 물이 새는 파이프 — a ____________ pipe
6. 완전한 변화 — a ____________ change

B 우리말에 알맞은 말을 골라 문장을 완성하세요.

1. (Fasten / Unfasten) your seatbelts, please. 안전벨트를 매 주세요.
2. My watch has (broke / broken). 내 시계가 고장 났어.
3. The roof is being (repair / repaired). 지붕은 수리(되고 있는) 중이다.
4. My car (broke down / broken down) on the highway. 내 차가 고속도로에서 고장이 났다.
5. I am busy (clean / cleaning) the house. 나는 집을 청소하느라 바쁘다.

Build Up

A Write the correct word for each definition.

firmly	lift	chore	lawn	repair	tap

1. 

a small job that you do regularly

____

2. 

an area of grass in a garden

____

3. 

strongly and tightly

____

4. 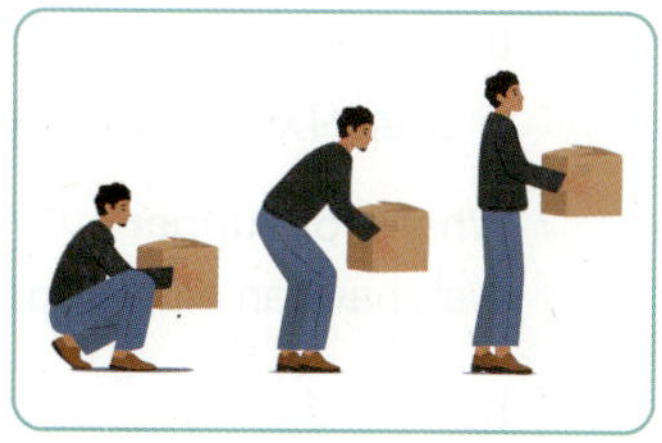

to raise something to a higher position

____

5. 

a device that controls the flow of water

____

6. 

to fix something

____

B Write the correct word or phrase next to each definition.

household	shut	pause	break	task	leak

1. all the people living together in a house ______________________
2. a piece of work (that someone has to do) ______________________
3. to allow liquid or gas to pass through a small hole ______________________
4. to close something; to become closed ______________________
5. to separate or become separated into pieces ______________________
6. to stop talking or doing something for a short time ______________________

141 **hunger**
[hʌ́ŋgər]
hungry 형 배고픈

the feeling caused by a need to eat; lack of food
명 1. 배고픔, 굶주림 2. (~에 대한) 갈구 동 굶주리다, 갈망하다 ((for))

I always feel **hunger** after exercising. 운동 후에 나는 늘 배고픔을 느낀다.
a **hunger for** knowledge 지식에 대한 갈구
They **hunger for** change. 그들은 변화를 갈망하고 있다.

142 **thirst**
[θəːrst]
thirsty 형 목이 마른

the feeling of needing or wanting a drink
명 1. 목마름, 갈증 2. 갈망 ((for))

She woke up with a severe **thirst**. 그녀는 심한 갈증에 잠이 깼다.
a **thirst for** adventure 모험에 대한 갈망[목마름]

143 **supper**
[sʌ́pər]

the evening meal
명 저녁 식사, 가벼운 만찬 *dinner보다는 덜 격식적

What's for **supper**? 저녁 메뉴는 뭐예요?
We'll have an early **supper** today. 우리는 오늘 일찍 저녁을 먹을 것이다.

144 **flavor**
[fléivər]

how food tastes
명 1. 맛, 풍미 2. 조미료, 향신료 = flavoring

The soup has a rich **flavor**. 이 수프는 풍부한 맛이 난다.
natural **flavors** 천연 조미료[향신료]

145 **swallow**
[swálou]

to make food go down your throat and into your stomach
동 (음식 등을) 삼키다 *chew 씹다 명 제비

Always chew food well before **swallowing** it. 음식을 삼키기 전에 반드시 잘 씹어라.
a little **swallow** 작은 제비 한 마리

146 **digest**
[daidʒést]
digestion 명 소화

to break down food
동 1. (음식을) 소화하다; 소화되다 2. 이해하다

I can't **digest** milk well. 나는 우유를 잘 소화하지 못한다.
It took a while to **digest** the information. 그 정보를 이해하는 데 시간이 좀 걸렸다.

147 **tender**
[téndər]
tenderness 명 부드러움, 다정함

easy to cut and chew; not tough
형 1. (음식이) 연한 2. 다정한, 상냥한

This steak is so **tender**. 이 스테이크는 정말 연하다.
Her voice was **tender** and soft. 그녀의 목소리는 다정하고 부드러웠다.

148 **tough**
[tʌf]

difficult to cut or chew; not tender
형 1. (고기가) 질긴 2. 강인한, 거친 3. 힘든, 어려운

This meat is very **tough**. 이 고기는 매우 질기다.
a **tough** guy 강인한[거친] 남자
He had a **tough** time at work. 그는 직장에서 힘든 시간을 보냈다.

149 **raw**
[rɔː]

not cooked
형 1. 익히지 않은, 날것의 2. 가공하지 않은

Do you eat **raw** fish? 너는 생선회를 먹니?
raw sugar (가공하지 않은) 원당

150 **flesh**
[fleʃ]
fleshy 형 살집이 있는; 과육이 많은

the soft part between the skin and bones of animal or human bodies
명 1. (사람·동물의) 살, 고기 2. (식물의) 속, 과육

The **flesh** of this fish is tender. 이 생선의 살은 부드럽다.
the **flesh** of a melon 멜론의 과육

151 **pour**
[pɔːr]

to make a liquid flow from a container
동 1. 따르다, 붓다 2. (비 등이) 마구 쏟아지다, 퍼붓다

She **poured** the milk into a glass. 그녀는 유리컵에 우유를 따랐다.
Tears **poured** down her cheeks. 눈물이 그녀의 뺨 위로 마구 흘러내렸다.
It's **pouring** outside. 밖에는 비가 퍼붓고 있다.

152 **spill**
[spil]

to cause (something) to fall or flow from a container, often accidentally
동 쏟다, 엎지르다; 엎질러지다 명 유출(물)

Be careful not to **spill** the coffee. 커피를 쏟지 않도록 조심해라.
Milk **spilled** onto the table. 우유가 탁자 위로 쏟아졌다.
It's no use crying over **spilled** milk. 엎질러진 우유에 울어 봤자 소용없다(이미 엎질러진 물이다).
an oil **spill** 기름 유출

153 **chop**
[tʃɑp]

to cut something into smaller pieces
동 작게 썰다, 다지다 = chop up

Chop the carrots **up** into small pieces. 당근을 잘게 디지세요.

154 **crush**
[krʌʃ]

to press something so hard that it is made flat or broken into pieces
동 1. 눌러 부수다, 찌그러뜨리다 2. 으깨다, 빻다 *squeeze (눌러) 짜다, 짜내다

He **crushed** an empty can. 그는 빈 캔을 찌그러뜨렸다.
crush garlic 마늘을 빻다

155 **peel**
[piːl]

to remove skin from fruit or vegetables
동 1. (과일 등의) 껍질을 벗기다 2. 벗겨지다

Peel and chop the potatoes. 감자 껍질을 벗기고 잘게 써세요.
The wallpaper was beginning to **peel**. 벽지가 벗겨지기 시작하고 있었다.

156 **slice**
[slais]

a thin, flat piece of food cut from something
명 (얇게 썬) 조각 ((of)) 유 piece 조각 동 얇게 썰다 = slice up

a **slice of** pizza 피자 한 조각
Cut the tomatoes into **slices**. 토마토를 얇게(슬라이스로) 자르세요.
Slice up the onions. 양파를 얇게 써세요.

157 **steam**
[stiːm]

to cook or heat something with steam

동 1. 찌다 2. 김을 내뿜다 *boil 끓다; 끓이다 명 김, (수)증기

Steam the vegetables lightly. 야채들을 살짝 찌세요.
The kettle began to **steam.** 주전자가 김을 내뿜기 시작했다.
Steam rose from the hot soup. 뜨거운 수프에서 김이 올라왔다.

158 **stir**
[stəːr]

to mix food or liquid

동 젓다, 휘젓다 *stir-fry 볶다

Stir the soup until it is thick. 수프가 걸쭉해질 때까지 저으세요.
She **stirred** her coffee with a spoon. 그녀는 숟가락으로 커피를 저었다.

159 **eat out**

to have a meal at a restaurant
외식하다

We often **eat out** on weekends. 우리는 주말에 종종 외식을 한다.
We decided to **eat out** tonight. 우리는 오늘 밤 외식하기로 했다.

160 **pass down**

to hand down
~을 물려주다, ~을 전해 주다

My mom **passed down** family recipes to me. 엄마는 내게 가족 요리법을 물려주셨다.
It has been **passed down** from mother to daughter. 그것은 어머니에게서 딸에게로 전해져 왔다.

Check Up

A 우리말에 맞게 빈칸에 알맞은 말을 넣으세요.

1. 지식에 대한 갈구 a ______________ for knowledge
2. 천연 조미료[향신료] natural ______________
3. 저녁을 먹다 have ______________
4. 생선회 ______________ fish
5. 피자 한 조각 a ______________ of pizza
6. 가족 요리법을 물려주다 ______________ family recipes

B 우리말에 알맞은 말을 골라 문장을 완성하세요.

1. I can't (**digest** / **swallow**) milk well. 나는 우유를 잘 소화하지 못한다.
2. She (**spilled** / **poured**) the milk into a glass. 그녀는 유리컵에 우유를 따랐다.
3. He (**chopped** / **crushed**) an empty can. 그는 빈 캔을 찌그러뜨렸다.
4. We often (**go out** / **eat out**) on weekends. 우리는 주말에 종종 외식을 한다.
5. It has been (**pass down** / **passed down**) from mother to daughter.
그것은 어머니에게서 딸에게로 전해져 왔다.

Build Up

A Write the correct word for each definition.

1. 

the feeling caused by a need to eat

____

2. 

the feeling of needing a drink

____

3. 

easy to cut and chew

____

4. 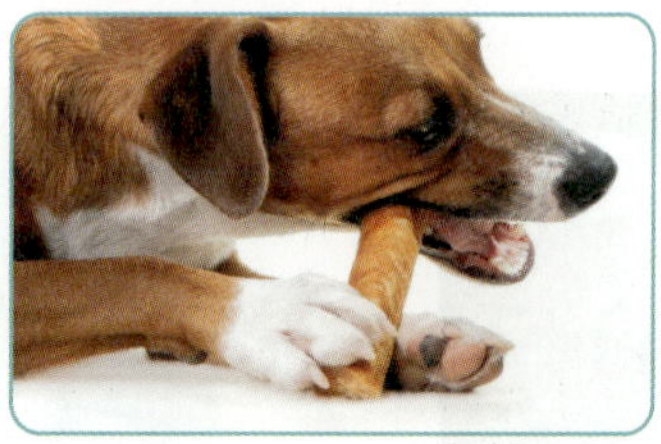

difficult to cut or chew

____

5. 

to cause something to fall or flow from a container

____

6. 

to mix food or liquid

____

hunger
tender
thirst
tough
stir
spill

B Write the correct word or phrase next to each definition.

chop	steam	swallow	pour	digest	eat out

1. to make food go down your throat and into your stomach __________________
2. to break down food __________________
3. to make a liquid flow from a container __________________
4. to cut something into smaller pieces __________________
5. to cook or heat something with steam __________________
6. to have a meal at a restaurant __________________

Review Test 02 DAY 05-08

A 그림을 보고, 빈칸에 알맞은 단어를 넣으세요.

pour　　ladder　　leak　　detector　　lawn　　exhausted

1. 
____

2. 
____

3. 
____

4. 
____

5. 
____

6. 
____

B 그림에 알맞은 문장을 골라 표시하세요.

1. 
- ☐ There is a stain on the floor.
- ☐ There's a lot of dirt on the floor.

2. 
- ☐ Be careful not to break the glass.
- ☐ Milk spilled onto the table.

3. 
- ☐ The building is shut for repairs.
- ☐ The building is being repaired.

4. 
- ☐ She is fastening the tap tightly.
- ☐ She is fastening her seatbelt.

C 우리말 뜻에 맞게 빈칸에 알맞은 말을 넣으세요.

escape	in case	detect	plenty of
routine	break	slice	chores

1. ____________ a gas leak 가스 누수를 감지하다
2. ____________ from an emergency 비상 상황에서 탈출하다
3. my morning ____________ 나의 아침 일과
4. just ____________ ~할 경우에 대비하여
5. get ____________ sleep 충분한 수면을 취하다
6. do the household ____________ 집안일을 하다
7. take a ____________ 잠시 쉬다
8. a ____________ of pizza 피자 한 조각

D 우리말 뜻에 맞게 빈칸에 알맞은 말을 넣으세요.

lack of	emergency	disgusting	stayed up	realized	maintain

1. In an ____________, call this number. 비상시에는 이 번호로 전화하세요.
2. Try to ____________ a positive mind. 긍정적인 마음을 유지하려고 노력해라.
3. I'm tired from a ____________ sleep. 나는 수면 부족으로 피곤하다.
4. What a ____________ smell! 정말 역겨운 냄새야!
5. He ____________ his dream of becoming a doctor. 그는 의사가 되는 꿈을 이뤘다.
6. I ____________ late to finish my homework. 나는 숙제를 끝내기 위해 늦게까지 깨어 있었다.

E 밑줄 친 단어와 비슷한 뜻을 가진 단어를 고르세요.

1. The event was <u>organized</u> by a party planner.

   a. completed　　b. recognized　　c. arranged

2. He had to <u>rush</u> to catch the bus.

   a. skip　　b. hurry　　c. escape

3. In this <u>instance</u>, you should ask for help.

   a. example　　b. emergency　　c. case

4. At night, it looked <u>completely</u> different.

   a. quite　　b. briefly　　c. totally

F 밑줄 친 단어와 반대의 뜻을 가진 단어를 고르세요.

1. The fire was <u>visible</u> from 5 kilometers away.

   a. impossible　　b. invisible　　c. seen

2. I was <u>awake</u> all night.

   a. exhausted　　b. sleep　　c. asleep

3. 1, 3, and 5 are <u>odd</u> numbers.

   a. strange　　b. flat　　c. even

4. This meat is very <u>tough</u>.

   a. tender　　b. strong　　c. raw

G 주어진 영영풀이에 알맞은 단어를 고르세요.

1. a serious or dangerous situation (that needs immediate action)

   a. escape b. emergency c. instance

2. to continue to exist; to be left

   a. remain b. maintain c. arrange

3. to know who someone is (or what something is)

   a. realize b. organize c. recognize

4. to stop talking or doing something for a short time

   a. pause b. break c. skip

5. to remove skin from fruit or vegetables

   a. chop b. crush c. peel

6. a small job that you do regularly

   a. chore b. task c. work

H 빈칸에 알맞은 동사 형태를 넣어 문장을 완성하세요.

1. The detector goes off as soon as smoke is ______________. (detect)
2. Why are you ______________ at me like that? (stare)
3. My car ______________ on the highway yesterday. (break down)
4. It has been ______________ from mother to daughter. (pass down)

DAY 09

161 **emotional**
[imóuʃənl]
emotion 명 (희로애락의) 감정

relating to emotions
형 1. 감정의, 정서의 2. 감정적인

emotional music 정서적인 음악
He gave an **emotional** response to the news. 그는 그 소식에 감정적인 반응을 보였다.

162 **mood**
[mu:d]

the way you feel at a particular time
명 1. (일시적인) 기분 2. 분위기

She is in a good **mood** today. 그녀는 오늘 기분이 좋다.
The whole town is in a festive **mood**. 도시 전체가 축제 분위기이다.

163 **amaze**
[əméiz]

to surprise someone very much
동 (대단히) 놀라게 하다, 경탄하게 하다

The fireworks **amazed** the children. 불꽃놀이는 아이들을 놀라게 했다(감탄을 자아냈다).

164 **amazed**
[əméizd]
amazing 형 놀라운, 굉장한

very surprised
형 놀란, 경탄한

an **amazed** silence 놀라움에 찬 침묵
They were **amazed** by the fireworks. 그들은 불꽃놀이에 감탄했다.

165 **amuse**
[əmjú:z]

to make someone laugh or smile
동 즐겁게 하다, 재미있게 하다

His jokes **amused** all of us. 그의 농담은 우리 모두를 즐겁게 했다.
He made funny faces to **amuse** the kids. 그는 아이들을 즐겁게 하려고 웃기는 표정을 지었다.

166 **amused**
[əmjú:zd]
amusing 형 재미있는, 웃긴
amusement 명 재미, 즐거움

showing that you think something is funny
형 즐거워하는, 재미있어 하는

She gave him an **amused** smile. 그녀는 그에게 즐거워하는 미소를 지었다.
We were all **amused** by his funny dance. 우리는 모두 그의 재미있는 춤에 즐거워했다.

167 **entertain**
[èntərtéin]
entertainment 명 연예, 오락(물)
entertainer 명 연예인

to amuse people
동 즐겁게 해 주다

The comedian **entertained** the audience. 그 코미디언은 관객들을 즐겁게 했다.
His jokes always **entertain** people. 그의 농담은 항상 사람들을 즐겁게 한다.

168 **entertaining**
[èntərtéiniŋ]

interesting and amusing
형 재미있는, 즐거움을 주는

The movie was very **entertaining**. 그 영화는 매우 재미있었다.
an **entertaining** circus show 즐거운 서커스 쇼

169 **pure** [pjuər]

purely 부 순전히; 전적으로
purity 명 순수; 깨끗함

not mixed with anything else
형 1. 순수한 2. 맑은, 깨끗한 반 impure 불순물이 섞인, 더러운

a ring made of **pure** gold 순금으로 만들어진 반지
a bottle of **pure** water 깨끗한 물 한 병

170 **interest** [íntərəst]

interested 형 관심 있는, 흥미 있는
interesting 형 흥미로운, 재미있는

the feeling of wanting to know more about something
명 1. 관심, 흥미 ((in)) 2. 관심사 동 관심을 끌다

He **has an interest in** art. 그는 예술에 관심이 있다.
a common **interest** 공통의 관심사
Politics doesn't **interest** me. 정치는 내 관심을 끌지 못한다(관심사가 아니다).

171 **pride** [praid]

a feeling that you are proud of something
명 1. 자랑스러움, 자부심 2. 자존심; 자만심

I take **pride** in my work. 나는 내 일에 자부심을 가지고 있다.
He hurt my **pride**. 그는 내 자존심을 상하게 했다.

172 **proud** [praud]

feeling very pleased about something you have done; feeling pride
형 1. 자랑스러워하는, 자랑스러운 ((of)) 2. 거만한, 오만한

I feel **proud of** myself. 나는 나 자신이 자랑스럽다.
He is too **proud** to admit his mistake. 그는 자신의 실수를 인정하기에는 너무 오만하다.

173 **expose** [ikspóuz]

exposure 명 노출; 폭로

to show something that is usually hidden or covered
동 1. 드러내다, 노출시키다 2. 폭로하다 ((to)) = uncover

She **exposed** her emotions in the diary. 그녀는 일기에 자신의 감정을 드러냈다.
Don't **expose** your skin **to** the sun. 피부를 햇빛에 노출시키지 마세요.
expose a secret 비밀을 폭로하다

174 **reveal** [rivíːl]

to make something known to someone
동 (비밀 등을) 드러내 보이다, 밝히다 ((to)) = disclose

She **revealed** her secret **to** her best friend. 그녀는 절친에게 자신의 비밀을 털어놓았다.

175 **prefer** [prifə́ːr]

preference 명 선호

to like one thing better than another
동 (…보다) ~을 더 좋아하다, 선호하다 ((to))

Which do you **prefer**, this or that? 이것과 저것 중 어느 것을 더 좋아하니?
I **prefer** winter **to** summer. 나는 여름보다 겨울을 더 좋아한다.

176 **rather** [rǽðər]

to some degree
부 1. 꽤, 약간, 상당히 2. 오히려, 차라리

It's **rather** cold outside. 밖이 꽤 춥다.
I would **rather** stay home today. 나는 오늘 차라리 집에 있겠다.

177 **attitude**
[ǽtitjùːd]

the way that you think and feel about something

명 태도, 자세

He has a positive **attitude** toward life. 그는 삶에 대해 긍정적인 태도를 가지고 있다.

178 **position**
[pəzíʃən]

pose 동 포즈를 취하다 명 포즈, 자세

the place where someone or something is located

명 1. (자리 잡고 있는) 위치 2. (몸의) 자세 3. 입장, 처지 4. 직책 *location 장소

The **position** of the sun changes each day. 태양의 위치는 매일 달라진다.
fall asleep in a sitting **position** 앉은 자세로 잠이 들다
He is in a very difficult **position**. 그는 아주 어려운 입장에 처해 있다.
apply for a manager **position** 관리직에 지원하다

179 **be in the mood for[to]**

to feel like

~하고 싶다, ~할 기분이다

I'm in the mood for dancing. 나는 춤추고 싶은 기분이다.
She **is** not **in the mood to** talk now. 그녀는 지금 말할 기분이 아니다.

180 **have (an) interest in / lose interest in**

to be interested in / to no longer be interested in

~에 관심이 있다 / ~에 흥미를 잃다

She **has an interest in** science. 그녀는 과학에 관심이 있다.
Soon, she **lost interest in** her studies. 곧 그녀는 학업에 흥미를 잃었다.

Check Up

A 우리말에 맞게 빈칸에 알맞은 말을 넣으세요.

1. 기분이 좋다 — be in a good ____________
2. 깨끗한 물 한 병 — a bottle of ____________ water
3. 자존심을 상하게 하다 — hurt one's ____________
4. 비밀을 폭로하다 — ____________ a secret
5. 긍정적인 태도 — a positive ____________
6. 음악에 관심이 있다 — have an ____________ in music

B 우리말에 알맞은 말을 골라 문장을 완성하세요.

1. The children were (**amazed / amazing**) by the fireworks. 아이들은 불꽃놀이에 감탄했다.
2. The movie was very (**entertaining / entertained**). 그 영화는 매우 재미있었다.
3. I take (**pride / proud**) in my work. 나는 내 일에 자부심을 가지고 있다.
4. I feel (**pride / proud**) of myself. 나는 나 자신이 자랑스럽다.
5. I would (**rather / prefer**) stay home today. 나는 오늘 차라리 집에 있겠다.

Build Up

A Write the correct word for each definition.

amazed | proud | position | entertain | pure | prefer

1. 

very surprised

____

2. 

to amuse people

____

3. 

not mixed with anything else

____

4. 

feeling pride

____

5. 

to like one thing better than another

____

6. 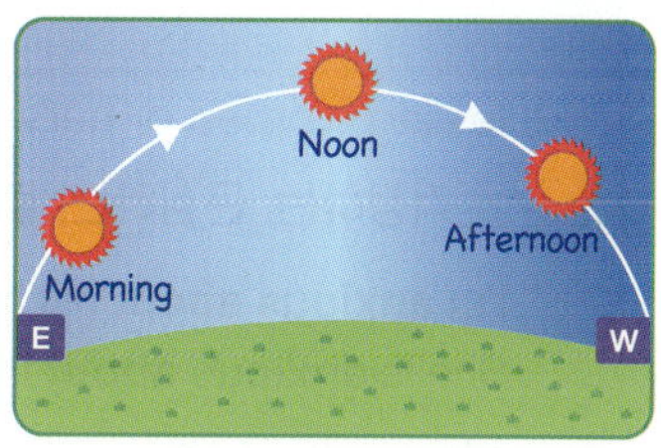

the place where something is located

____

B Write the correct word or phrase next to each definition.

amaze | amuse | emotional | have (an) interest in | expose | attitude

1. relating to emotions ________________
2. to surprise someone very much ________________
3. to make someone laugh or smile ________________
4. to show something that is usually hidden or covered ________________
5. the way that you think and feel about something ________________
6. to be interested in ________________

181 **fascinate**
[fǽsənèit]
fascination 명 매혹, 매료(됨)

to attract or interest someone very much
동 마음을 사로잡다, 매혹하다, 매료시키다

Alaska has always **fascinated** me. 알래스카는 항상 내 마음을 사로잡아 왔다.
Dolphins **fascinate** her. 돌고래는 그녀를 매료시킨다.

182 **fascinated**
[fǽsənèitid]
fascinating 형 마음을 사로잡는, 매혹적인

extremely interested
형 마음을 빼앗긴, 매료된

I was **fascinated** by his voice. 나는 그의 목소리에 마음을 빼앗겼다.
The children were **fascinated** by the game. 아이들은 그 게임에 매료되었다.

183 **refresh**
[rifréʃ]
refreshed 형 상쾌해진
refreshing 형 상쾌하게 하는

to make someone feel less tired or less hot
동 생기를 되찾게 하다, 상쾌하게 하다 *fresh 신선한, 상쾌한

The long sleep **refreshed** her. 긴 잠을 자고 나니 그녀는 생기를 되찾았다.
A shower will **refresh** you. 샤워를 하면 상쾌해질 거야.

184 **recharge**
[riːtʃɑ́ːrdʒ]
rechargeable 형 재충전되는

to fill a battery with electricity
동 1. (전기를) 재충전하다 2. (휴식으로) 재충전하다 유 charge 충전하다

recharge the phone battery 휴대폰 배터리를 재충전하다
She took a trip to **recharge** her batteries. 그녀는 재충전을 위해 여행을 갔다.

185 **anxious**
[ǽŋkʃəs]

feeling worried or nervous
형 걱정하는, 근심하는, 불안해하는 ((about))

I'm **anxious about** his health. 나는 그의 건강이 걱정된다.
She is **anxious about** the interview. 그녀는 면접에 대해 불안해하고 있다.

186 **anxiety**
[æŋzáiəti]

the feeling of being very worried
명 걱정, 불안(감) ((about))

I have **anxiety about** his health. 나는 그의 건강이 걱정된다.
She felt **anxiety about** her future. 그녀는 자신의 미래에 대해 불안감을 느꼈다.

187 **concern**
[kənsə́ːrn]

a feeling of worry, usually shared by many people
명 1. 우려, 걱정 ((about/for)) 2. 관심사 동 1. 걱정시키다 2. 관련이 있다

concern about the environment 환경에 대한 우려
our main **concern** 우리의 주된 관심사
What **concerns** you the most? 당신이 가장 걱정하는 것은 무엇인가요?
The problem **concerns** us all. 그 문제는 우리 모두와 관련이 있다(영향을 미친다).

188 **concerned**
[kənsə́ːrnd]

worried about something
형 1. 걱정하는, 염려하는 ((about/for)) 2. 관련이 있는, 관심이 있는 ((with))

I am **concerned about** climate change. 나는 기후 변화에 대해 걱정한다.
The problem is **concerned with** the environment. 그 문제는 환경과 관련이 있다.

189 **confuse**
[kənfjúːz]

to make someone uncertain (or unable to understand)
동 1. 혼란스럽게 하다 2. 혼동하다 ((confuse A with B))

Her explanation **confused** me. 그녀의 설명이 나를 혼란스럽게 했다.
I **confused** him **with** his brother. 나는 그를 그의 형과 혼동했다.

190 **confused**
[kənfjúːzd]

confusing 형 혼란스럽게 하는

unable to understand or think clearly
형 혼란스러운, 헷갈리는 ((about))

a **confused** look 혼란스러운 표정
I'm **confused about** what to do next. 나는 다음에 무엇을 해야 할지 혼란스럽다.

191 **depress**
[diprés]

depression 명 우울증, 우울함; 불경기

to make someone feel sad or unhappy
동 우울하게 하다

Stress can **depress** your mood. 스트레스는 기분을 우울하게 할 수 있다.
The sad news **depressed** everyone. 그 슬픈 소식이 모두를 우울하게 했다.

192 **depressed**
[diprést]

depressing 형 우울하게 만드는

very sad and unhappy
형 1. 우울한, 의기소침한 2. 불경기의

He felt **depressed** after failing the exam. 그는 시험에 실패한 후 우울함을 느꼈다.
a **depressed** market 침체된 시장

193 **fright**
[frait]

a sudden feeling of shock and fear
명 (섬뜩하게) 놀람, 공포

cry out **in fright** 놀라서 비명을 지르다
She was shaking **with fright**. 그녀는 놀라서 떨고 있었다.

194 **frighten**
[fráitn]

frightened 형 겁먹은, 두려워하는
frightening 형 무서운, 겁나는

to make someone feel afraid
동 깜짝 놀라게 하다, 겁먹게 하다

You **frightened** me. Don't do that again. 깜짝 놀랐잖아. 다시는 그러지 마.
I was **frightened** by the scream. 나는 비명 소리에 깜짝 놀랐다.

195 **satisfy**
[sǽtisfài]

satisfied 형 만족한, 만족해하는
satisfying 형 만족시키는, 만족스러운
satisfaction 명 만족(감), 충족

to make someone pleased by doing what they want
동 만족시키다, (요구 등을) 충족시키다 ((with))

His explanation **satisfied** everyone. 그의 설명은 모두를 만족시켰다.
He was **satisfied with** his exam results. 그는 시험 결과에 만족했다.
The meal didn't **satisfy** my hunger. 그 식사는 나의 배고픔을 충족시키지 못했다.

196 **disappoint**
[dìsəpɔ́int]

disappointed 형 실망한
disappointing 형 실망스러운
disappointment 명 실망

to make someone feel unhappy; to let down
동 실망시키다; [수동형으로] 실망하다 ((with/at/about))

I didn't want to **disappoint** you. 나는 너를 실망시키고 싶지 않았다.
We are **disappointed with** the food. 우리는 그 음식에 실망했다.

197 **annoy**
[ənɔ́i]

annoyed 형 짜증이 난
annoying 형 짜증 나게 하는

to make someone slightly angry
동 짜증 나게 하다, 귀찮게 하다

Her stupid questions **annoyed** me. 그녀의 바보 같은 질문들이 나를 짜증 나게 했다.
Stop **annoying** me. 짜증 나게 하지 마. / 귀찮게 하지 마.

198 **frustrate**
[frʌ́streit]

frustrated 형 좌절감을 느끼는
frustrating 형 좌절감을 주는
frustration 명 좌절

to make someone feel angry, disappointed, or discouraged
동 좌절감을 주다, 좌절시키다

She felt **frustrated** with the results. 그녀는 그 결과에 좌절감을 느꼈다.
Their plan was **frustrated** by bad weather. 그들의 계획은 악천후로 좌절되었다.

199 **get over**

to overcome
1. (곤란을) 극복하다 2. (병 등에서) 회복하다

She never **got over** the shock. 그녀는 결코 그 충격에서 벗어나지 못했다.
how to **get over** a cold quickly 감기에서 빨리 낫는 방법

200 **be concerned with**

to be interested in; to relate to
1. ~에 관심이 있다 2. ~와 관련되다 *be concerned about ~에 대해 걱정하다

They **are** not **concerned with** the issue. 그들은 그 문제에 대해 관심이 없다.
This documentary **is concerned with** climate change.
이 다큐멘터리는 기후 변화에 관한 것이다.

Check Up

A 우리말에 맞게 빈칸에 알맞은 말을 넣으세요.

1. 휴대폰 배터리를 재충전하다 ____________ the phone battery
2. 환경에 대한 우려[걱정] ____________ about the environment
3. 혼란스러운 표정 a ____________ look
4. 침체된 시장 a ____________ market
5. 놀라서 비명을 지르다 cry out in ____________
6. 감기에서 빨리 낫는 방법 how to ____________ a cold quickly

B 우리말에 알맞은 말을 골라 문장을 완성하세요.

1. Alaska has always (fascinate / fascinated) me. 알래스카는 항상 내 마음을 사로잡아 왔다.
2. I'm (anxious / anxiety) about his health. 나는 그의 건강이 걱정된다.
3. I am (concern / concerned) about climate change. 나는 기후 변화에 대해 걱정한다.
4. We are (disappointing / disappointed) with the food. 우리는 그 음식에 실망했다.
5. She felt (frustrating / frustrated) with the results. 그녀는 그 결과에 좌절감을 느꼈다.

Build Up

A Write the correct word for each definition.

recharge
refresh
satisfy
frighten
confused
anxious

1. 

to make someone feel less tired

____

2. 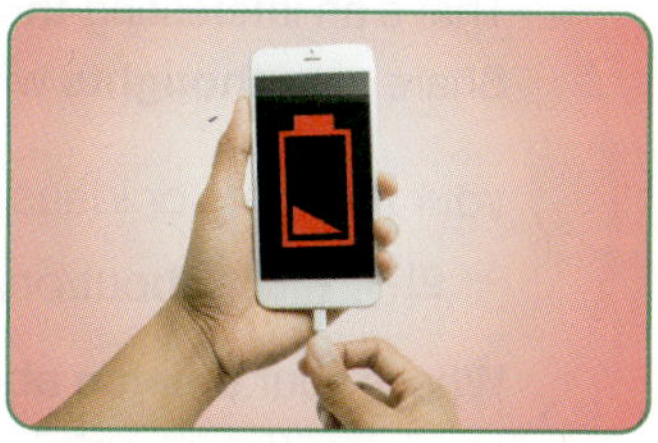

to fill a battery with electricity

____

3. 

feeling worried or nervous

____

4. 

unable to understand or think clearly

____

5. 

to make someone pleased

____

6. 

to make someone feel afraid

____

B Write the correct word or phrase next to each definition.

disappoint	annoy	concern	fascinate	confuse	get over

1. to attract or interest someone very much ______________
2. a feeling of worry, usually shared by many people ______________
3. to make someone uncertain or unable to understand ______________
4. to make someone feel unhappy; to let down ______________
5. to make someone slightly angry ______________
6. to overcome ______________

201 **thought** [θɔːt]
think 동 생각하다

something that you think of
명 생각, 의견 = idea; opinion

That's an interesting **thought**. 그거 흥미로운 생각이다.
Share your **thoughts** with others. 너의 생각을 다른 사람들과 공유해라.

202 **opinion** [əpínjən]

your thoughts or ideas about something
명 의견, 견해 ((about/on/of)) = view

What's your **opinion about** the matter? 그 문제에 대해 당신의 의견은 무엇인가요?
I have a different **opinion on** the issue. 나는 그 문제에 대해 다른 견해를 갖고 있다.
in my **opinion** 내 생각에는

203 **comment** [kάment]

something that you say or write to give your opinion
명 논평, 의견 동 논평하다, 견해를 밝히다 ((about/on))

He made a **comment about** the movie. 그는 그 영화에 대해 논평했다.
No **comment**. 드릴 말씀이 없습니다. / 노코멘트 하겠습니다.
I don't want to **comment on** it. 나는 그것에 대해 논평하고 싶지 않다.

204 **theory** [θíːəri]
theoretical 형 이론의, 이론적인

an idea or set of ideas that are suggested to explain something
명 이론, 학설

He tried to prove the **theory**. 그는 그 이론을 증명하려고 노력했다.

205 **pretty** [príti]

to some extent
부 꽤, 제법 = fairly 형 예쁜

His comment was **pretty** impressive. 그의 논평은 꽤 인상적이었다.
It's **pretty** cold today. 오늘은 꽤 춥다.

206 **quite** [kwait]

to a great degree
부 상당히, 꽤, 매우 = very; really

The exam was **quite** difficult. 그 시험은 상당히 어려웠다.
The news was **quite** a shock. 그 뉴스는 꽤 충격적이었다.

207 **aware** [əwɛ́ər]
awareness 명 인식, 의식

knowing or realizing something; conscious of something
형 1. 알고 있는, 인식하고 있는 2. 알아차린 ((of)) 반 unaware 눈치채지 못하는

I am **aware of** the rules of the game. 나는 그 게임의 규칙을 알고 있다.
They were **aware of** the noise outside. 그들은 밖의 소음을 알아차렸다.

208 **conscious** [kάnʃəs]
consciousness 명 의식, 자각

noticing or realizing something
형 1. 의식하는, 알고 있는 ((of)) 2. 의식이 있는
반 unconscious 의식하지 못하는; 의식이 없는

They were **conscious of** the noise outside. 그들은 밖의 소음을 의식하고 있었다.
The patient is not **conscious** yet. 그 환자는 아직 의식이 없다.

209 **remind**
[rimáind]
reminder 명 상기시키는 것

to help someone remember something
동 상기시키다, 생각나게 하다 ((remind A of B))

Remind me to buy some eggs. 계란을 사야 한다고 내게 상기시켜 줘.
This song **reminds** me **of** my childhood. 이 노래는 내 어린 시절을 생각나게 한다.

210 **recall**
[rikɔ́:l]

to remember something
동 1. 기억해 내다, 상기하다 2. 생각나게 하다

She could not **recall** his name. 그녀는 그의 이름이 기억나지 않았다.
I can still **recall** our last summer. 나는 아직도 우리의 지난 여름을 기억한다.
His paintings **recall** the style of Picasso. 그의 그림은 피카소 스타일을 생각나게 한다.

211 **unlike**
[ənláik]

different from someone or something
전 1. ~와 다른 2. ~답지 않은 3. ~와 달리 반 like ~와 비슷한, ~처럼

His work is **unlike** other paintings. 그의 작품은 다른 그림들과는 다르다.
It's **unlike** him to be so late. 그렇게 늦는 것은 그답지 않다.
Unlike her, Liz is very shy. 그녀와 달리 리즈는 아주 수줍음이 많다.

212 **likely**
[láikli]

probably going to happen; expected
형 1. ~할 것 같은 ((to)) 2. 있을 법한, 그럴듯한 반 unlikely ~할 것 같지 않은

She is **likely to** arrive late. 그녀는 늦게 도착할 것 같다.
the most **likely** cause of the delay 지연의 가장 그럴듯한 이유

213 **consider**
[kənsídər]
consideration 명 사려, 고려; 배려

to think about something carefully
동 1. 잘 생각하다, 숙고하다 2. ~로 여기다[생각하다] 3. 고려하다

We're **considering** buy**ing** a new car. 우리는 새 차 구입을 생각 중이다.
He is **considered** an expert. 그는 전문가로 여겨진다.
You should **consider** other people. 너는 다른 사람들을 고려해야 한다.

214 **considerable**
[kənsídərəbl]

large in size, amount, or degree
형 상당한, 많은

spend a **considerable** amount of money 상당한 금액의 돈을 쓰다
The storm caused **considerable** damage. 그 폭풍은 많은 피해를 입혔다.

215 **steady**
[stédi]

happening at a gradual, regular rate
형 1. 꾸준한 2. 변함없는, 고정적인

The model is a **steady** seller. 그 모델은 꾸준히 잘 팔린다(스테디셀러이다).
a **steady** income 고정적인 수입
Slow and **steady** wins the race. 느려도 꾸준히 하면 경주에서 이긴다.

216 **stable**
[stéibl]

firmly fixed; not likely to move, change, or fail
형 1. 안정된, 안정적인 2. 견고한 반 unstable 불안정한

Gas prices are **stable**. 가솔린 가격(유가)은 안정적이다.
The chair doesn't look very **stable**. 그 의자는 별로 견고해 보이지 않는다.

217 **comfort**

[kʌ́mfərt]

comfortable ⓗ 편안한, 안락한

the state of being relaxed and free from pain

명 1. 안락, 편안함 2. 위로, 위안 동 위로하다, 위안하다

a **comfort** chair 편안한 의자, 안락의자

What's your **comfort** food? 당신에게 위안이 되는 음식(소울푸드)은 무엇입니까?

She tried to **comfort** her friend. 그녀는 친구를 위로하려 애썼다.

218 **awkward**

[ɔ́:kwərd]

making you feel embarrassed

형 1. 어색한, 불편한 2. 곤란한

There was an **awkward** silence. 어색한 침묵이 감돌았다.

Don't ask **awkward** questions. 곤란한 질문들은 하지 마라.

219 **remind A of B**

to make A think of B

A에게 B를 떠올리게 하다[생각나게 하다]

Her smile **reminds** me **of** her mother. 그녀의 미소는 내게 그녀의 어머니를 떠올리게 한다.

The smell of fresh cookies **reminded** her **of** home.
갓 구운 쿠키의 냄새가 그녀에게 집을 생각나게 했다.

220 **be aware of**

to be conscious of

~을 알고 있다, ~을 눈치채고 있다

We **are** well **aware of** the rules. 우리는 그 규칙을 잘 알고 있다.

He **was** not **aware of** the change at first. 그는 처음에는 변화를 눈치채지 못했다.

Check Up

A 우리말에 맞게 빈칸에 알맞은 말을 넣으세요.

1. 논평하다 — make a ____________
2. 규칙을 알고 있다 — be ____________ of the rules
3. 상당한 금액의 돈을 쓰다 — spend a ____________ amount of money
4. 꾸준히 잘 팔리는 제품 — a ____________ seller
5. 편안한 의자, 안락의자 — a ____________ chair
6. 어색한 침묵 — an ____________ silence

B 우리말에 알맞은 말을 골라 문장을 완성하세요.

1. I have a different (opinion / theory) on the issue. 나는 그 문제에 대해 다른 견해를 갖고 있다.
2. We were (conscious / consider) of the noise outside. 우리는 밖의 소음을 의식하고 있었다.
3. This song (recalls / reminds) me of my childhood. 이 노래는 내 어린 시절을 생각나게 한다.
4. It's (like / unlike) him to be so late. 그렇게 늦는 것은 그답지 않다.
5. We're (considering / considered) buying a new car. 우리는 새 차 구입을 생각 중이다.

Build Up

A Write the correct word for each definition.

steady	aware	opinion	recall	comfort	consider

1. 

your thoughts or ideas

____

2. 

knowing or realizing something

____

3. 

to remember something

____

4. 

to think about something carefully

____

5. 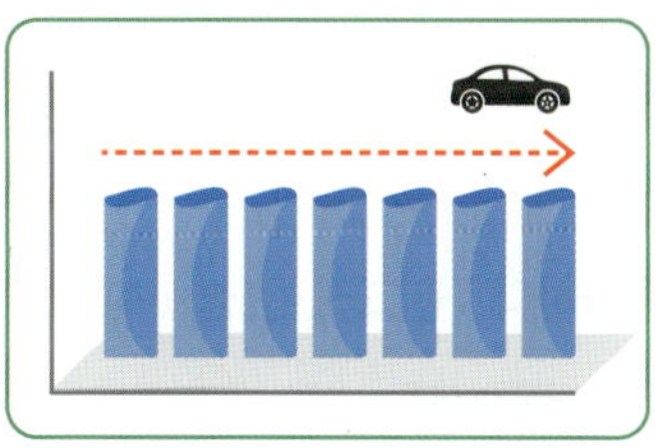

happening at a gradual, regular rate

____

6. 

the state of being relaxed

____

B Write the correct word or phrase next to each definition.

quite	stable	considerable	thought	remind A of B	awkward

1. something that you think of ______________
2. to a great degree ______________
3. large in size, amount, or degree ______________
4. firmly fixed; not likely to move, change, or fail ______________
5. making you feel embarrassed ______________
6. to make A think of B ______________

221 **believe**
[bilí:v]
believer 명 믿는 사람, 신자

to accept something as true
동 1. 믿다 2. (~라고) 생각하다[여기다]
Don't **believe** everything you read. 네가 읽는 것을 모두 다 믿지는 마라.
I **believed** (that) he was honest. 나는 그가 정직하다고 생각했다.

222 **belief**
[bilí:f]

a strong feeling (that) something is true or real
명 믿음, 신념 ((in)) 반 disbelief 불신(감)
He has a firm **belief in** success. 그는 성공에 대한 확고한 믿음을 가지고 있다.
religious **beliefs** 종교적 신념

223 **faith**
[feiθ]
faithful 형 충실한, 믿을 수 있는

a strong belief or trust (in someone or something)
명 1. 믿음, 신뢰 2. 신념 3. 신앙(심) ((in)) 반 unfaith 불신
I have great **faith in** him. 나는 그를 굉장히 신뢰한다.
She lost her **faith in** God. 그녀는 신앙심을 잃었다.

224 **trust**
[trʌst]
trustworthy 형 신뢰할 수 있는

the belief (that) someone or something is good or honest
명 신뢰, 신임 동 1. 신뢰하다 2. (무엇이 옳다고) 믿다 반 distrust 불신; 불신하다
a lack of **trust** among members 멤버들 간의 신뢰 부족
I can't **trust** you anymore. 나는 더 이상 너를 신뢰할 수 없다.
Do you **trust** the news? 너는 그 뉴스를 믿니?

225 **regard**
[rigá:rd]

to think about someone or something in a particular way
동 1. (~로) 여기다, 간주하다 ((as)) 2. 평가하다 명 고려, 관심 ((to))
She **regards** him **as** a mentor. 그녀는 그를 멘토로 여긴다.
They **regarded** his opinion highly. 그들은 그의 의견을 높이 평가했다.
With **regard to** the matter, I have a question. 그 문제와 관련하여 질문이 있습니다.

226 **regardless**
[rigá:rdlis]

without being affected by something
부 상관없이, 개의치 않고 ((of))
We will go hiking **regardless of** the weather. 우리는 날씨에 상관없이 하이킹을 갈 것이다.

227 **vision**
[víʒən]

the ability to see
명 1. 시력 = sight 2. 전망, 비전, 통찰력
have good **vision** 좋은 시력을 갖고 있다, (미래에 대한) 좋은 비전을 가지고 있다
He has a clear **vision** for the future. 그는 미래에 대한 명확한 비전을 가지고 있다.

228 **visual**
[víʒuəl]

relating to seeing
형 (눈으로) 보는, 시각의, 시각적인
The movie has dramatic **visual** effects. 그 영화는 극적인 시각 효과를 가지고 있다.
They use **visual** aids in class. 그들은 수업 시간에 시각 자료를 사용한다.

229 **suppose**
[səpóuz]

to think (that) something is true or possible
동 1. 추측하다, 생각하다 유 guess 추측하다 2. 가정하다

I **suppose** (that) she is late. 내 생각에 그녀는 늦을 것 같다.
Suppose we miss the train, what should we do? 기차를 놓친다면, 우리는 어떻게 해야 할까?

230 **assume**
[əsúːm]

to think (that) something is true, although you have no proof
동 추정하다, 가정하다

I **assumed** (that) she was coming to the party. 나는 그녀가 파티에 올 거라고 생각했다.
Let's **assume** the plan succeeds. 그 계획이 성공한다고 가정해 보자.

231 **decide**
[disáid]

to make a choice to do something
동 결정하다, 결심하다 ((to))

She **decided to** take the job. 그녀는 그 일을 맡기로 결정했다.
I haven't **decided** yet. 나는 아직 결정을 못했어.

232 **decision**
[disíʒən]
decisive 형 결정적인; 결단력 있는

a choice you make about something
명 결정, 판단

make a **decision** 결정하다
It was the right **decision**. 그것은 옳은 결정이었다.

233 **regret**
[rigrét]
regretful 형 후회하는, 유감스런

to feel sorry about something you have done
동 후회하다 명 후회, 유감

I don't **regret** my decision. 나는 내 결정을 후회하지 않는다.
He has no **regrets** about leaving the city. 그는 그 도시를 떠난 것에 대해 후회가 없다.

234 **moment**
[móumənt]

a very short period of time
명 1. 잠깐, 잠시 2. (특정한) 순간, 시점

I thought for a **moment**. 나는 잠시 생각했다.
I won't regret a **moment**. 나는 한 순간도 후회하지 않을 것이다.
That was the best **moment** of my life. 그것은 내 인생 최고의 순간이었다.

235 **grateful**
[gréitfəl]

feeling or showing thanks
형 감사하는, 고맙게 여기는 ((for)) = thankful

I'm really **grateful for** your help. 도와주셔서 정말 감사드립니다.

236 **jealous**
[dʒéləs]
jealousy 명 질투(심)

feeling unhappy because you want something that someone else has
형 질투하는, 시기하는, 시샘하는 ((of)) 유 envious 부러워하는

feel **jealous** 질투를 느끼다
He was **jealous of** my success. 그는 나의 성공을 시기했다.
I'm **jealous of** your new car. 나는 네 새 차가 부럽다.

237 **admire**

[ædmáiər]

admiration 명 존경, 감탄
admirable 형 존경[감탄]스러운

to respect someone

동 1. 존경하다 2. 감탄하며 바라보다

I really **admire** your courage. 나는 당신의 용기를 정말 존경합니다.
She **admired** the beautiful painting. 그녀는 그 아름다운 그림을 감탄하며 바라봤다.

238 **appreciate**

[əprí:ʃièit]

appreciation 명 감상; 감사

to recognize the worth of something

동 1. (진가를) 알아보다, 인정하다 2. 감사하다

No one **appreciated** the value of the work. 아무도 그 작품의 가치를 알아보지 못했다.
I really **appreciate** your help. 도와주셔서 정말 감사드립니다.

239 **be supposed to**

to be expected to do something

~하기로 되어 있다, ~해야 한다

I **am supposed to** meet him today. 나는 오늘 그를 만나기로 되어 있다.
You **were supposed to** be here by 12:00. 너는 12시까지 여기 왔어야 했다.
You **are** not **supposed to** smoke in here. 여기서 담배를 피우면 안 됩니다.

240 **decide to**

to make a decision

~하기로 결심하다[결정하다]

She **decided to** tell the truth. 그녀는 진실을 말하기로 결심했다.
I have **decided** not **to** take the job. 나는 그 일을 맡지 않기로 결정했다.

Check Up

A 우리말에 맞게 빈칸에 알맞은 말을 넣으세요.

1. 성공에 대한 확고한 믿음 — a firm ______________ in success
2. 그 문제와 관련하여 — with ______________ to the matter
3. 좋은 시력을 갖고 있다 — have good ______________
4. 극적인 시각 효과 — dramatic ______________ effects
5. 결정하다 — make a ______________
6. 질투를 느끼다 — feel ______________

B 우리말에 알맞은 말을 골라 문장을 완성하세요.

1. I can't (trust / faith) you anymore. 나는 더 이상 너를 신뢰할 수 없다.
2. We will go hiking (regard / regardless) of the weather. 우리는 날씨에 상관없이 하이킹을 갈 것이다.
3. I haven't (decide / decided) yet. 나는 아직 결정을 못했어.
4. I really (grateful / appreciate) your help. 도와주셔서 정말 감사드립니다.
5. I am (suppose / supposed) to meet him today. 나는 오늘 그를 만나기로 되어 있다.

Build Up

A Write the correct word for each definition.

1. 

to accept something as true

____

2. 

to make a choice

____

3. 

to feel sorry about something you have done

____

4. 

a very short period of time

____

5. 

feeling or showing thanks

____

6. 

to respect someone

____

believe
regret
decide
grateful
admire
moment

B Write the correct word or phrase next to each definition.

decide to	regardless	faith	appreciate	assume	be supposed to

1. a strong belief or trust (in someone or something) ____________________
2. without being affected by something ____________________
3. to make a decision ____________________
4. to be expected to do something ____________________
5. to recognize the worth of something ____________________
6. to think (that) something is true, although you have no proof ____________________

Review Test 03 DAY 09-12

A 그림을 보고, 빈칸에 알맞은 단어를 넣으세요.

consider position anxious amused admire recall

1. 

____

2. 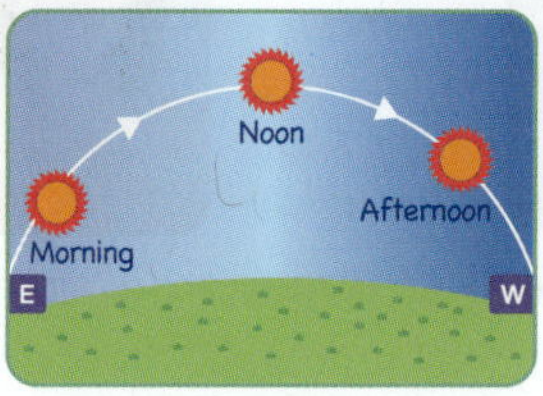

____

3. 

____

4. 

____

5. 

____

6. 

____

B 그림에 알맞은 문장을 골라 표시하세요.

1. 

- ☐ The fireworks frightened the children.
- ☐ The fireworks amazed the children.

2. 

- ☐ She has an interest in science.
- ☐ She lost interest in science.

3. 

- ☐ The chair looks quite stable.
- ☐ The chair looks pretty unstable.

4. 

- ☐ You don't need to recharge your batteries.
- ☐ The phone battery is recharging.

C 우리말 뜻에 맞게 빈칸에 알맞은 말을 넣으세요.

interest	mood	pure	depressed
regardless of	steady	decision	get over

1. be in a good ________________ 기분이 좋다
2. a bottle of ________________ water 깨끗한 물 한 병
3. have a common ________________ 공통의 관심사를 가지다
4. feel ________________ (기분이) 우울하다
5. ________________ a shock 충격을 극복하다
6. a ________________ seller 꾸준히 잘 팔리는 제품
7. ________________ the weather 날씨에 상관없이
8. make a ________________ 결정하다

D 우리말 뜻에 맞게 빈칸에 알맞은 말을 넣으세요.

proud of	confused ~ with	supposed to	rather	prefer ~ to	reminds ~ of

1. I feel ________________ myself. 나는 나 자신이 자랑스럽다.
2. I ____________ winter ____________ summer. 나는 여름보다 겨울을 더 좋아한다.
3. I ____________ him ____________ his brother. 나는 그를 그의 형과 혼동했다.
4. I would ________________ stay home today. 나는 오늘 차라리 집에 있겠다.
5. This song ____________ me ____________ my childhood. 이 노래는 내 어린 시절을 생각나게 한다.
6. I am ________________ meet him today. 나는 오늘 그를 만나기로 되어 있다.

E 밑줄 친 단어와 비슷한 뜻을 가진 단어를 고르세요.

1. She <u>exposed</u> her emotions in the diary.

   a. covered　　b. revealed　　c. closed

2. I am <u>concerned</u> about climate change.

   a. worried　　b. interested　　c. annoyed

3. The exam was <u>quite</u> difficult.

   a. slightly　　b. a little　　c. very

4. They were <u>conscious</u> of the noise outside.

   a. anxious　　b. concerned　　c. aware

F 밑줄 친 단어와 반대의 뜻을 가진 단어를 고르세요.

1. He was <u>satisfied</u> with his exam results.

   a. frustrated　　b. disappointed　　c. depressed

2. She is <u>likely</u> to arrive late.

   a. supposed　　b. assumed　　c. unlikely

3. There was an <u>awkward</u> silence.

   a. confused　　b. comfort　　c. comfortable

4. The movie was very <u>entertaining</u>.

   a. disappointing　　b. boring　　c. bored

G 주어진 영영풀이에 알맞은 단어를 고르세요.

1. the way that you think and feel about something

   a. position　　b. quality　　c. attitude

2. to make someone feel less tired or less hot

   a. charge　　b. fresh　　c. refresh

3. a feeling of worry, usually shared by many people

   a. concern　　b. anxiety　　c. theory

4. unable to understand or think clearly

   a. concerned　　b. confused　　c. depressed

5. to make someone feel unhappy; to let down

   a. assume　　b. disappoint　　c. frustrate

6. to feel sorry about something you have done

   a. remind　　b. recall　　c. regret

H 빈칸에 알맞은 동사 형태를 넣어 문장을 완성하세요.

1. Alaska has always ________________ me. (fascinate)
2. She felt ________________ with the results. (frustrate)
3. They were ________________ by the scream. (frighten)
4. We're ________________ buying a new car. (consider)

241 **communicate**
[kəmjúːnəkèit]

to exchange information or have a conversation with others
동 1. 의사소통을 하다, 연락하다 2. 전하다, 전달하다

We **communicate** mostly by email. 우리는 주로 이메일로 연락한다.
He **communicated** his idea clearly to them.
그는 그들에게 자신의 아이디어를 명확하게 전달했다.

242 **communication**
[kəmjùːnəkéiʃən]

the act of communicating with other people
명 1. 의사소통 2. 전달, 보도 3. 통신

He has good **communication** skills. 그는 훌륭한 의사소통 능력을 가지고 있다.
mass **communication** 대중 전달, 매스컴
communication system 통신 체계

243 **mention**
[ménʃən]

to speak or write about something (or someone) briefly
동 (간단히) 언급하다, 거론하다 명 언급, 거론

He **mentioned** nothing about it. 그는 그것에 대해 아무것도 언급하지 않았다.
make a **mention** 언급하다

244 **remark**
[rimáːrk]

to say or write a comment about something (or someone)
동 언급하다, 발언하다, 논평하다 ((on)) 명 발언, 언급

He **remarked on** the new design of the website.
그는 그 웹사이트의 새 디자인에 대해 언급했다.
make a funny **remark** 재미있는 발언을 하다

245 **vocabulary**
[voukǽbjulèri]

all the words in a particular language
명 어휘, 어휘력 유 word 단어

Reading will increase your **vocabulary**. 독서는 너의 어휘력을 키울 것이다.

246 **accent**
[ǽksent]

the way that someone speaks, showing where he or she comes from
명 1. 말투, 억양 2. (단어의) 강세 3. 강조, 역점 ((on)) = emphasis

She has a strong British **accent**. 그녀는 강한 영국 억양을 가지고 있다.
The new design put an **accent on** simplicity. 그 새 디자인은 단순함에 역점을 두었다.

247 **pronounce**
[prənáuns]

to make the sound of a letter or word
동 발음하다

How do you **pronounce** this word? 이 단어는 어떻게 발음하나요?
The "k" in "know" is not **pronounced**. 'know'의 'k'는 발음되지 않는다.

248 **pronunciation**
[prənʌ̀nsiéiʃən]

how words are pronounced
명 발음

Your **pronunciation** is excellent. 너의 발음은 아주 훌륭하다.

249 **phrase**
[freiz]

a group of words that are often used together
명 구; 문구, 구절 *sentence 문장 *idiom 숙어, 관용구

What does this **phrase** mean? 이 구절은 무슨 의미인가요?

250 **proverb**
[právəːrb]

a famous phrase or sentence that gives you advice
명 속담, 격언 = saying

an old Korean **proverb** 옛날 한국 속담
My favorite **proverb** is "Better late than never."
내가 좋아하는 속담은 '늦더라도 안 하는 것보다는 낫다'이다.

251 **term**
[təːrm]

a word or phrase that is used to mean a particular thing
명 1. 용어 2. 학기 = (미) semester 3. (일정한) 기간, 기한

a scientific **term** 과학 용어
The school **term** starts next week. 학교 학기는 다음 주에 시작된다.
In the long **term**, it's very useful. 장기적으로 (보면) 그것은 매우 유용하다.

252 **clearly**
[klíərli]

clear 형 분명한; 맑은

in a clear manner
부 1. 또렷하게 2. 명확히, 알기 쉽게

Please speak more **clearly**. 좀 더 또렷하게 말씀해 주세요.
He explained the term very **clearly**. 그는 그 용어를 아주 명확히 설명해 주었다.

253 **define**
[difáin]

definition 명 (단어·개념의) 정의, 의미

to say exactly what something means
동 1. (단어의 뜻을) 정의하다 2. 규정하다, 분명히 밝히다

The term is difficult to **define**. 그 용어는 정의하기가 어렵다.
We need to **define** the task clearly. 우리는 그 작업을 명확히 규정할 필요가 있다.

254 **definite**
[défənit]

definitely 부 분명히, 확실히

sure or certain
형 명확한, 확실한

We need a **definite** answer by tomorrow. 우리는 내일까지 명확한 답이 필요하다.
Let's fix a **definite** date. 확실한 날짜를 정하자.

255 **significant**
[signífikənt]

significantly 부 상당히, 의미심장하게

important or noticeable
형 중요한, 의미 있는 = meaningful

make a **significant** discovery 중요한 발견을 하다
He gave me a **significant** smile. 그는 내게 의미심장한 미소를 지었다.

256 **gesture**
[dʒéstʃər]

a movement you make with your body (to show a feeling or message)
명 1. 몸짓, 제스처 2. (감정·의사의) 표현, 표시 동 제스처를 하다 ((to))

make a friendly **gesture** 다정한 제스처를 취하다
I bowed deeply **in a gesture of** respect. 나는 존경의 표시로 고개를 깊이 숙여 인사했다.
She **gestured** for us **to** follow her. 그녀는 우리에게 자신을 따라오라는 제스처를 했다.

257 **envelope**
[énvəlòup]

a flat paper container used for sending letters in
명 (편지) 봉투
writing paper and **envelopes** 편지지와 편지 봉투

258 **stamp**
[stæmp]

a small piece of paper (that) you stick on an envelope
명 1. 우표 2. 도장, 스탬프
She put a **stamp** on the envelope. 그녀는 봉투에 우표를 붙였다.
Make sure to get a **stamp** on your ticket. 네 표에 스탬프 받는 것 잊지 마.

259 **be likely to / be unlikely to**

to probably will / to probably won't
~할 것 같다 / ~할 것 같지 않다
It'**s likely to** rain tomorrow. 내일 비가 올 것 같다.
She **is unlikely to** arrive early. 그녀는 일찍 도착할 것 같지 않다.

260 **be willing to**

to be prepared or open to do something
기꺼이 ~하다, ~할 의향이 있다
I'**m willing to** help you. 저는 기꺼이 당신을 도와드리겠습니다.
They **are willing to** volunteer for the event. 그들은 그 행사에 자원봉사할 의향이 있다.

Check Up

A 우리말에 맞게 빈칸에 알맞은 말을 넣으세요.

1. 대중 전달, 매스컴 — mass ________________
2. 재미있는 발언을 하다 — make a funny ________________
3. 강한 영국 억양을 가지고 있다 — have a strong British ________________
4. 옛날 한국 속담 — an old Korean ________________
5. 확실한 날짜를 정하다 — fix a ________________ date
6. 다정한 제스처를 취하다 — make a friendly ________________

B 우리말에 알맞은 말을 골라 문장을 완성하세요.

1. We (communicate / communication) mostly by email. 우리는 주로 이메일로 연락한다.
2. Your (pronounce / pronunciation) is excellent. 너의 발음은 아주 훌륭하다.
3. The term is difficult to (define / definite). 그 용어는 정의하기가 어렵다.
4. It's (likely / unlikely) to rain tomorrow. 내일 비가 올 것 같지 않다.
5. I'm (will / willing) to help you. 저는 기꺼이 당신을 도와드리겠습니다.

Build Up

A Write the correct word for each definition.

gesture	vocabulary	communication	envelope	significant	stamp

1. 

the act of communicating with others

____

2. 

all the words in a language

____

3. 

a movement you make with your body

____

4. 

important or noticeable

____

5. 

a flat paper container
used for sending letters in

____

6. 

a small piece of paper
you stick on an envelope

____

B Write the correct word or phrase next to each definition.

pronounce	phrase	mention	definite	be likely to	proverb

1. to speak or write about something (or someone) briefly ______________________
2. to make the sound of a letter or word ______________________
3. a group of words that are often used together ______________________
4. a famous phrase or sentence that gives you advice ______________________
5. sure or certain ______________________
6. to probably will ______________________

261 **praise**
[preiz]

to say that someone or something is very good
동 칭찬하다 명 칭찬, 찬사, 찬양 ((for))

The coach **praised** the team **for** their hard work. 코치는 팀의 노고를 칭찬했다.
She was **praised** by her teacher. 그녀는 선생님에게 칭찬받았다.
songs of **praise** 찬송가

262 **blame**
[bleim]

to say that a person or thing is responsible for (something bad)
동 비난하다, ~을 탓하다 ((for)) 명 책임, 탓 ((on))

Don't **blame** me. 나를 탓하지 마.
He **blamed** his bad luck **for** losing the game. 그는 경기에 진 것을 불운 탓으로 돌렸다.
Don't put the **blame on** me. 내게 책임을 돌리지 마.

263 **punish**
[pʌ́niʃ]
punishment 명 벌, 처벌

to make someone suffer (because they have done something wrong)
동 처벌하다, 벌주다 ((for))

She was **punished for** breaking the rules. 그녀는 규칙을 어겨서 벌을 받았다.

264 **complain**
[kəmpléin]
complaint 명 불평, 항의

to say that you are unhappy or not satisfied (about something)
동 불평하다, 항의하다 ((about/to))

She **complained about** the punishment. 그녀는 그 처벌에 대해 불평했다.
They **complained to** the manager **about** the poor service.
그들은 매니저에게 형편없는 서비스에 대해 항의했다.

265 **accept**
[æksépt]
acceptance 명 받아들임, 수락

to take or receive something that is offered
동 1. (기꺼이) 받아들이다 2. (동의하여) 수락하다, 인정하다

She didn't **accept** his invitation. 그녀는 그의 초대를 받아들이지 않았다.
They **accepted** the court's decision. 그들은 법원의 결정을 받아들였다.

266 **refuse**
[rifjúːz]
refusal 명 거절, 거부

to say that you will not do or accept something
동 (요청·부탁 등을) 거절하다, 거부하다

She **refused** the offer. 그녀는 그 제안을 거절했다.
They **refused** him a visa. 그들은 그의 비자 발급을 거부했다.

267 **reject**
[ridʒékt]
rejection 명 거부, 거절

to refuse to accept something
동 (주장·요구·제안 등을) 거부하다, 받아들이지 않다

His offer was **rejected**. 그의 제안은 받아들여지지 않았다.

268 **deny**
[dinái]
denial 명 부인; 거부

to say that something is not true
동 1. 부인하다 2. 거부하다, 허락하지 않다

He **denied** taking the money. 그는 돈을 가져간 것을 부인했다.
He was **denied** access to the data. 그는 그 데이터에 대한 접근을 거부당했다.

269 **admit**
[ædmít]

to agree unwillingly that something is true
동 1. 인정하다, 시인하다 2. (입장 등을) 허락하다 반 deny 부인하다, 거부하다

He **admitted** all his mistakes. 그는 자신의 모든 실수를 인정했다.
Only members are **admitted** to the club. 회원들만 그 클럽에 입장할 수 있다.

270 **admission**
[ædmíʃən]

the act of agreeing that something is true
명 1. 시인, 인정 ((of)) 2. 가입, 입장, 입학 3. 입장료

make an **admission of** failure 실패를 인정하다
No **admission** after 10:00 PM. 오후 10시 이후에는 입장 불가.
What's the **admission**? 입장료가 얼마인가요?

271 **oppose**
[əpóuz]
opposition 명 반대

to disagree with a plan or activity and try to stop it
동 (계획·정책 등에) 반대하다 반 agree 동의하다

They strongly **opposed** the plan. 그들은 강력히 그 계획에 반대했다.

272 **resist**
[rizíst]
resistance 명 저항, 저항력

to refuse to accept or be changed by something
동 1. 저항하다, 대항하다 2. (열·손상 등에) 강하다 3. 참다, 견디다

People often **resist** change. 사람들은 흔히 변화에 저항한다.
This paint can **resist** heat and moisture. 이 페인트는 열과 습기에 강하다.
I just can't **resist** chocolate. 나는 초콜릿이라면 참지를 못한다.

273 **suggest**
[səgdʒést]
suggestion 명 제안; 시사

to tell someone your ideas about what they should do
동 1. 제안하다 = propose 2. 추천하다 = recommend 3. 시사하다, 암시하다 = hint

She **suggested** going out to eat. 그녀는 외식을 하자고 제안했다.
Can you **suggest** a nice restaurant? 좋은 식당을 추천해 주시겠어요?
As the name **suggests**, it's a French restaurant. 이름에서 알 수 있듯이, 이곳은 프랑스 식당이다.

274 **recommend**
[rèkəménd]
recommendation 명 추천; 권고

to tell someone that something is good or useful
동 1. 추천하다 2. 권(장)하다 유 advise 조언하다

recommend a good movie 좋은 영화를 추천하다
I **recommend** (that) he see a doctor. 나는 그가 진찰을 받아 보기를 권합니다.

275 **propose**
[prəpóuz]

to suggest a plan or action
동 1. 제안하다 2. 청혼하다 ((to))

propose a new project 새 프로젝트를 제안하다
He **proposed to** her on her birthday. 그는 그녀의 생일에 그녀에게 청혼했다.

276 **proposal**
[prəpóuzəl]

a formal suggestion or plan
명 1. 제안, 제의 2. 청혼, 프러포즈

His **proposal** was not accepted. 그의 제안은 받아들여지지 않았다.
make a **proposal** 제안을 하다, 청혼을 하다

277 **contract**
[kɑ́ntrækt]

an official agreement

명 계약(서) 동 [kəntrǽkt] 계약하다 ((with)) *agreement 협정, 동의

sign a **contract** 계약서에 서명하다, 계약을 하다

He **contracted with** the agency for a one-year term. 그는 그 에이전시와 1년 계약을 했다.

278 **signature**
[sígnətʃər]

sign 동 서명하다

a person's name written in that person's handwriting

명 1. 서명 2. 특징

Please put your **signature** here. 여기에 서명해 주세요.

the chef's **signature** dish 그 셰프의 대표(특징적인) 요리

279 **put off (V-ing)**

to delay doing something

미루다, 연기하다

He **put off** signing the contract. 그는 계약서에 서명하는 것을 미루었다.

They **put off** the meeting until next week. 그들은 회의를 다음 주로 연기했다.

280 **make up one's mind**

to decide to

결심하다, 마음을 정하다

I **made up my mind** to refuse the proposal. 나는 그 제안을 거절하기로 결심했다.

He **made up his mind** to leave. 그는 떠나기로 마음먹었다.

Check Up

A 우리말에 맞게 빈칸에 알맞은 말을 넣으세요.

1. ~에게 책임을 돌리다, ~ 탓을 하다 put the ________________ on
2. 실패를 인정하다 make an ________________ of failure
3. 좋은 영화를 추천하다 ________________ a good movie
4. 제안을 하다, 청혼을 하다 make a ________________
5. 계약서에 서명하다, 계약을 하다 sign a ________________
6. 결심하다, 마음을 정하다 ________________ one's mind

B 우리말에 알맞은 말을 골라 문장을 완성하세요.

1. She was (blamed / punished) for breaking the rules. 그녀는 규칙을 어겨서 벌을 받았다.
2. She (accepted / refused) the offer. 그녀는 그 제안을 거절했다.
3. He (admitted / denied) all his mistakes. 그는 자신의 모든 실수를 인정했다.
4. They strongly (opposed / proposed) the plan. 그들은 강력히 그 계획에 반대했다.
5. I just can't (reject / resist) chocolate. 나는 초콜릿이라면 참지를 못한다.

Build Up

A Write the correct word for each definition.

complain
accept
praise
contract
punish
reject

1. 

to say that someone is very good

____

2. 

to make someone suffer

____

3. 

to say that you are not satisfied

____

4. 

to take or receive something

____

5. 

to refuse to accept

____

6. 

an official agreement

____

B Write the correct word or phrase next to each definition.

oppose	deny	propose	blame	put off	signature

1. to say that a person or thing is responsible for (something bad) __________
2. to say that something is not true __________
3. to disagree with a plan or activity and try to stop it __________
4. to suggest a plan or action __________
5. a person's name written in that person's handwriting __________
6. to delay doing something __________

DAY 15

281 **discuss**
[diskʌ́s]

to talk about something with someone
동 논의하다, 토론하다 ((with))

Have you **discussed** the problem **with** anyone? 그 문제를 누구와 논의해 봤니?
This issue will be **discussed** at the meeting. 이 문제는 회의에서 논의될 것이다.

282 **discussion**
[diskʌ́ʃən]

the act of discussing something
명 논의, 토의, 토론 ((about))

have a **discussion about** the proposal 그 제안에 대해 논의하다
The **discussion** lasted for over an hour. 그 토의는 한 시간 넘게 계속되었다.

283 **debate**
[dibéit]

to discuss a subject formally
동 토론하다, 논쟁하다 명 토론, 논쟁

They **debated** the issue openly. 그들은 그 문제에 대해 공개적으로 토론했다.
a heated **debate** 열띤 논쟁

284 **argue**
[ɑ́ːrgjuː]

argument 명 언쟁, 말다툼

to speak angrily to someone (because you disagree with them)
동 1. 언쟁을 하다, 말다툼을 하다 ((with)) 2. 주장하다

They're always **arguing with** each other about money. 그들은 항상 돈 문제로 서로 다툰다.
He **argued** (that) he needed a car. 그는 차가 필요하다고 주장했다.

285 **insist**
[insíst]

to say firmly that something is true
동 주장하다, 우기다, 고집하다

Chris **insisted** (that) he was right. 크리스는 자신이 옳다고 주장했다.
He **insisted** I should take a taxi. 그는 내가 택시를 타야 한다고 우겼다.

286 **claim**
[kleim]

to say that something is true, even though it has not been proved
동 1. 주장하다 2. 요구하다, 청구하다 명 1. 주장 2. 청구 ((for))

He **claimed** (that) the dog attacked him. 그는 그 개가 자신을 공격했다고 주장했다.
a **claim for** damages 손해 배상 청구

287 **demonstrate**
[démənstrèit]

demonstration 명 설명; 입증; 시위

to show or prove something clearly
동 1. 증명하다 = prove 2. (사용법을) 설명하다, 보여 주다 3. 시위[데모]를 하다

It **demonstrates** (that) our plan is working. 그것은 우리의 계획이 효과가 있음을 증명한다.
demonstrate how to use the new software 새 소프트웨어 사용법을 보여 주다
demonstrate against a war 전쟁 반대 시위를 하다

288 **criticize**
[krítəsàiz]

critical 형 비판적인
criticism 명 비난, 비판; 비평

to say that someone or something is bad
동 1. 비난[비판]하다 ((for)) 반 praise 칭찬하다 2. 비평하다

She **criticized** him **for** his behavior. 그녀는 그의 행동을 비난했다.
criticize a poem 시를 비평하다

289 **context** [kántekst]

the parts of a text that help to understand its meaning

명 1. (글의) 문맥 2. (어떤 일의) 정황, 맥락

Guess the meaning from the **context**. 문맥에서 의미를 추측해 보세요.
from the historical **context** 역사적 맥락에서 볼 때

290 **content** [kántent]

the things that are contained in something

명 1. 속에 든 것들, 내용물 2. 목차 형 [kəntént] 만족하는

The **contents** of the box were surprising. 그 상자의 내용물은 놀라웠다.
online **content** providers 온라인 콘텐츠 제공 회사들
a table of **contents** (책의) 목차
feel **content** 만족감을 느끼다

291 **translate** [trænsléit]

to change written or spoken words into another language

동 번역하다, 통역하다 ((into))

Her books have been **translated into** 28 languages. 그녀의 책들은 28개 언어로 번역되었다.

292 **translator** [trænsléitər]

translation 명 번역, 번역물

a person who translates from one language into another

명 1. 번역가, 통역가 2. 번역기

He works as a freelance **translator**. 그는 프리랜서 번역가로 일한다.
use a **translator** 번역기를 사용하다

293 **interpret** [intə́ːrprit]

interpretation 명 통역; 해석

to translate spoken words from one language into another

동 1. 통역하다 2. 해석하다, 이해하다 ((as))

He couldn't speak English, so I **interpreted** for him.
그는 영어를 할 수 없어서 내가 통역을 했다.
I **interpreted** his silence **as** a positive sign. 나는 그의 침묵을 긍정적인 신호로 해석했다.

294 **interpreter** [intə́ːrpritər]

someone who changes spoken words from one language into another

명 통역사

She works as an **interpreter**. 그녀는 통역사로 일한다.
a sign language **interpreter** 수화 통역사

295 **particular** [pərtíkjulər]

particularly 부 특히, 특별히

special or single

형 특정한, 특별한 *certain 어떤, 특정한

Is there a **particular** city you want to visit? 너는 방문하고 싶은 특정한 도시가 있니?
pay **particular** attention 특히 주의하다, 특별히 신경 쓰다

296 **specific** [spəsífik]

specifically 부 특별히; 구체적으로

connected with one particular thing only

형 1. 특정한 = particular 2. 구체적인, 명확한

Do you prefer a **specific** brand of shoes? 너는 특정 브랜드의 신발을 선호하니?
provide **specific** guidelines 구체적인 지침을 제공하다

297 **bet**
[bet]

to risk money on the result of a race or game **(bet–bet)**
동 1. (내기 등에) 돈을 걸다 2. 장담하다 명 내기, 내기 돈

He **bet** $50 on the game. 그는 그 게임에 50달러를 걸었다.
I **bet** he'll lose the **bet** again. 나는 그가 내기에서 또 질 거라고 장담한다.
win a **bet** / lose a **bet** 내기에서 이기다 / 내기에서 지다

298 **slightly**
[sláitli]

slight 형 약간의, 조금의

a little; a bit
부 약간, 다소, 조금

The result was **slightly** lower than expected. 결과는 예상보다 약간 낮았다.
It **slightly** missed the target. 그것은 과녁을 살짝 빗나갔다.

299 **be content with**

to be happy with; to be satisfied with
~에 만족하다

She **is content with** her job. 그녀는 자신의 일에 만족한다.
He **was** not **content with** living in the city. 그는 도시에서 사는 것에 만족하지 않았다.

300 **insist on**

to keep doing something, even if it annoys other people
~을 고집하다, ~을 주장하다

He **insisted on** coming with us. 그는 우리와 함께 가겠다고 우겼다.
He **insisted on** having a meeting about the issue. 그는 그 문제에 대해 회의를 하자고 주장했다.

Check Up

A 우리말에 맞게 빈칸에 알맞은 말을 넣으세요.

1. ~에 대해 논의하다 — have a ______________ about
2. 손해 배상 청구 — a ______________ for damages
3. 소프트웨어 사용법을 보여 주다[설명하다] — ______________ how to use the software
4. 시를 비평하다 — ______________ a poem
5. 번역기를 사용하다 — use a ______________
6. 구체적인 지침을 제공하다 — provide ______________ guidelines

B 우리말에 알맞은 말을 골라 문장을 완성하세요.

1. They (**debated** / **argued**) the issue openly. 그들은 그 문제에 대해 공개적으로 토론했다.
2. They're always (**discussing** / **arguing**) with each other. 그들은 항상 서로 다툰다.
3. She works as an (**interpret** / **interpreter**). 그녀는 통역사로 일한다.
4. She is (**context** / **content**) with her job. 그녀는 자신의 일에 만족한다.
5. He (**insisted** / **claimed**) on coming with us. 그는 우리와 함께 가겠다고 우겼다.

Build Up

A Write the correct word for each definition.

translate	translator	argue	discuss	particular	context

1. 

to talk about something with someone

____

2. 

to speak angrily to someone

____

3. 

the parts of a text that help to understand its meaning

____

4. 

to change written or spoken words into another language

____

5. 

a person who translates

____

6. 

special or single

____

B Write the correct word or phrase next to each definition.

debate	content	bet	criticize	interpret	specific

1. to discuss a subject formally ______________________
2. to say that someone or something is bad ______________________
3. the things that are contained in something ______________________
4. to translate spoken words from one language into another ______________________
5. connected with one particular thing only ______________________
6. to risk money on the result of a race or game ______________________

DAY 16

301 **committee** [kəmíti]

a group of people who are chosen to do a particular job
명 위원회

the International **Committee** of the Red Cross 국제 적십자 위원회
The **committee** rejected the new proposal. 위원회는 그 새 제안을 거절했다.

302 **session** [séʃən]

a period of time used for a particular activity
명 1. (특정한 활동을 하는) 기간, 시간 2. (의회 등의) 회기, 회의

have a Q&A **session** 질의 응답 시간을 갖다
The committee is now **in session**. 위원회가 현재 개회 중이다.

303 **determine** [ditə́:rmin]
determination 명 결정

to officially decide something
동 1. (공식적으로) 결정하다, 확정하다 2. 파악하다, 밝히다

The committee will **determine** the new rules. 위원회가 새 규칙을 결정할 것이다.
determine the cause of an accident 사고의 원인을 밝히다

304 **confirm** [kənfə́:rm]
confirmation 명 확인, 확정

to say or show that something is true or correct
동 확인하다, 확정하다

He refused to **confirm** the news. 그는 그 뉴스를 확인해 주기를 거부했다.
confirm one's reservation 예약을 확인하다[확정하다]

305 **approve** [əprú:v]
approval 명 인정, 승인

to allow or officially agree to something
동 1. 승인하다 2. 찬성하다 ((of)) 반 disapprove 찬성하지 않다

The committee **approved** the budget. 위원회는 그 예산안을 승인했다.
I don't **approve of** smoking. 나는 흡연을 찬성하지 않는다.

306 **conclude** [kənklú:d]
conclusion 명 결론, 결말
conclusive 형 결정적인, 확실한

to decide something (after studying all the information about it)
동 1. 결론을 내리다 2. 끝내다; 끝나다 ((with))

The report **concluded** that the drug was safe. 그 보고서는 그 약이 안전하다는 결론을 내렸다.
The event **concluded with** a fireworks display. 그 행사는 불꽃놀이로 끝났다.

307 **conflict** [kánflikt]

a serious disagreement or argument
명 갈등, 충돌 동 [kənflíkt] 상충하다, 충돌하다 ((with))

a **conflict** between two cultures 두 문화 간의 충돌
These two ideas **conflict with** each other. 이 두 아이디어는 서로 상충한다.

308 **accuse** [əkjú:z]
accusation 명 비난; 고발

to say that someone has done something wrong
동 1. 비난하다 2. 고발하다, 고소하다 ((of))

She **accused** him **of** lying. 그녀는 그가 거짓말을 했다고 비난했다.
He was **accused of** stealing. 그는 도둑질을 한 혐의로 고발되었다.

309 **urge**
[əːrdʒ]

to strongly suggest (someone) to do something
동 (강력히) 권고하다, 촉구하다 ((to)) 명 (강한) 충동, 욕구 ((to))

They **urged** people **to** wear masks. 그들은 사람들에게 마스크를 쓰라고 촉구했다.
I felt a sudden **urge to** cry. 나는 갑자기 울고 싶은 충동을 느꼈다.

310 **urgent**
[ə́ːrdʒənt]

urgency 명 긴급, 절박함
urgently 부 긴급히

very important and needing to be dealt with immediately
형 긴급한, 다급한

receive an **urgent** call 긴급한 전화를 받다, 긴급 호출을 받다
Her voice sounded **urgent**. 그녀의 목소리는 다급하게 들렸다.

311 **desire**
[dizáiər]

desirable 형 바람직한
desirous 형 바라는, 원하는

a strong wish to have or do something
명 욕구, 갈망 ((for/to)) 동 원하다 ((to))

a **desire for** power 권력욕
a strong **desire to** win 이기고 싶은 강한 욕구
He **desires to** become a famous actor. 그는 유명한 배우가 되기를 원한다.

312 **eager**
[íːgər]

eagerness 명 간절함, 갈망

wanting to do or have something very much
형 갈망[열망]하는, 간절히 바라는 ((for/to)) = keen

eager for success 성공을 갈망하는
He is **eager to** become an actor. 그는 배우가 되기를 간절히 바란다.

313 **drive**
[draiv]

driver 명 운전자

to force someone to act in a particular way **(drove-driven)**
동 1. (~하게) 만들다, 몰아가다 ((to)) 2. 운전하다

His desire for success **drives** him **to** work hard.
성공에 대한 그의 갈망이 그를 열심히 일하게 만든다.

314 **force**
[fɔːrs]

forceful 형 강력한, 강압적인

to make someone do something (that they do not want to do)
동 억지로 ~을 시키다, 강요하다 ((to)) 명 1. 힘 2. 무력, 폭력

The manager **forced** him **to** work late. 매니저는 그가 늦게까지 일하도록 강요했다.
They used **force** to open the door. 그들은 문을 열기 위해 힘을 사용했다.
with the use of **force** 무력을 사용하여

315 **persuade**
[pərswéid]

persuasion 명 설득
persuasive 형 설득력 있는

to make someone do or believe something
동 1. (~하도록) 설득하다 ((to)) 2. 납득시키다

Try to **persuade** him **to** accept the proposal. 그 제안을 받아들이도록 그를 설득해 봐라.
It will be difficult to **persuade** him. 그를 납득시키기는 어려울 것이다.

316 **convince**
[kənvíns]

convincing 형 설득력 있는
convinced 형 확신하는

to make someone believe that something is true
동 1. 납득시키다, 확신시키다 2. 설득하다 ((to))

Convince him there is no other choice. 다른 선택이 없다는 것을 그에게 납득시켜라.
I **convinced** him **to** see a dentist. 나는 그가 치과에 가도록 설득했다.

317 **inspire**
[inspáiər]

inspiration 명 영감, 영감을 주는 것
inspirational 형 영감을 주는

to make someone feel that they want to do something

동 1. 고무하다, 격려하다 2. 영감을 주다 유 encourage 격려하다

Her courage has **inspired** us. 그녀의 용기는 우리를 고무시켰다.
His paintings were **inspired** by Monet's work. 그의 그림들은 모네의 작품으로부터 영감을 받은 것이다.

318 **generation**
[dʒènəréiʃən]

all the people who were born at about the same time

명 세대(비슷한 연령층), 대(代)

His speech inspired the younger **generation**. 그의 연설은 젊은 세대에게 영감을 주었다.
stories passed down from **generation** to **generation** 대대로 전해져 온 이야기들

319 **force (someone) to do (something)**

to make (someone) do (something) against their will

~에게 …하기를 강요하다

They **forced** him **to** sign the document. 그들은 그에게 문서에 서명하도록 강요했다.
The heavy rain **forced** us **to** cancel the picnic. 폭우로 인해 우리는 소풍을 취소할 수밖에 없었다.

320 **be forced to**

to have no choice but to do

~할 수밖에 없다

He **was forced to** sign the document. 그는 그 문서에 서명할 수밖에 없었다.
We **were forced to** cancel the picnic because of the weather.
우리는 날씨 때문에 소풍을 취소할 수밖에 없었다.

Check Up

A 우리말에 맞게 빈칸에 알맞은 말을 넣으세요.

1. 질의 응답 시간을 갖다 — have a Q&A ______________
2. 예약을 확인하다[확정하다] — ______________ one's reservation
3. 긴급한 전화를 받다, 긴급 호출을 받다 — receive an ______________ call
4. 성공을 갈망하는 — ______________ for success
5. 무력을 사용하여 — with the use of ______________
6. 대대로 전해 주다 — pass down from ______________ to ______________

B 우리말에 알맞은 말을 골라 문장을 완성하세요.

1. She (accused / approved) him of lying. 그녀는 그가 거짓말을 했다고 비난했다.
2. They (urgent / urged) people to wear masks. 그들은 사람들에게 마스크를 쓰라고 촉구했다.
3. Her courage has (inspired / persuaded) us. 그녀의 용기는 우리를 고무시켰다.
4. I (convinced / drove) him to see a dentist. 나는 그가 치과에 가도록 설득했다.
5. He (forced / was forced) to sign the document. 그는 그 문서에 서명할 수밖에 없었다.

Build Up

A Write the correct word for each definition.

desire	approve	conflict	urge	determine	force

1. 

to officially decide something

____

2. 

to allow or officially agree to something

____

3. 

a serious disagreement or argument

____

4. 

to strongly suggest someone to do something

____

5. 

a strong wish to have or do something

____

6. 

to make someone do something

____

B Write the correct word or phrase next to each definition.

persuade	generation	committee	eager	drive	conclude

1. a group of people who are chosen to do a particular job ______________________
2. to decide something (after studying all the information about it) ______________________
3. wanting to do or have something very much ______________________
4. to force someone to act in a particular way ______________________
5. to make someone do or believe something ______________________
6. all the people who were born at about the same time ______________________

Review Test 04 DAY 13-16

A 그림을 보고, 빈칸에 알맞은 단어를 넣으세요.

approve　signature　translator　envelope　contract　argue

1. 
____

2. 
____

3. 
____

4. 
____

5. 
____

6. 
____

B 그림에 알맞은 문장을 골라 표시하세요.

1. 

☐ She is likely to arrive early.
☐ She is unlikely to arrive early.

2. 

☐ No admission after 10:00 PM.
☐ Only members are admitted to the club.

3. 

☐ He is denying taking the money.
☐ They are accusing him of lying.

4. 

☐ He has a strong desire to win.
☐ He is eager to become a singer.

C 우리말 뜻에 맞게 빈칸에 알맞은 말을 넣으세요.

blame	accent	urgent	significant
conflict	confirm	make up	accused of

1. put an ______________ on ~에 역점을 두다
2. make a ______________ discovery 중요한 발견을 하다
3. put the ______________ on ~에게 책임을 돌리다
4. ______________ one's mind to leave 떠나기로 마음을 정하다
5. ______________ one's reservation 예약을 확인하다[확정하다]
6. a ______________ between two cultures 두 문화 간의 충돌
7. receive an ______________ call 긴급한 전화를 받다, 긴급 호출을 받다
8. be ______________ stealing 도둑질을 한 혐의로 고발당하다

D 우리말 뜻에 맞게 빈칸에 알맞은 말을 넣으세요.

content with	put off	willing to	insisted on	convinced ~ to	blamed ~ for

1. I'm ______________ help you. 저는 기꺼이 당신을 도와드리겠습니다.
2. He ______________ his bad luck __________ losing the game. 그는 경기에 진 것을 불운 탓으로 돌렸다.
3. He ______________ signing the contract. 그는 계약서에 서명하는 것을 미루었다.
4. He was not ______________ living in the city. 그는 도시에서 사는 것에 만족하지 않았다.
5. He ______________ coming with us. 그는 우리와 함께 가겠다고 우겼다.
6. I ______________ him __________ see a dentist. 나는 그가 치과에 가도록 설득했다.

E 밑줄 친 단어와 비슷한 뜻을 가진 단어를 고르세요.

1. We need a <u>definite</u> answer by tomorrow.

   a. certain　　b. particular　　c. rapid

2. He <u>proposed</u> a new project.

   a. hinted　　b. demonstrated　　c. suggested

3. They <u>debated</u> the issue openly.

   a. argued　　b. discussed　　c. remarked

4. Do you prefer a <u>specific</u> brand of shoes?

   a. popular　　b. significant　　c. particular

F 밑줄 친 단어와 반대의 뜻을 가진 단어를 고르세요.

1. She didn't <u>accept</u> his invitation.

   a. refuse　　b. resist　　c. recommend

2. He <u>admitted</u> all his mistakes.

   a. disagreed　　b. denied　　c. blamed

3. They strongly <u>opposed</u> the plan.

   a. agreed　　b. disagreed　　c. rejected

4. She <u>criticized</u> him for his behavior.

   a. blamed　　b. complained　　c. praised

G 주어진 영영풀이에 알맞은 단어를 고르세요.

1. to exchange information or have a conversation with others

   a. remark　　b. oppose　　c. communicate

2. a famous phrase or sentence that gives you advice

   a. term　　b. proverb　　c. pronunciation

3. a movement you make with your body (to show a feeling or message)

   a. admission　　b. gesture　　c. behavior

4. to make someone suffer (because they have done something wrong)

   a. punish　　b. blame　　c. resist

5. to officially decide something

   a. confirm　　b. recommend　　c. determine

6. to strongly suggest (someone) to do something

   a. conclude　　b. define　　c. urge

H 빈칸에 알맞은 동사 형태를 넣어 문장을 완성하세요.

1. She ________________ by her teacher yesterday. (praise)
2. Her books have been ________________ into 28 languages. (translate)
3. We ________________ to cancel the picnic because of the weather yesterday. (force)
4. Her courage has ________________ us. (inspire)

DAY 17

321 **recent**
[ríːsnt]

happening not long ago
형 최근의

a **recent** event 최근의 사건[일]
There have been many changes in **recent** years. 최근 몇 년 동안 많은 변화가 있었다.

322 **recently**
[ríːsntli]

not long ago
부 최근에 유 lately 최근에, 요즘

I received an email from him **recently**. 나는 최근에 그로부터 이메일을 받았다.
Recently, they had a baby. 최근에 그들은 아기를 낳았다.

323 **pregnant**
[prégnənt]
pregnancy 명 임신

having a baby developing inside the body
형 (사람·포유 동물이) 임신한

My wife is **pregnant**. 제 아내가 임신을 했어요.
She's six months **pregnant**. 그녀는 임신 6개월이에요.

324 **due**
[djuː]

expected to happen
형 1. ~하기로 되어 있는[예정된] 2. ~로 인한, ~ 때문에 ((to))

When is the baby **due**? 출산 예정일이 언제예요?
The report is **due** by the end of the week. 그 보고서는 주말까지 제출해야 한다.
due to bad weather 악천후로 인하여

325 **birth**
[bəːrθ]

the time when a baby is born; the process of being born
명 1. 탄생, 출생 반 death 죽음 2. 출산 *be born 태어나다

She **gave birth to** a baby boy last week. 그녀는 지난주에 아들을 낳았다.
Our country's **birth** rate has decreased. 우리 나라의 출산율이 감소했다.

326 **newborn**
[núːbɔrn]

recently born
형 갓 태어난 명 신생아 유 infant 갓난아기, 유아

a **newborn** baby 갓난아기

327 **breath**
[breθ]

the air that you take into your lungs and send out again
명 1. 호흡 2. 입김, 숨

She **took a** deep **breath**. 그녀는 숨을 한 번 깊이 들이쉬었다(심호흡을 했다).
bad **breath** 입내, 구취

328 **breathe**
[briːð]

to take air into your lungs and send it out again
동 숨을 쉬다, 호흡하다

breathe in / **breathe** out 숨을 들이쉬다 / 숨을 내쉬다
She **breathed** deeply before speaking. 그녀는 말을 하기 전에 심호흡을 했다.

329 **breed**
[bri:d]

to produce young animals **(bred-bred)**

동 1. (동물이) 새끼를 낳다, 번식하다 2. 사육하다, 번식시키다 유 raise 키우다, 기르다

Many animals **breed** in spring. 많은 동물들은 봄에 번식을 한다.
The dogs are **bred** for hunting. 그 개들은 사냥을 위해 사육된다.

330 **feed**
[fi:d]

to give food to a person or an animal **(fed-fed)**

동 밥을 먹이다, 먹이를 주다

Let's **feed** the children first. 먼저 아이들에게 밥을 먹입시다.
Have you **fed** the cat? 고양이에게 밥 줬니?

331 **chest**
[ʧest]

the front part of your body between your neck and waist

명 가슴, 흉부

a man with a broad **chest** and shoulders 넓은 가슴과 어깨를 가진 남자
I have **chest** pains. 나는 가슴 통증이 있다.

332 **breast**
[brest]

one of the two soft, round parts on a woman's chest

명 1. 가슴, 유방 2. (새·동물의) 가슴살 *breast-feeding 모유 수유

drink **breast** milk 모유를 먹다
She put the baby to her **breast** to feed. 그녀가 아기에게 젖을 물렸다.
chicken **breast** 닭 가슴살

333 **develop**
[divéləp]

development 명 발달, 성장; 개발

to gradually grow or become bigger

동 1. 성장[발달]하다; 성장[발달]시키다 2. 개발하다

The child is **developing** normally. 그 아이는 정상적으로 성장하고 있다.
The new software was **developed** by Samsung. 그 새 소프트웨어는 삼성에 의해 개발되었다.

334 **survive**
[sərváiv]

survival 명 생존
survivor 명 생존자

to continue to live or exist

동 1. 살아남다, 생존하다 2. (위기 등을) 견뎌 내다

He **survived** the car crash. 그는 그 자동차 충돌 사고에서 살아남았다.
The plant **survived** the harsh winter. 그 식물은 혹독한 겨울을 견뎌 냈다.

335 **absolute**
[ǽbsəlù:t]

complete and total

형 1. 완벽한, 완전한 2. 절대적인, 무제한의 반 relative 상대적인

a book for **absolute** beginners 완전 초보자들을 위한 책
absolute power 절대(적인) 권력
Her love for her family is **absolute**. 그녀의 가족에 대한 사랑은 절대적이다.

336 **absolutely**
[ǽbsəlu:tli]

completely; totally

부 1. 전적으로, 완전히 2. 전혀 (~ 않다)

I **absolutely** agree with you. 나는 전적으로 네게 동의한다.
He did **absolutely** no work. 그는 전혀 아무 일도 안 했다.

337 **either**
[íːðər]

one or the other of two (things or people)
대 (둘 중) 어느 하나 부 1. [부정문] ~도 또한 2. ~거나, ~든 ((or))

Either is fine with me. 나는 어느 쪽이든 좋다.
I don't eat meat, **either.** 나도 고기를 먹지 않는다.
You can choose **either** tea **or** coffee. 차나 커피 중에서 선택할 수 있다.

338 **neither**
[níːðər]

not one or the other of two (things or people)
대 (둘 중) 어느 것도 ~ 아니다 부 1. [부정문] ~도 또한 2. ~도 …도 아니다 ((nor))

Neither of us has a car. 우리 둘 다 차가 없다.
I don't eat meat, and **neither** does my sister. 나는 고기를 먹지 않고 내 누나도 그렇다.
I like **neither** coffee **nor** tea. 나는 커피도 차도 좋아하지 않는다.

339 **due to**

because of
~ 때문에, ~로 인해

Due to the storm, the flight was canceled. 폭풍우로 비행기가 취소되었다.
I was late **due to** heavy traffic. 나는 교통 체증 때문에 늦었다.

340 **according to**

as reported by someone or something
~에 따르면, ~에 따라서

According to the weather report, it will snow today. 일기 예보에 따르면 오늘 눈이 올 것이다.
Everything went **according to** plan. 모든 것이 계획대로 진행되었다.

Check Up

A 우리말에 맞게 빈칸에 알맞은 말을 넣으세요.

1. 악천후로 인하여 ________________ to bad weather
2. 아기를 낳다 give ________________ to a baby
3. 숨을 한 번 깊이 들이쉬다(심호흡을 하다) take a deep ________________
4. 모유를 먹다 drink ________________ milk
5. 완전 초보자들을 위한 책 a book for ________________ beginners
6. 일기 예보에 따르면 ________________ the weather report

B 우리말에 알맞은 말을 골라 문장을 완성하세요.

1. There have been many changes in (**recent** / **recently**) years. 최근 몇 년 동안 많은 변화가 있었다.
2. Many animals (**breed** / **breathe**) in spring. 많은 동물들은 봄에 번식을 한다.
3. The child is (**developing** / **developed**) normally. 그 아이는 정상적으로 성장하고 있다.
4. (**Either** / **Neither**) is fine with me. 나는 어느 쪽이든 좋다.
5. I like (**either** / **neither**) coffee nor tea. 나는 커피도 차도 좋아하지 않는다.

Build Up

A Write the correct word for each definition.

newborn	pregnant	feed	due	survive	develop

1. 

having a baby developing inside the body

____

2. 

expected to happen

____

3. 

recently born

____

4. 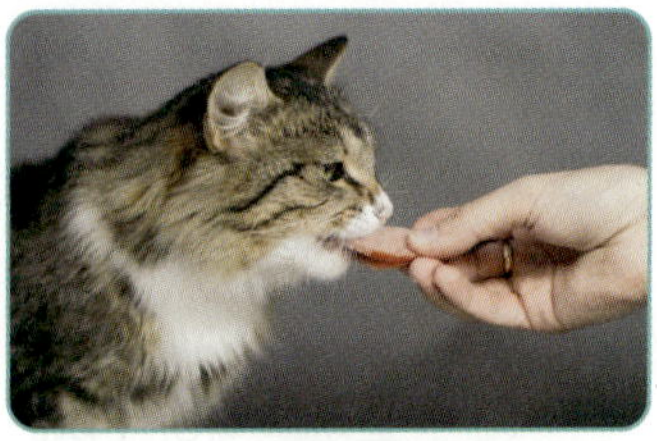

to give food

____

5. 

to gradually grow

____

6. 

to continue to live or exist

____

B Write the correct word or phrase next to each definition.

breed	absolute	birth	due to	chest	breathe

1. the time when a baby is born; the process of being born ______________
2. to take air into your lungs and send it out again ______________
3. the front part of your body between your neck and waist ______________
4. to produce young animals ______________
5. complete and total ______________
6. because of ______________

341 **medical**
[médikəl]
medicine 명 약, 의약품

related to the treatment of disease or injury
형 의학의, 의료의

study **medical** science 의학을 공부하다
He received **medical** treatment in the hospital. 그는 병원에서 (의료) 치료를 받았다.

342 **vital**
[váitl]

extremely important; essential
형 1. 필수적인, 극히 중요한 2. 생명의, 생명 유지에 필요한

A medical checkup is **vital** for your health. 건강 검진은 당신의 건강에 필수적이다.
check one's **vital** signs 생명 징후를 체크하다 *혈압/체온/호흡/맥박 등의 측정

343 **injury**
[índʒəri]

a wound or damage to someone's body (in an accident or attack)
명 (사고로 인한) 부상, 상해 ((to))

His leg **injury** was quite serious. 그의 다리 부상은 꽤 심각했다.
He had a serious **injury to** his leg. 그는 다리에 심한 부상[중상]을 입었다.

344 **injured**
[índʒərd]
injure 동 부상을 입다[입히다]

having an injury
형 1. 부상을 당한, 다친 2. (the injured) 부상자들

Luckily, she wasn't **injured**. 다행히 그녀는 다치지 않았다.
take **the injured** to a hospital 부상자들을 병원으로 옮기다

345 **wound**
[wuːnd]
wounded 형 부상을 입은, 다친

an injury, especially one (that is) made by a knife or bullet
명 (칼·총과 같은 흉기로 인한) 상처, 부상 동 상처[부상]를 입히다 ((in)) = injure

a leg **wound** 다리 부상
He was badly **wounded in** his leg during the war. 그는 전쟁 중에 다리에 심한 부상을 입었다.

346 **damage**
[dǽmidʒ]
damaged 형 손상을 입은

harm or injury
명 손상, 피해, 훼손 동 손상을 입히다, 피해를 주다 유 harm 해를 입히다; 해

cause severe **damage** 심한 손상을 초래하다
The fire badly **damaged** the building. 그 화재로 건물이 심하게 훼손되었다.

347 **blind**
[blaind]

not able to see
형 1. 눈이 먼, 맹인의 2. (the blind) 맹인들 동 눈이 멀게 만들다

Guide dogs help people who are **blind**. 안내견은 시각 장애인들을 돕는다.
She was **blinded** in a car crash. 그녀는 자동차 충돌 사고로 시력을 잃었다.

348 **deaf**
[def]

unable to hear or unable to hear very well
형 1. 귀가 먹은, 청각 장애가 있는 2. (the deaf) 청각 장애인들

go **deaf** / become **deaf** 귀가 먹게 되다, 청각을 잃다
Many **deaf** people use sign language. 많은 청각 장애인들은 수화를 사용한다.
a school for **the deaf** 청각 장애인들을 위한 학교

349 **cancer**
[kǽnsər]

a serious disease
명 암

get **cancer** 암에 걸리다
He died of **cancer** last month. 그는 지난달에 암으로 죽었다.

350 **flu**
[flu:]

an illness like a very bad cold that causes pains and fever
명 (흔히 the flu) 독감 유 cold 감기

I had **the flu** last week. 나는 지난주에 독감에 걸렸다.
The whole family has **the flu**. 가족 모두가 독감에 걸렸다(걸려 있다).

351 **prevent**
[privént]
prevention 명 예방, 방지

to stop someone doing something; to stop something from happening
동 1. 막다, 방해하다 ((from)) 2. 예방하다, 방지하다

The vaccine **prevents** the flu **from** spreading. 백신은 독감의 확산을 막는다.
prevent an accident 사고를 방지하다

352 **poison**
[pɔizn]
poisonous 형 유독한, 독(성)이 있는

a substance that can kill you if you eat or drink it
명 독, 독약 동 독을 넣다, 독살하다

a deadly **poison** 치명적인 독
He tried to **poison** the king. 그는 왕을 독살하려고 했다.

353 **scratch**
[skrætʃ]

to rub your skin with your nails
동 긁다, 할퀴다 명 긁힌 자국

Try not to **scratch**. 긁지 않도록 해라.
Don't worry; it's only a **scratch**. 걱정하지 마. 그냥 긁힌 것뿐이야.

354 **scream**
[skri:m]

to give a loud, high cry
동 비명을 지르다, 소리치다 명 비명 유 yell, shout 소리치다

She **screamed** with pain. 그녀는 고통으로 비명을 질렀다.
I thought I heard a **scream**. 나는 비명을 들은 것 같았다.

355 **suffer**
[sʌ́fər]
suffering 명 고통

to experience physical or mental pain
동 1. (질병 등에) 시달리다, 고통받다 ((from)) 2. (부상·고통 등을) 겪다

She often **suffers from** stress. 그녀는 종종 스트레스에 시달린다.
suffer a heart attack 심장 마비를 겪다

356 **operate**
[ápərèit]
operation 명 작동; 수술

to use and control a machine or make it work
동 1. (기계를) 가동[조작]하다; 가동[작동]되다 2. 수술하다 ((on))

The machine is **operating** smoothly. 기계는 원활하게 작동되고 있다.
The doctor will **operate on** him next week. 의사가 다음 주에 그를 수술할 것이다.

357 **recover**
[rikʌ́vər]
recovery 명 회복

to get well again after being sick, hurt, etc.
동 회복되다; 회복하다, 되찾다 ((from)) = get well, get over

He is still **recovering from** his operation. 그는 아직 수술에서 회복 중이다.
recover one's health 건강을 회복하다

358 **overcome**
[ouvərkʌ́m]

to succeed in dealing with a problem (overcame-overcome)
동 1. 극복하다, 이겨 내다 = get over 2. [수동형으로] ~에 압도당하다 ((with/by))

He finally **overcame** the illness. 그는 마침내 그 병을 이겨 냈다.
His parents were **overcome with** joy. 그의 부모님은 기쁨에 겨워하셨다.

359 **prevent A from V-ing**

to stop[keep] A from doing something
A가 ~하는 것을 막다

He **prevented** the fire **from** spreading. 그는 불길이 퍼지는 것을 막았다.
The snow **prevented** him **from** going out. 눈 때문에 그는 나갈 수가 없었다.

360 **pass away / die of**

to die
사망하다, 돌아가시다 / ~로 죽다

My grandmother **passed away** last year. 우리 할머니는 작년에 돌아가셨다.
She **died of** cancer. 그녀는 암으로 사망했다.

Check Up

A 우리말에 맞게 빈칸에 알맞은 말을 넣으세요.

1. 생명 징후를 체크하다 — check one's __________ signs
2. 귀가 먹게 되다, 청각을 잃다 — go __________
3. 암에 걸리다 — get __________
4. 사고를 방지하다 — __________ an accident
5. 치명적인 독 — a deadly __________
6. 암으로 죽다 — __________ cancer

B 우리말에 알맞은 말을 골라 문장을 완성하세요.

1. Luckily, she wasn't (**injury / injured**). 다행히 그녀는 다치지 않았다.
2. He was badly (**wound / wounded**) in his leg. 그는 다리에 심한 부상을 입었다.
3. The fire caused severe (**damage / damaged**) to the building. 그 화재는 건물에 심각한 피해를 주었다.
4. She was (**blinding / blinded**) in a car crash. 그녀는 자동차 충돌 사고로 시력을 잃었다.
5. The vaccine (**prevents / overcomes**) the flu from spreading. 백신은 독감의 확산을 막는다.

Build Up

A Write the correct word for each definition.

injury	scratch	medical	recover	scream	operate

1. 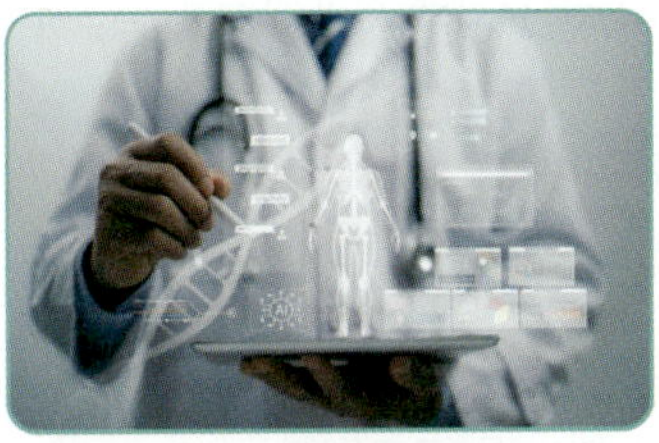

related to the treatment of disease

____

2. 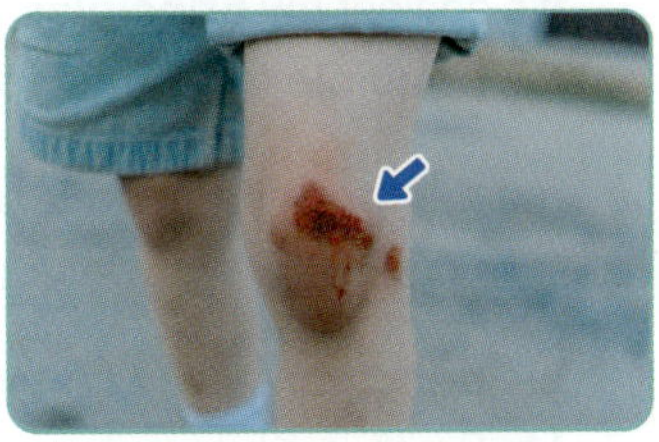

a wound or damage

____

3. 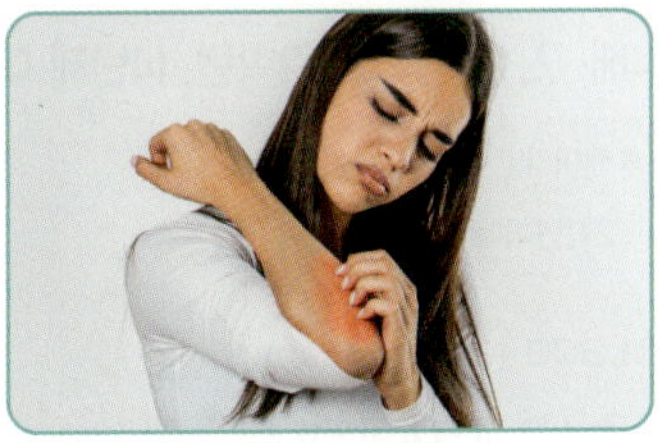

to rub your skin with your nails

____

4. 

to give a loud, high cry

____

5. 

to use and control a machine

____

6. 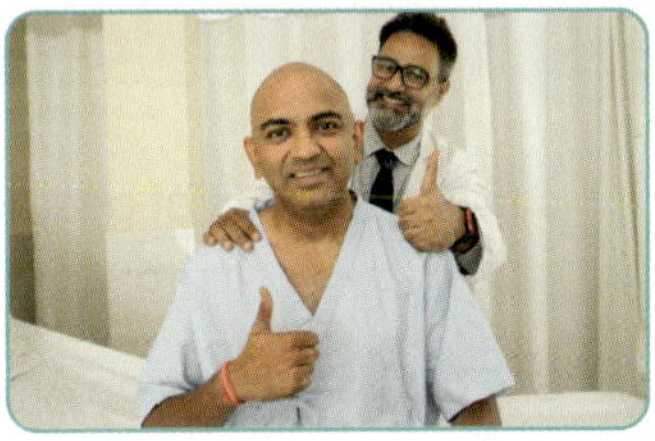

to get well again after being sick

____

B Write the correct word or phrase next to each definition.

the flu	pass away	vital	overcome	suffer	damage

1. extremely important; essential ________________
2. harm or injury ________________
3. an illness like a very bad cold that causes pains and fever ________________
4. to experience physical or mental pain ________________
5. to succeed in dealing with a problem ________________
6. to die ________________

DAY 19

361 **principle**
[prínsəpl]

a rule or belief that influences your behavior

명 1. (개인의) 신념, 원칙 2. (기본이 되는) 원리, 원칙 *discipline 규율, 훈육

It's against my **principles** to lie. 거짓말을 하는 것은 내 신념에 어긋난다.
the **principle** of writing reports 리포트 쓰기의 원칙

362 **principal**
[prínsəpəl]

most important; head teacher; chief

형 주요한, 주된 명 교장, (단체의) 장

the **principal** reason for the failure 실패의 주된 이유
Mr. Smith is a high school **principal**. 스미스 씨는 고등학교 교장이다.

363 **junior**
[dʒúːnjər]

low or lower in rank; younger in age

형 손아래의, 후배의 ((to)) 명 1. 손아랫사람, 후배 2. (고등학교) 2학년, (4년제 대학) 3학년

He is **junior to** me by a year. 그는 나보다 1년 후배이다.
She is a **junior** in high school. 그녀는 고등학교 2학년이다.

364 **senior**
[síːnjər]

having a higher position or rank; older in age

형 손위의, 선배의 ((to)) 명 1. 연장자, 선배 2. (고교·대학의) 상급생

a **senior** manager 선임 관리자
senior citizens 노인 시민들, 어르신들
high school **seniors** 고등학교 3학년(졸업반 학생들)

365 **lecture**
[léktʃər]

lecturer 명 강사, 강연자

a talk to a group of people about a subject

명 강의, 강연 동 강의하다 ((on)) 유 lesson 수업, 강습

She gave a **lecture on** American history. 그녀는 미국 역사에 대해 강의했다.
He **lectures on** modern art at the university. 그는 대학에서 현대 미술에 대해 강의한다.

366 **instruct**
[instrʌ́kt]

instruction 명 설명; 지시
instructor 명 강사

to teach or educate

동 1. 가르치다 2. 지시하다 유 order 지시하다

He **instructed** children on road safety. 그는 아이들에게 도로 안전에 대해 가르쳤다.
We were **instructed** to follow the safety rules. 우리는 안전 규칙을 따르라는 지시를 받았다.

367 **assign**
[əsáin]

assignment 명 과제, 임무, 배정

to give someone a particular job or responsibility

동 (일 등을) 맡기다, 부과하다, 배정하다 ((to))

The teacher **assigned** a task **to** us. 선생님은 우리에게 과제를 부과했다.
I was **assigned to** team B. 나는 B팀에 배정받았다.

368 **cope**
[koup]

to deal successfully with something difficult

동 대처하다, 대응하다 ((with))

I wasn't able to **cope with** stress. 나는 스트레스를 감당할 수 없었다.
It was hard to **cope with** the changes. 변화에 대처하기가 어려웠다.

369 **prime** [praim]

main; most important; excellent
형 1. 주된, 주요한 2. 최고의, 최상의

a **prime** issue 주요 문제, 가장 중요한 문제
a show on **prime**-time television 황금(주요) 시간대의 TV 프로
prime beef 최상급 쇠고기

370 **primary** [práimeri]

main; most important; most basic
형 1. 주된, 주요한 2. 최초의, 초기의

Our **primary** concern is safety. 우리의 주된 관심사는 안전이다.
the **primary** stage of the project 그 프로젝트의 초기 단계
primary school (영) 초등학교 = (미) elementary school

371 **purpose** [pə́ːrpəs]

the reason why something is done or used
명 1. 목적, 의도 ((of)) 2. (-s) 용도

What is the **purpose of** your visit? 당신의 방문 목적은 무엇입니까?
This is for medical **purposes** only. 이것은 의료 용도로만 사용된다.

372 **aim** [eim]

a goal or purpose that you try to achieve
명 1. 목적, 목표 ((of)) 2. 겨냥, 조준 동 1. 목표로 하다 ((to)) 2. 겨냥하다 ((at))

the **aim of** this course 이 강좌의 목표
We **aim to** improve your reading skills. 우리는 여러분의 읽기 능력을 향상시키는 것을 목표로 합니다.
aim a gun **at** a target 총을 과녁에 겨누다

373 **object** [ɑ́bdʒikt]

objective 명 목표
objection 명 이의, 반대

a thing that you can see or touch
명 1. 물건, 물체 2. 목적 ((of)) = purpose 동 [əbdʒékt] 반대하다 ((to))

a small metal **object** 작은 금속 물체
the **object of** the meeting 회의의 목적
Sam **objected to** the plan. 샘은 그 계획에 반대했다.

374 **structure** [strʌ́ktʃər]

structural 형 구조의, 구조적인

the way that parts of something are arranged
명 1. (사물 등의) 구조 ((of)) 2. 구조물, 건축물

We studied the **structure of** the human body. 우리는 인체의 구조를 공부했다.
the **structure of** the building 그 건물의 구조
The Eiffel Tower is a steel **structure**. 에펠 탑은 철 구조물이다.

375 **enroll** [inróul]

enrollment 명 등록, 입학

to officially arrange to join a school or course
동 (강좌·학교 등에) 등록하다; 등록시키다 ((in))

enroll in a writing course 글쓰기 강좌에 등록하다
You need to **enroll** before the end of August. 8월말 이전에 등록해야 한다.

376 **register** [rédʒistər]

registration 명 등록

to record your name on an official list
동 등록하다 ((for)); (출생 등을) 신고하다 명 등록부, 명부

I have to **register for** classes this week. 나는 이번 주에 수강 신청을 해야 한다.
register a birth 출생 신고를 하다
a school **register** 학적부

377 **space**
[speis]
spacious 형 (공간이) 널찍한

an empty area that is free to be used
명 1. (비어 있는) 공간, 자리 = room 2. 우주

There is enough **space** for a desk. 책상을 놓을 수 있는 충분한 공간이 있다.
Astronauts travel into **space**. 우주 비행사들은 우주로 여행한다.

378 **blank**
[blæŋk]

empty; with no writing, pictures, or sound
형 빈, 공백의 명 빈칸, 공란

Sign your name in the **blank** space below. 아래 빈 공간에 서명하세요.
Please fill in the **blanks**. 빈칸을 채우세요.

379 **sign up for**

to enroll in or register for something
~을 신청하다, ~에 가입하다[등록하다]

She **signed up for** the summer camp. 그녀는 여름 캠프를 신청했다.
He **signed up for** the gym. 그는 헬스클럽에 등록했다.

380 **on purpose**

purposely; intentionally
고의로, 일부러

Someone set the fire **on purpose**. 누군가 고의로 불을 질렀다.
I didn't do it **on purpose**. It was an accident. 내가 일부러 그런 게 아니다. 그것은 사고였다.

Check Up

A 우리말에 맞게 빈칸에 알맞은 말을 넣으세요.

1. 리포트 쓰기의 원칙 the ________________ of writing reports
2. 과제를 부과하다 ________________ a task
3. 변화에 대처하다 ________________ with the changes
4. 황금(주요) 시간대의 TV 프로 a show on ________________-time television
5. 글쓰기 강좌에 등록하다 ________________ in a writing course
6. 여름 캠프를 신청하다 ________________ for a summer camp

B 우리말에 알맞은 말을 골라 문장을 완성하세요.

1. Mr. Smith is a high school (**principle** / **principal**). 스미스 씨는 고등학교 교장이다.
2. She is a (**junior** / **senior**) in high school. 그녀는 고등학교 2학년이다.
3. I have to (**register** / **enroll**) for classes this week. 나는 이번 주에 수강 신청을 해야 한다.
4. There is enough (**space** / **blank**) for a desk. 책상을 놓을 수 있는 충분한 공간이 있다.
5. Someone set the fire (**purpose** / **on purpose**). 누군가 고의로 불을 질렀다.

Build Up

A **Write the correct word for each definition.**

instruct	lecture	principal	aim	object	structure

1. 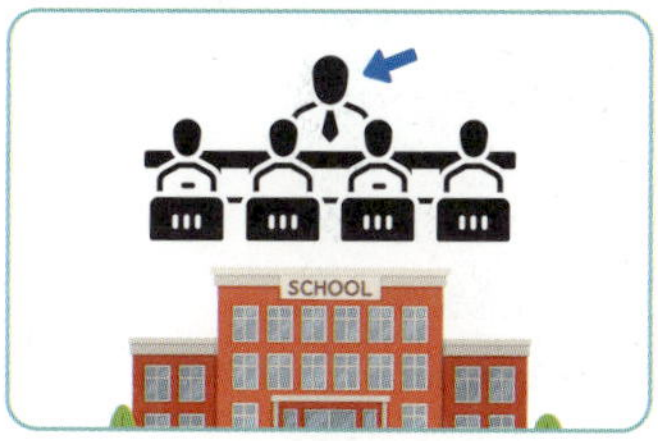

head teacher; chief

____

2. 

a talk to a group of people about a subject

____

3. 

to teach or educate

____

4. 

a thing that you can see or touch

____

5. 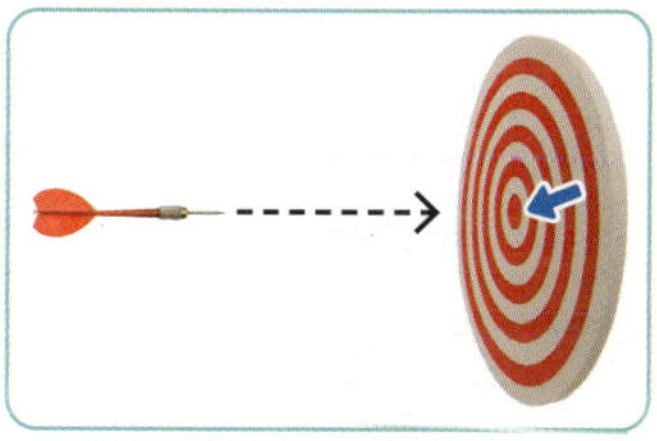

a goal or purpose that you try to achieve

____

6. 

the way that parts of something are arranged

____

B **Write the correct word or phrase next to each definition.**

primary	purpose	on purpose	sign up for	principle	cope

1. a rule or belief that influences your behavior ______________
2. to deal successfully with something difficult ______________
3. main; most important; most basic ______________
4. the reason why something is done or used ______________
5. to enroll in or register for something ______________
6. purposely; intentionally ______________

DAY 20

381 **emphasize**
[émfəsàiz]
emphasis 명 강조, 역점

to say something in a strong way
동 강조하다 = stress
She **emphasized** the importance of practice. 그녀는 연습의 중요성을 강조했다.

382 **concentrate**
[kάnsəntrèit]
concentration 명 집중

to give all your attention to something
동 집중하다 ((on)) = focus
I can't **concentrate on** my studies. 나는 공부에 집중할 수가 없다.
Turn off your phone, and you will **concentrate** better. 핸드폰을 끄면 더 잘 집중할 수 있을 거야.

383 **interrupt**
[ìntərʌ́pt]
interruption 명 방해; 중단

to stop someone while they are talking or doing something
동 1. (말·행동 등을) 방해하다, 가로막다 2. 중단시키다
Sorry to **interrupt**, but I have a question. 방해해서(말을 끊어서) 죄송하지만, 질문이 있습니다.
The game was **interrupted** by rain. 그 경기는 비로 중단되었다.

384 **disturb**
[distə́ːrb]
disturbance 명 방해, 소란

to interrupt what someone is doing
동 1. (일·수면 등을) 방해하다 2. 불안하게 하다 3. 어지럽히다
Don't **disturb** me when I'm studying. 내가 공부할 때는 방해하지 마.
The news **disturbed** us. 그 뉴스는 우리를 불안하게 했다.
The children **disturbed** the room. 아이들이 방을 어지럽혔다.

385 **examine**
[igzǽmin]
examination 명 조사; 검사; 시험 (= exam)

to look at something carefully
동 1. 조사하다, 검토하다 2. 검사하다, 진찰하다 3. 시험을 실시하다 ((on/in))
examine a proposal 제안을 검토하다
The doctor **examined** my eyes. 의사가 내 눈을 검사했다.
We will be **examined on** world history. 우리는 세계 역사에 대해 시험을 볼 것이다.

386 **refer**
[rifə́ːr]
reference 명 언급; 참조, 참고

to mention or speak about something
동 1. 참고[참조]하다 2. 지시하다, 나타내다 3. 언급하다 ((to))
Please **refer to** the guidebook. 안내 책자를 참고하세요.
The symbol **refers to** a tree. 그 기호는 나무를 나타낸다.
Don't **refer to** the matter again. 그 문제를 다시는 언급하지 마라.

387 **progress**
[prάgres]
progressive 형 진보적인, 점진적인

the process of getting better (at doing something)
명 진전, 진보 동 [prəgrés] 진행되다, 진척되다 *process 과정, 절차; 처리하다
He is making rapid **progress** in math. 그는 수학에서 빠른 진전을 보이고 있다.
The project **progressed** smoothly. 그 프로젝트는 순조롭게 진행되었다.

388 **advance**
[ədvǽns]
advanced 형 앞선, 선진의

progress or the forward movement of something
명 1. 진전, 발전 2. (군대의) 전진 동 1. (기술 등이) 진보하다 2. 전진하다
the **advance** of technology 기술의 발전
Science and technology have **advanced** rapidly. 과학 기술이 빠르게 향상되어 왔다.
The army **advanced** slowly. 그 군대는 천천히 진격했다.

389 **achieve**
[ətʃíːv]
achievement 명 업적, 성취

to succeed in reaching a goal, especially by working hard
동 이루다, 달성하다, 성취하다 = accomplish

achieve one's goal 목표를 이루다
I worked hard to **achieve** my dreams. 나는 꿈을 이루기 위해 열심히 노력했다.

390 **deserve**
[dizə́ːrv]
deserved 형 응당한, 당연한

to have earned something by good or bad actions
동 ~을 받을 만하다, ~할 자격이 있다, ~해야 마땅하다 ((to))

You **deserve** it. 너는 마땅히 그럴 자격이 있어. / 너는 그래도 싸다. (부정적 의미)
He **deserves to** be praised. 그는 칭찬받아 마땅하다.

391 **hardly**
[hɑ́ːrdli]

almost not, or only a very small amount
부 거의 ~ 아니다[없다], 거의 ~하지 않다

I was so excited that I could **hardly** speak. 나는 너무 흥분해서 거의 말을 할 수 없었다.
She **hardly** studied for the exam. 그녀는 시험 공부를 거의 하지 않았다.

392 **barely**
[béərli]

only just
부 1. 간신히, 가까스로 2. 거의 ~ 않다

She **barely** passed the exam. 그녀는 가까스로 시험을 통과했다.
He **barely** spoke during the meeting. 그는 회의 중에 거의 말을 하지 않았다.

393 **intense**
[inténs]

extreme or very strong
형 1. 극심한, 강렬한 2. 치열한

the **intense** heat of summer 여름의 극심한 더위
The game was **intense**. 그 게임은 치열했다.

394 **intend**
[inténd]
intended 형 의도된, 고의의

to have a plan or purpose
동 의도하다, (~하려고) 생각하다 ((to)) 유 mean 의도하다, 뜻하다

It took longer than we had **intended**. 우리가 의도했던 것보다 시간이 더 걸렸다.
I didn't **intend to** hurt you. 너를 상처 주려고 한 건 아니었어.

395 **intention**
[inténʃən]

what you intend or plan to do; your aim
명 의사, 의도, 목적 ((of))

I had no **intention of** harming anyone. 나는 누구에게도 해를 끼칠 의도가 없었다.
His **intention** was clear from the beginning. 그의 의도는 처음부터 명확했다.

396 **intentional**
[inténʃənl]
intentionally 부 고의로

planned or intended
형 의도적인, 고의로 한

Sorry, it wasn't **intentional**. 미안, 고의로 그런 것이 아니야.

397 **prove**
[pru:v]
proof 명 증거

to show that something is true by providing facts, etc.
동 1. 증명하다, 입증하다 2. (~임이) 드러나다, 판명되다 = turn out

Can you **prove** it? 너는 그것을 증명할 수 있어?
The task **proved** to be impossible. 그 작업은 불가능한 것으로 판명되었다.

398 **indicate**
[índikèit]

to show that something is true or exists
동 1. 나타내다, 보여 주다 2. 가리키다

His low voice **indicates** he is upset. 그의 낮은 목소리는 그가 화가 났음을 보여 준다.
He **indicated** a place on the map. 그는 지도에서 한 장소를 가리켰다.

399 **in advance**

ahead of time
미리, 사전에

Book **in advance** if you want good seats. 좋은 자리를 원한다면 미리 예약하세요.
Thank you **in advance** for your help. 당신의 도움에 미리 감사드립니다.

400 **intend to**

to mean to; to plan to
~하려고 의도하다, ~할 작정이다

I didn't **intend to** disturb your studying. 네 공부를 방해할 생각은 없었어.
We **intend to** finish the project by Friday. 우리는 금요일까지 그 프로젝트를 끝낼 작정이다.

Check Up

A 우리말에 맞게 빈칸에 알맞은 말을 넣으세요.

1. 공부에 집중하다 ____________ on studying
2. 제안을 검토하다 ____________ a proposal
3. 안내 책자를 참고하다 ____________ to a guidebook
4. 목표를 이루다[달성하다] ____________ one's goal
5. 가까스로 시험을 통과하다 ____________ pass the exam
6. 미리[사전에] 예약하다 book ____________

B 우리말에 알맞은 말을 골라 문장을 완성하세요.

1. The game was (interrupted / disturbed) by rain. 그 경기는 비로 중단되었다.
2. You (deserve / prove) it. 너는 마땅히 그럴 자격이 있어.
3. I didn't (intend / intention) to hurt you. 너를 상처 주려고 한 건 아니었어.
4. I had no (intend / intention) of harming anyone. 나는 누구에게도 해를 끼칠 의도가 없었다.
5. The task (proved / indicated) to be impossible. 그 작업은 불가능한 것으로 판명되었다.

Build Up

A Write the correct word for each definition.

progress	examine	emphasize	intense	disturb	achieve

1. 

to say something in a strong way

____

2. 

to interrupt what someone is doing

____

3. 

to look at something carefully

____

4. 

the process of getting better

____

5. 

to succeed in reaching a goal

____

6. 

extreme or very strong

____

B Write the correct word or phrase next to each definition.

indicate	prove	intend to	intentional	concentrate	hardly

1. to give all your attention to something ________________
2. almost not, or only a very small amount ________________
3. planned or intended ________________
4. to show that something is true by providing facts, etc. ________________
5. to show that something is true or exists ________________
6. to mean to; to plan to ________________

Review Test 05 DAY 17-20

A 그림을 보고, 빈칸에 알맞은 단어를 넣으세요.

recover	lecture	survive	due	progress	object

1. 
____

2. 
____

3. 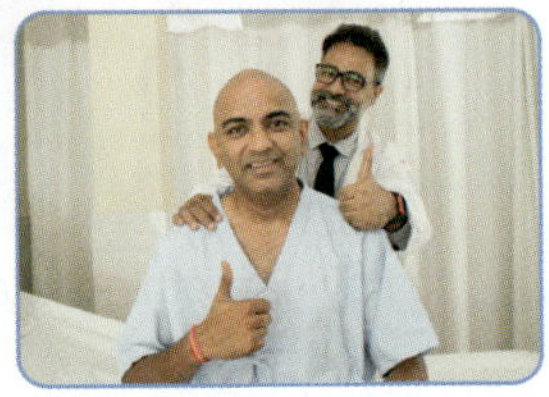
____

4. 
____

5. 
____

6. 
____

B 그림에 알맞은 문장을 골라 표시하세요.

1. 

☐ The woman is pregnant.

☐ She gave birth to a baby.

2. 

☐ Either is fine with me.

☐ I like neither coffee nor tea.

3. 

☐ The children disturbed the room.

☐ The rain prevented them from going out.

4. 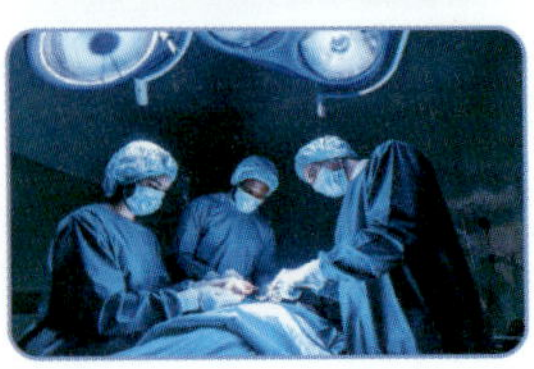

☐ They are operating a machine.

☐ They are operating on a patient.

C 우리말 뜻에 맞게 빈칸에 알맞은 말을 넣으세요.

damage	vital	newborn	according to
due to	cancer	cope with	achieve

1. ____________ bad weather 악천후로 인하여
2. a ____________ baby 갓난아기
3. ____________ the weather report 일기 예보에 따르면
4. check one's ____________ signs 생명 징후를 체크하다
5. cause severe ____________ 심한 손상을 초래하다
6. get ____________ 암에 걸리다
7. ____________ one's goal 목표를 이루다
8. ____________ the changes 변화에 대처하다

D 우리말 뜻에 맞게 빈칸에 알맞은 말을 넣으세요.

blind	aim to	on purpose	deserve to	intend to	suffers from

1. Guide dogs help people who are ____________. 안내견은 시각 장애인들을 돕는다.
2. He often ____________ stress. 그는 종종 스트레스에 시달린다.
3. We ____________ improve your reading skills.
   우리는 여러분의 읽기 능력을 향상시키는 것을 목표로 합니다.
4. You ____________ be praised. 너는 칭찬받아 마땅하다.
5. Someone set the fire ____________. 누군가 고의로 불을 질렀다.
6. I didn't ____________ disturb your studying. 네 공부를 방해할 생각은 없었어.

E 밑줄 친 단어와 비슷한 뜻을 가진 단어를 고르세요.

1. The vaccine <u>prevents</u> the flu from spreading.

   a. stops　　b. copes　　c. harms

2. My grandmother <u>passed away</u> last year.

   a. survived　　b. lived　　c. died

3. He finally <u>overcame</u> the illness.

   a. got over　　b. suffered　　c. prevented

4. What is the <u>purpose</u> of your visit?

   a. poison　　b. aim　　c. principle

F 밑줄 친 단어와 반대의 뜻을 가진 단어를 고르세요.

1. Our country's <u>birth</u> rate has decreased.

   a. chest　　b. death　　c. breath

2. Her love for her family is <u>absolute</u>.

   a. relative　　b. primary　　c. devoted

3. He is <u>junior</u> to me by a year.

   a. older　　b. higher　　c. senior

4. <u>Either</u> is fine with me.

   a. Both　　b. Neither　　c. Nor

G 주어진 영영풀이에 알맞은 단어를 고르세요.

1. the air that you take into your lungs and send out again

   a. breath b. breathe c. breast

2. to produce young animals

   a. raise b. feed c. breed

3. related to the treatment of disease or injury

   a. medicine b. technology c. medical

4. a wound or damage to someone's body (in an accident or attack)

   a. injure b. injured c. injury

5. unable to hear or unable to hear very well

   a. deaf b. blind c. damaged

6. to record your name on an official list

   a. register b. intend c. sign

H 빈칸에 알맞은 동사 형태를 넣어 문장을 완성하세요.

1. Have you ________________ the cat? (feed)
2. The new software was ________________ by Samsung. (develop)
3. We were ________________ to follow the safety rules. (instruct)
4. Science and technology have ________________ rapidly. (advance)

DAY 21

401 **closet**
[klázit]

a small room or space in a wall used for storing things

명 벽장, (붙박이) 옷장 *wardrobe 옷장

The **closet** is full of beautiful clothes. 그 옷장은 아름다운 옷으로 가득 차 있다.

402 **drawer**
[drɔːr]

a container like a box that is part of a piece of furniture

명 서랍

I keep my socks in the **drawer**. 나는 내 양말들을 서랍에 보관한다.
a desk **drawer** 책상 서랍

403 **cotton**
[kátn]

cloth or thread (that is) made from the cotton plant

명 1. 솜, 면직물 2. 목화 *cloth 천, 옷감 *thread 실 *fabric 천, 직물

a **cotton** shirt 면 셔츠
The towels are 100% pure **cotton**. 그 수건들은 백 퍼센트 순면이다.
cotton fields 목화밭

404 **costume**
[kástjuːm]

a set of clothes worn to show a particular character, time period, or style

명 (특정 지역이나 시대의) 의상, 복장

The children were dressed in Halloween **costumes**. 아이들은 핼러윈 의상을 입고 있었다.
wear a stage **costume** 무대 의상을 입다

405 **quality**
[kwáləti]

how good or bad something is

명 질, 품질 ((of))

The **quality of** the cotton is excellent. 그 면의 품질은 뛰어나다.

406 **quantity**
[kwántəti]

the amount or number of something

명 (세거나 잴 수 있는) 양, 수량, 분량 ((of))

They produce goods in large **quantities**. 그들은 대량으로 상품을 생산한다.
a small **quantity of** sugar 소량의 설탕

407 **bare**
[bɛər]

not covered by clothes

형 맨살을 드러낸

He walked around in **bare** feet. 그는 맨발로 돌아다녔다.
wear a dress with **bare** legs 맨다리에 드레스를 입다

408 **naked**
[néikid]

not wearing any clothes

형 (완전히) 벌거벗은, 아무것도 걸치지 않은

The baby was **naked** after taking a bath. 아기는 목욕 후 벌거벗은 상태였다.
with the **naked** eye 육안으로, 맨눈으로

409 **sew**
[sou]

to use a needle and thread to make or repair clothes **(sewed-sewed, sewn)**
동 **바느질하다, 꿰매다** *knit 뜨개질하다

She learned to **sew** at school. 그녀는 학교에서 바느질하는 법을 배웠다.
sew a button on the shirt 셔츠에 단추를 달다

410 **suitable**
[súːtəbl]
suit 동 잘 맞다, 적합하다

acceptable or right for someone or something
형 **적절한, 적합한, 알맞은** ((for)) 반 unsuitable 부적합한

This dress is **suitable for** the party. 이 드레스는 그 파티에 어울린다.
The movie is not **suitable for** children. 그 영화는 아이들에게 적합하지 않다.

411 **plain**
[plein]

simple and not complicated
형 **1. 꾸미지 않은, 평범한 2. 분명한** = clear 명 **평지, 평원**

a **plain** but elegant dress 소박하지만 우아한 드레스
It's **plain** that she needs help. 그녀가 도움이 필요하다는 것은 분명하다.
the Great **Plains** (미국의) 대평원

412 **fancy**
[fǽnsi]

complicated or having a lot of decoration
형 **1. 화려한, 장식이 많은 2. 값비싼, 고급의**

That dress is too **fancy** for a little girl. 저 드레스는 어린 소녀에게는 너무 화려하다.
a **fancy** restaurant 고급 식당

413 **amount**
[əmáunt]

a quantity of something such as time or money
명 **1. (시간·물질 등의) 양 2. (돈의) 액수, 총액** ((of))

They ate a huge **amount of** food. 그들은 엄청난 양의 음식을 먹었다.
spend a large **amount of** money 많은 액수의 돈을 쓰다

414 **bit**
[bit]

a small amount or piece of something
명 **한 조각** 부 **1. (a bit) 조금, 약간 2. (a bit) 잠시**

a **bit** of bread 빵 한 조각, 약간의 빵
These pants are **a bit** tight. 이 바지는 조금 꽉 낀다.
Wait **a bit**, please. 잠시만 기다려 주세요.

415 **alter**
[ɔ́ːltər]
alteration 명 변화, 개조; 수선

to change or to make someone or something change
동 **1. 바꾸다, 변경하다; 바뀌다 2. (옷을) 고치다**

We had to **alter** our plans due to bad weather. 우리는 악천후로 우리의 계획을 변경해야 했다.
She had the dress **altered**. 그녀는 드레스를 수선했다(수선시켰다).

416 **mend**
[mend]

to fix or repair something
동 **1. 수리하다, 고치다 2. (옷 등을) 수선하다, 꿰매다**

The repairman is **mending** the roof. 수리공이 지붕을 수리하고 있다.
I need to **mend** the hole in my sweater. 나는 내 스웨터의 구멍을 수선해야 한다.

417 **ignore**
[ignɔ́ːr]
ignorance 명 무지, 무식함

to intentionally pay no attention to something
동 1. 무시하다 2. (사람을) 못 본 척하다

She **ignored** his advice. 그녀는 그의 충고를 무시했다.
She **ignored** him and kept walking. 그녀는 그를 못 본 척하고 계속 걸었다.

418 **pretend**
[priténd]

to behave as if something is true
동 1. ~인 척하다 ((to)) 2. ~라고 가장하다[상상하다]

She **pretended to** be happy at the party. 그녀는 파티에서 행복한 척했다.
Let's **pretend** (that) we are pirates. 우리 해적 놀이 하자(우리가 해적이라고 가장하자).

419 **prefer A to B**

to like A more than B
B보다 A를 더 좋아하다[선호하다]

I **prefer** quality **to** quantity. 나는 양보다 질을 선호한다.
She **prefers** pizza **to** chicken. 그녀는 치킨보다 피자를 더 좋아한다.

420 **would rather A (than B)**

to prefer A to B
(B하느니) 차라리 A하고 싶다, (B보다) A하는 게 낫다

I **would rather** read books **than** watch TV. 나는 TV를 보느니 차라리 책을 읽고 싶다.
She **would rather** have tea **than** coffee. 그녀는 커피보다 차를 마실 것이다.

Check Up

A 우리말에 맞게 빈칸에 알맞은 말을 넣으세요.

1. 무대 의상을 입다 — wear a stage ____________
2. 육안으로, 맨눈으로 — with the ____________ eye
3. 아이들에게 적합하다 — be ____________ for children
4. 엄청난 양의 음식을 먹다 — eat a huge ____________ of food
5. 상품을 대량으로 생산하다 — produce goods in large ____________
6. 치킨보다 피자를 더 좋아하다 — ____________ pizza to chicken

B 우리말에 알맞은 말을 골라 문장을 완성하세요.

1. The (quantity / quality) of the cotton is excellent. 그 면의 품질은 뛰어나다.
2. He walked around in (bare / naked) feet. 그는 맨발로 돌아다녔다.
3. These pants are (a bit / a bit of) tight. 이 바지는 조금 꽉 낀다.
4. She (pretended / preferred) to be happy. 그녀는 행복한 척했다.
5. I would (rather / alter) read books than watch TV. 나는 TV를 보느니 차라리 책을 읽고 싶다.

Build Up

A Write the correct word for each definition.

costume	cotton	plain	bare	drawer	closet

1. 

a small room or space in a wall used for storing things

____

2. 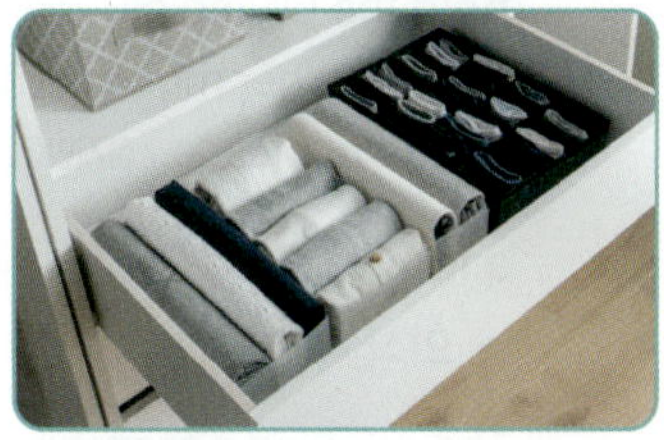

a container that is part of a piece of furniture

____

3. 

cloth made from the cotton plant

____

4. 

a set of clothes worn to show a character

____

5. 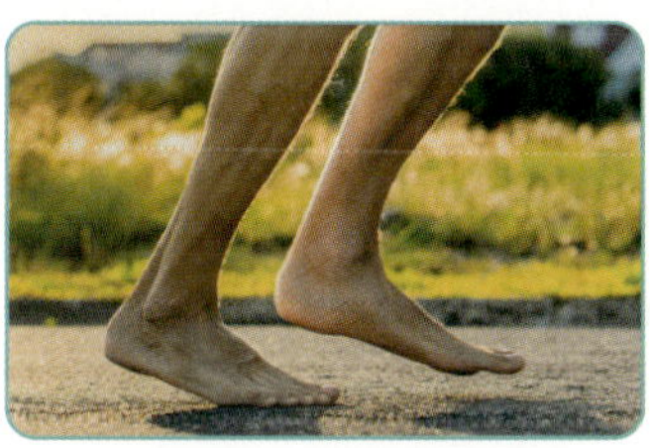

not covered by clothes

____

6. 

simple and not complicated

____

B Write the correct word or phrase next to each definition.

naked	fancy	quantity	ignore	prefer A to B	alter

1. the amount or number of something ________________
2. not wearing any clothes ________________
3. complicated or having a lot of decoration ________________
4. to change or to make someone or something change ________________
5. to intentionally pay no attention to something ________________
6. to like A more than B ________________

DAY 22

421 **hold**
[hould]

to organize an event **(held-held)**
동 1. (행사 등을) 열다, 개최하다 2. 잡다, 들다, 안다 3. 버티다, 유지하다

hold the Olympics 올림픽을 개최하다
She **held** her mother's hand tightly. 그녀는 엄마의 손을 꽉 잡았다.
Hold on, please. 잠시만(끊지 말고) 기다려 주세요.

422 **ceremony**
[sérəmòuni]

a formal event
명 의식, 예식

The opening **ceremony** will be held at 9:00 AM. 개막식은 오전 9시에 열릴 것이다.
a wedding **ceremony** 결혼식

423 **athlete**
[ǽθliːt]
athletic 형 운동 경기의

a person who competes in sports
명 운동선수

Olympic **athletes** 올림픽 선수들
He is a talented **athlete** in track and field. 그는 육상에서 재능 있는 운동선수이다.

424 **sweat**
[swet]
sweaty 형 땀에 젖은

the liquid that is on your skin when you are hot
명 땀 동 땀을 흘리다

He wiped the **sweat** from his face. 그는 얼굴의 땀을 닦았다.
He **sweats** a lot when he exercises. 그는 운동할 때 땀을 많이 흘린다.

425 **compete**
[kəmpíːt]
competitive 형 경쟁을 하는, 경쟁력 있는

to try to win a competition
동 1. 경쟁하다, 겨루다 ((for/with/against)) 2. (경기 등에) 참가하다 ((in))

They will **compete for** Olympic medals. 그들은 올림픽 메달을 놓고 경쟁할 것이다.
compete against each other 서로 경쟁하다
compete in a marathon 마라톤에 참가하다

426 **competition**
[kàmpətíʃən]

the activity of competing or the contest itself
명 1. 경쟁 2. 대회, 시합 유 contest 대회, 경연

They enjoyed the intense **competition**. 그들은 치열한 경쟁을 즐겼다.
win a **competition** 시합에서 이기다

427 **bounce**
[bauns]

to move up or away after hitting a surface
동 (공 등이) 튀다, 튀어 오르다

The ball **bounced** off the goalpost. 공은 골대를 맞고 튕겨 나왔다.

428 **leap**
[liːp]

to jump high or far
동 (높이) 뛰어오르다, 뛰어넘다 명 높이뛰기, 도약

The athlete **leaped** over the high jump bar. 그 선수는 높이뛰기 바를 뛰어넘었다.
The horse made a **leap** over the hurdle. 그 말은 장애물을 뛰어넘었다.
Sales took a huge **leap**. 매출이 크게 늘었다.

429 **slide** [slaid]

to move smoothly along a surface **(slid-slid)**

동 **미끄러지다, 미끄러지듯이 움직이다** 명 **미끄럼틀**

The skiers **slid** down the slope. 스키어들이 슬로프를 미끄러져 내려갔다.
slide down the **slide** 미끄럼틀을 타고 내려가다

430 **slippery** [slípəri]

slip 동 미끄러지다

difficult to stand or move on (because something is smooth or wet)

형 **미끄러운, 미끈거리는**

slippery roads 미끄러운 도로
Caution: **Slippery** When Wet 주의: 젖으면(비 올 때) 미끄러움

431 **row** [rou]

a straight line of people or things

명 **1. (죽 늘어선) 열, 줄 2. (극장 등의 좌석) 줄** 동 **노를 젓다**

line up in a **row** 일렬로 줄을 서다
We sat in the first **row**. 우리는 첫 번째 줄에 앉았다.
row a boat 배를 젓다

432 **aloud** [əláud]

loud 형 소리가 큰, 시끄러운

in a voice that other people can hear

부 **1. 소리 내어 2. 큰 소리로, 크게** = out loud, loudly

read **aloud** 소리 내어 읽다
They cheered and shouted **aloud**. 그들은 환호하며 큰 소리로 외쳤다.

433 **beat** [biːt]

to hit (someone or something) repeatedly, usually very hard **(beat-beaten)**

동 **1. (세게 계속) 때리다, 두드리다 2. 이기다 3. (심장이) 뛰다**

beat a drum 북을 치다
Our team **beat** Japan 3 to 1. 우리 팀이 일본을 3대 1로 이겼다.
My heart **beat** fast with joy. 내 심장은 기쁨으로 빠르게 뛰었다.

434 **defeat** [difíːt]

to win against someone (in a war or competition)

동 **패배시키다, 물리치다, 이기다** 명 **패배**

We **defeated** them in the finals. 우리는 결승전에서 그들을 물리쳤다.
admit **defeat** 패배를 인정하다

435 **lost** [lɔːst]

lose 동 (길을) 잃다; (무엇을) 잃어버리다; (시합에서) 지다

unable to find your way

형 **1. 길을 잃은 2. 잃어버린, 분실된**

get **lost** 길을 잃다, 어찌할 바를 모르다
find a **lost** puppy 잃어버린 강아지를 찾다

436 **loss** [lɔːs]

the state of no longer having something

명 **1. 분실, 상실 2. (금전적) 손실** 반 profit 이익 **3. 패배**

a **loss** of confidence 자신감 상실
make a **loss** of 10 million dollars 1천만 달러의 손실을 보다
three wins and four **losses** 3승 4패

437 **award**
[əwɔ́ːrd]

a prize given to someone (for something they have achieved)
명 상 유 prize 상, 상품 동 (상 등을) 수여하다, 주다

an **award** ceremony 시상식
win an **award** 상을 받다

438 **reward**
[riwɔ́ːrd]

a deserved outcome or result
명 보상 동 보상하다, 보답하다

If you work hard, you will get your **reward**. 열심히 일하면 너는 보상을 받을 것이다.
Our efforts were finally **rewarded**. 우리의 노력이 마침내 보상을 받았다.

439 **be held**

to take place
(행사 등이) 열리다, 개최되다

The next Olympics will **be held** in Los Angeles. 다음 올림픽은 로스앤젤레스에서 열릴 것이다.
The festival **was held** in August. 그 축제는 8월에 열렸다.

440 **take place**

to happen, to occur; to be held
(사건 등이) 일어나다; (행사 등이) 열리다

When did the accident **take place**? 그 사고가 언제 일어났습니까?
The film festival **takes place** in October. 그 영화제는 10월에 열린다.

Check Up

A 우리말에 맞게 빈칸에 알맞은 말을 넣으세요.

1. 올림픽을 개최하다 ______________ the Olympics
2. 개막식 the opening ______________
3. 서로 경쟁하다 ______________ against each other
4. 미끄럼틀을 타고 내려가다 ______________ down the slide
5. 일렬로 줄을 서다 line up in a ______________
6. 길을 잃다, 어찌할 바를 모르다 get ______________

B 우리말에 알맞은 말을 골라 문장을 완성하세요.

1. The athlete (**bounced** / **leaped**) over the high jump bar. 그 선수는 높이뛰기 바를 뛰어넘었다.
2. Our team (**bet** / **beat**) Japan 3 to 1. 우리 팀이 일본을 3대 1로 이겼다.
3. We (**defeated** / **competed**) them in the finals. 우리는 결승전에서 그들을 물리쳤다.
4. Our efforts were finally (**awarded** / **rewarded**). 우리의 노력이 마침내 보상을 받았다.
5. The festival was (**hold** / **held**) in August. 그 축제는 8월에 열렸다.

Build Up

A **Write the correct word for each definition.**

row	award	ceremony	compete	athlete	slippery

1. 

a formal event

____

2. 

a person who competes in sports

____

3. 

to try to win a competition

____

4. 

a straight line of people or things

____

5. 

difficult to stand or move on

____

6. 

a prize given to someone

____

B **Write the correct word or phrase next to each definition.**

sweat	aloud	reward	loss	take place	competition

1. the liquid that is on your skin when you are hot ______________
2. the activity of competing or the contest itself ______________
3. in a voice that other people can hear ______________
4. the state of no longer having something ______________
5. a deserved outcome or result ______________
6. to happen, to occur; to be held ______________

DAY 23

441 **abroad**
[əbrɔ́:d]

in or to a foreign country
부 해외에(서), 해외로, 외국으로

She will study **abroad** next year. 그녀는 내년에 해외에서 공부할 것이다.
travel **abroad** 해외로 여행 가다

442 **overseas**
[ouvərsí:z]

in or to a foreign country that is across the sea
부 해외에[로], 외국에[으로] 형 해외의, 외국의

He worked **overseas** for a year. 그는 1년간 해외에서 일했다.
travel **overseas** 해외로 여행 가다
overseas markets 해외 시장

443 **harbor**
[há:rbər]

an area of water near the coast where ships are kept
명 항구, 항만

The **harbor** is busy with boats. 항구는 배로 붐빈다.
They plan to leave the **harbor** soon. 그들은 곧 항구를 떠날 계획이다.

444 **sail**
[seil]
sailor 명 선원

to travel in a ship or boat
동 항해하다 명 (배의) 돛

They will **sail** across the Pacific Ocean. 그들은 태평양을 가로질러 항해할 것이다.
raise the **sails** 돛을 올리다

445 **compass**
[kʌ́mpəs]

a device that is used to find direction
명 1. 나침반 2. (제도용) 컴퍼스

The **compass** is essential for sailing. 나침반은 항해에 필수적이다.
Draw a circle with a **compass**. 컴퍼스로 원을 그려라.

446 **needle**
[ni:dl]

a small, thin piece of steel
명 1. (바느질용) 바늘 2. (주사) 바늘 3. (계기의) 바늘

a sharp **needle** 날카로운 (주사) 바늘
The compass **needle** always points north. 나침반의 바늘은 항상 북쪽을 가리킨다.

447 **deck**
[dek]

the top outside floor of a ship or boat
명 1. (배의) 갑판 2. (이층 버스의) 층

relax on the **deck** 갑판에서 휴식을 취하다
We sat on the top **deck** of the double-decker bus. 우리는 이층 버스의 위층(2층)에 앉았다.

448 **section**
[sékʃən]

one of the parts that something is divided into
명 부분, 구획

Let's sit in the front **section** of the deck. 갑판의 앞쪽 부분에 앉자.
I like the travel **section** in the newspaper. 나는 신문에서 여행 섹션을 좋아한다.

449 **wrap**
[ræp]
wrapper 명 포장지

to cover something or someone with paper, cloth, etc.
동 1. 싸다, 포장하다 2. 두르다 반 unwrap 풀다, 벗기다

wrap a present 선물을 포장하다
She **wrapped** a scarf around her neck. 그녀는 목에 스카프를 둘렀다.

450 **tie**
[tai]

to fasten something with string, rope, etc.
동 묶다, 매다 명 넥타이

She **tied** a ribbon around the gift box. 그녀는 선물 상자에 리본을 묶었다.
wear a **tie** 넥타이를 매다

451 **national**
[nǽʃənl]
nation 명 국가, 나라
nationality 명 국적

relating to one particular nation; related to a whole nation
형 1. 국가의, 전국적인 2. 국립의

a **national** holiday 국경일
Every year, many tourists visit the **national** park.
해마다 많은 관광객들이 그 국립공원을 방문한다.

452 **international**
[ìntərnǽʃənəl]

relating to more than one nation
형 국제적인, 국가 간의

They arrived at Incheon **International** Airport. 그들은 인천국제공항에 도착했다.

453 **passenger**
[pǽsəndʒər]

a person who rides in a vehicle, such as a bus, boat, or plane
명 승객, 여객

The flight can carry 500 **passengers**. 이 항공편은 500명의 승객을 수송할 수 있다.
a **passenger** plane 여객기

454 **destination**
[dèstənéiʃən]

the place that someone or something is going to
명 1. 목적지 2. (물품의) 도착지

Our **destination** is New York City. 우리의 목적지는 뉴욕 시이다.
Please confirm your **destination** address. 도착지 주소를 확인해 주세요.

455 **transport**
[trænspɔ́:rt]
transportation 명 운송, 교통수단

to carry (someone or something) from one place to another
동 수송[운송]하다, 실어 나르다

transport goods overseas 물품을 해외로 운송하다
The airline **transports** passengers to various destinations.
그 항공사는 승객들을 다양한 목적지로 실어 나른다.

456 **baggage**
[bǽgidʒ]

all the cases and bags that you take with you (when you travel)
명 (여행용) 짐, 수화물 = luggage

Baggage claim is on the first floor. 수화물 찾는 곳은 1층에 있다.

457 **ease**
[iːz]

easy 형 쉬운
easily 부 쉽게

the state of being comfortable
명 쉬움, 편안함 동 (고통 등을) 완화하다; 편해지다

She found her baggage **with ease.** 그녀는 쉽게 자신의 짐을 찾았다.
She felt **at ease** once she arrived home. 그녀는 집에 도착하자 편안함을 느꼈다.
The medication **eased** her pain. 약이 그녀의 통증을 완화시켰다.

458 **tension**
[ténʃən]

tense 형 긴박한, 긴장된

a feeling that you are nervous, worried, and not relaxed
명 1. (심리적) 긴장 2. (관계 등의) 긴장 상태

I tried to ease my **tension.** 나는 긴장을 풀려고 노력했다.
high **tension** between the two countries 두 나라 간의 높은 긴장 상태

459 **take off**

to leave the ground and begin to fly
1. 이륙하다 반 land 착륙하다 2. (옷 등을) 벗다 반 put on 입다, 쓰다, 걸치다

The airplane **took off** smoothly. 비행기가 부드럽게 이륙했다.
Please **take off** your shoes before you come in. 들어오기 전에 신발을 벗어 주세요.

460 **make it**

to be successful at something
1. 성공하다, 해내다 2. (늦지 않게) 도착하다

After many tries, I finally **made it.** 여러 번의 시도 끝에 마침내 나는 해냈다.
If we run, we should **make it.** 뛰어가면 (시간 내에) 도착할 수 있을 거야.

Check Up

A 우리말에 맞게 빈칸에 알맞은 말을 넣으세요.

1. 해외로 여행 가다 — travel __________
2. 돛을 올리다 — raise the __________
3. 갑판에서 휴식을 취하다 — relax on the __________
4. 국경일 — a __________ holiday
5. 물품을 해외로 운송하다 — __________ goods overseas
6. 수화물 찾는 곳 — __________ claim

B 우리말에 알맞은 말을 골라 문장을 완성하세요.

1. They arrived at Incheon (**national** / **International**) Airport. 그들은 인천국제공항에 도착했다.
2. Our (**destination** / **tension**) is New York City. 우리의 목적지는 뉴욕 시이다.
3. The airplane (**took off** / **landed**) smoothly. 비행기가 부드럽게 이륙했다.
4. She felt at (**easy** / **ease**). 그녀는 편안함을 느꼈다.
5. After many tries, I finally (**make** / **made**) it. 여러 번의 시도 끝에 마침내 나는 해냈다.

Build Up

A **Write the correct word for each definition.**

abroad	transport	compass	harbor	wrap	passenger

1. 

in or to a foreign country

______

2. 

an area of water where ships are kept

______

3. 

a device used to find direction

______

4. 

to cover something with paper

______

5. 

a person who rides in a vehicle

______

6. 

to carry from one place to another

______

B **Write the correct word or phrase next to each definition.**

needle	sail	take off	destination	section	tension

1. to travel in a ship or boat ______
2. a small, thin piece of steel ______
3. one of the parts that something is divided into ______
4. the place that someone or something is going to ______
5. a feeling that you are nervous, worried, and not relaxed ______
6. to leave the ground and begin to fly ______

DAY 24

461 **society**
[səsáiəti]
social 형 시회의, 사회적인

a large group of people who live in the same country or area
명 1. 사회 2. 협회, 단체

We live in a multicultural **society**. 우리는 다문화 사회에 살고 있다.
the American Cancer **Society** 미국 암 협회

462 **identity**
[aidéntəti]
identification 명 신원 확인 (=ID)
identify 동 (신원 등을) 확인하다, 알아보다

who someone is
명 1. 신원, 신분 2. 정체성, 독자성 *ID: identity 혹은 identification의 약어

Can I see your **identity[ID]** card? 신분증을 보여 주시겠어요?
a sense of **identity** as a Korean 한국인으로서의 정체성

463 **diverse**
[daivə́ːrs]
diversity 명 다양성

very different from each other
형 다양한, 여러 가지의 = various

people from **diverse** cultures 다양한 문화권 출신의 사람들
We offer **diverse** activities for children. 우리는 아이들을 위한 다양한 활동을 제공한다.

464 **majority**
[mədʒɔ́ːrəti]
major 형 주요한, 중대한

most of the people or things in a group
명 대부분, 대다수, 다수 반 minority 소수

the **majority** of workers 대부분의 노동자들
The **majority** of people prefer peace to war. 대다수의 사람들은 전쟁보다 평화를 더 좋아한다.

465 **aid**
[eid]

money or food that is sent to help a country (or group of people)
명 1. 원조, 지원 2. 도움 = help

provide emergency **aid** 긴급 원조를 제공하다
He finished the work **with the aid of** the Internet. 그는 인터넷의 도움으로 작업을 끝냈다.

466 **necessary**
[nésəsèri]
necessity 명 필수품, 필요(성)

needed in order to do something; essential
형 필요한, 필수적인 ((for)) 반 unnecessary 불필요한

Water is **necessary for** all living things. 물은 모든 생명체에게 필요하다.
International aid is **necessary for** the country. 그 나라에는 국제 원조가 필요하다.

467 **appoint**
[əpɔ́int]

to officially choose someone for a position
동 1. 임명하다, 지명하다 ((as)) 2. (시간·장소 등을) 정하다

The committee **appointed** him **as** chairman. 위원회는 그를 의장으로 임명했다.
Let's **appoint** a date for the meeting. 회의 날짜를 정합시다.

468 **appointment**
[əpɔ́intmənt]

a formal arrangement to meet or visit someone
명 1. (공식적인) 약속, (진찰 등의) 예약 2. 임명, 지명

an **appointment** for an interview 면접 약속
make an **appointment** with a dentist 치과 예약을 하다
the **appointment** of a new chairman 새로운 의장의 임명

469 **donate**
[dóuneit]

donation 명 기부
donor 명 기부자, 기증자

to give money or goods to a person or organization
동 1. 기부하다, 기증하다 2. 헌혈하다; (장기를) 기증하다 ((to))

He **donated** $100 **to** the local animal shelter. 그는 지역 동물 보호소에 100달러를 기부했다.
donate blood 헌혈하다

470 **contribute**
[kəntríbju:t]

contribution 명 기부(금); 기여

to give something to help someone or something
동 1. 기부[기증]하다 2. 기여하다; (~의) 원인이 되다 ((to))

contribute money **to** the homeless shelter 노숙자 쉼터에 돈을 기부하다
Everyone **contributed to** the success of the project. 모두가 그 프로젝트의 성공에 기여했다.

471 **fund**
[fʌnd]

an amount of money that is collected for a purpose
명 기금, 자금

raise **funds** 기금을 모으다
set up a **fund** for local artists 지역 예술가들을 위한 기금을 조성하다

472 **charity**
[ʧǽrəti]

charitable 형 자선의

an organization for helping people in need
명 1. 자선 단체, 구호 단체 2. 자선

She is volunteering at a **charity**. 그녀는 자선 단체에서 자원봉사를 하고 있다.
a **charity** concert 자선 음악회

473 **obtain**
[əbtéin]

to get something, especially by making an effort
동 (노력 끝에) 얻다, 획득하다

obtain permission 허가를 받다
They hope to **obtain** funding for charity. 그들은 자선 기금을 마련하기를 희망한다.

474 **devote**
[divóut]

devoted 형 헌신적인
devotion 명 헌신, 몰두

to use time or energy for a particular purpose or person
동 (시간·노력 등을) 바치다, 쏟다 ((to)) 유 dedicate 바치다, 헌신하다

She **devoted** her life **to** helping others. 그녀는 다른 사람들을 돕는 데 자신의 삶을 바쳤다.
They **devote** their weekends **to** volunteering. 그들은 주말을 자원봉사에 바친다.

475 **depend**
[dipénd]

dependent 형 의존[의지]하는
dependence 명 의존, 의지

to be decided by; to change according to
동 1. (~에) 달려 있다 2. 의존하다, 의지하다 ((on, upon))

The choice **depends on** you. 선택은 너에게 달려 있다.
Young children **depend on** their parents. 어린 아이들은 그들의 부모에게 의지한다.

476 **rely**
[rilái]

reliable 형 믿을[신뢰할] 수 있는
reliance 명 의존, 의지

to depend on
동 1. (~에) 기대다, 의지하다 2. 믿다 ((on, upon))

You can **rely on** me at any time. 너는 언제든 내게 기대도 돼.
The shelter **relies on** volunteers. 그 쉼터는 자원봉사자들에게 의존한다.
You can **rely on** him to keep a secret. 그가 비밀을 지킬 거라고 믿어도 돼.

477 **adopt**

[ədάpt]

adoption 명 입양; 채택

to take someone else's child into your family

동 1. 입양하다 2. 채택하다

adopt a child 아이를 입양하다

They **adopted** a puppy from the shelter. 그들은 보호소에서 강아지를 입양했다.

adopt a new method 새로운 방법을 채택하다

478 **adapt**

[ədǽpt]

adaptation 명 적응

to change something to make it suitable for a new situation

동 적응하다, 익숙해지다 ((to))

adapt to a new environment 새로운 환경에 적응하다

It takes time to **adapt to** change. 변화에 적응하는 데는 시간이 걸린다.

479 **be devoted to**

to devote yourself to someone or something

~에게 헌신적이다

She **is devoted to** her family. 그녀는 가족에게 헌신적이다.

She has always **been devoted to** her children. 그녀는 항상 자녀들에게 헌신해 왔다.

480 **depend on**

to rely on someone or something

~에 의지[의존]하다, ~에 달려 있다

My brother and I **depend on** each other. 우리 형과 나는 서로 의지한다.

Whether we go or not **depends on** the weather. 우리가 가느냐 마느냐는 날씨에 달려 있다.

Check Up

A 우리말에 맞게 빈칸에 알맞은 말을 넣으세요.

1. 다문화 사회 — a multicultural ________
2. 긴급 원조를 제공하다 — provide emergency ________
3. 치과 예약을 하다 — make an ________ with a dentist
4. 헌혈하다 — ________ blood
5. 기금을 모으다 — raise ________
6. 새로운 환경에 적응하다 — ________ a new environment

B 우리말에 알맞은 말을 골라 문장을 완성하세요.

1. Can I see your (identity / diversity) card? 신분증을 보여 주시겠어요?
2. She (devoted / was devoted) her life to helping others. 그녀는 다른 사람들을 돕는 데 자신의 삶을 바쳤다.
3. She (devotes / is devoted) to her family. 그녀는 가족에게 헌신적이다.
4. The choice (relies / depends) on you. 선택은 너에게 달려 있다.
5. They (adopted / adapted) a puppy. 그들은 강아지를 입양했다.

Build Up

A Write the correct word for each definition.

majority	identity	diverse	obtain	appointment	donate

1. 

who someone is

____

2. 

very different from each other

____

3. 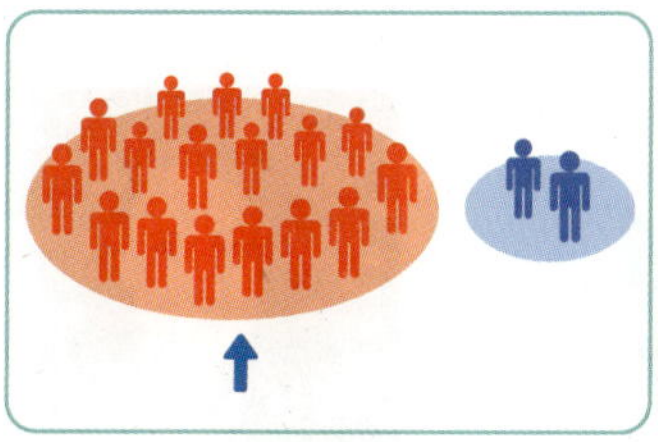

most of the people in a group

____

4. 

a formal arrangement to meet someone

____

5. 

to give money or goods to a person

____

6. 

to get something by making an effort

____

B Write the correct word or phrase next to each definition.

appoint	necessary	aid	depend on	charity	contribute

1. money or food that is sent to help a country ________________
2. needed in order to do something; essential ________________
3. to officially choose someone for a position ________________
4. to give something to help someone or something ________________
5. an organization for helping people in need ________________
6. to rely on someone or something ________________

Review Test 06 DAY 21-24

A 그림을 보고, 빈칸에 알맞은 단어를 넣으세요.

passenger	cotton	bare	award	identity	athlete

1. 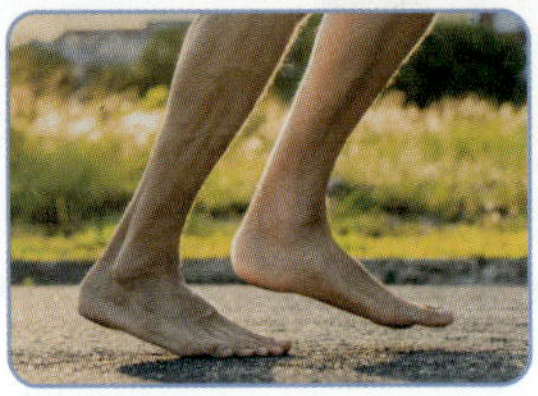 ______________

2. 

____

3.  ______________

4.  ______________

5.  ______________

6. 

____

B 그림에 알맞은 문장을 골라 표시하세요.

1. 

☐ The closet is full of clothes.

☐ The drawer is full of clothes.

2. 

☐ They are dressed in Halloween costumes.

☐ They are wearing stage costumes.

3. 

☐ The opening ceremony is being held now.

☐ A wedding ceremony is being held now.

4. 

☐ The surface of the road looks slippery.

☐ The skier is sliding down the slope.

C 우리말 뜻에 맞게 빈칸에 알맞은 말을 넣으세요.

compete	hold	slippery	amount of
lost	donate	funds	appointment

1. spend a large __________ money 많은 액수의 돈을 쓰다
2. __________ the Olympics 올림픽을 개최하다
3. __________ against each other 서로 경쟁하다
4. __________ roads 미끄러운 도로
5. find a __________ puppy 잃어버린 강아지를 찾다
6. make an __________ with a dentist 치과 예약을 하다
7. __________ blood 헌혈하다
8. raise __________ 기금을 모으다

D 우리말 뜻에 맞게 빈칸에 알맞은 말을 넣으세요.

naked	pretended to	suitable for
contributed ~ to	depend on	rather ~ than

1. The baby was __________ after taking a bath. 아기는 목욕 후 벌거벗은 상태였다.
2. The movie is not __________ children. 이 영화는 아이들에게 적합하지 않다.
3. She __________ be happy at the party. 그녀는 파티에서 행복한 척했다.
4. Young children __________ their parents. 어린 아이들은 그들의 부모에게 의지한다.
5. I would __________ read books __________ watch TV.
   나는 TV를 보느니 차라리 책을 읽고 싶다.
6. She __________ money __________ the homeless shelter.
   그녀는 노숙자 쉼터에 돈을 기부했다.

E 밑줄 친 단어와 비슷한 뜻을 가진 단어를 고르세요.

1. We <u>defeated</u> them in the finals.

   a. beat　　b. competed　　c. hit

2. When did the accident <u>take place</u>?

   a. take off　　b. happen　　c. make it

3. She will study <u>abroad</u> next year.

   a. local　　b. overseas　　c. outside

4. We offer <u>diverse</u> activities for children.

   a. suitable　　b. necessary　　c. various

F 밑줄 친 단어와 반대의 뜻을 가진 단어를 고르세요.

1. That dress is too <u>fancy</u> for a little girl.

   a. plain　　b. expensive　　c. suitable

2. They cheered and shouted <u>aloud</u>.

   a. loudly　　b. silently　　c. rapidly

3. They arrived at Incheon <u>International</u> Airport.

   a. foreign　　b. national　　c. abroad

4. The airplane <u>took off</u> smoothly.

   a. took on　　b. made it　　c. landed

G 주어진 영영풀이에 알맞은 단어를 고르세요.

1. a prize given to someone (for something they have achieved)

   a. award　　b. reward　　c. ceremony

2. a deserved outcome or result

   a. costume　　b. reward　　c. compass

3. the place that someone or something is going to

   a. passenger　　b. destination　　c. harbor

4. to take someone else's child into your family

   a. contribute　　b. adapt　　c. adopt

5. to use time or energy for a particular purpose or person

   a. devote　　b. donate　　c. depend

6. an organization for helping people in need

   a. donation　　b. fund　　c. charity

H 빈칸에 알맞은 동사 형태를 넣어 문장을 완성하세요.

1. The next Olympics will ____________________ in Los Angeles. (hold)
2. She had the dress ____________________. (alter)
3. After many tries, I finally ____________________. (make it)
4. She ____________________ pizza to chicken. (prefer)

481 **relate**
[riléit]

to connect (something) with (something else)
동 1. 관련시키다, 결부시키다 유 connect 연결하다 2. 이해하다, 공감하다 ((to))

He **related** the issue **to** everyday life. 그는 그 문제를 일상생활과 결부시켰다.
I can **relate to** your feelings. 나는 네 기분 이해해(네 감정에 공감할 수 있어).

482 **related**
[riléitid]

connected with something or someone
형 1. 관련된 2. 친척의 ((to))

These problems are closely **related**. 이 문제들은 밀접하게 연관되어 있다.
It is **related to** climate change. 그것은 기후 변화와 관련되어 있다.
Are you **related to** John? 너는 존과 친척이니?

483 **relationship**
[riléiʃənʃip]
relation 명 관계, 관련성

the way in which two things are connected
명 1. (사람·집단 사이의) 관계 ((with/between)) 2. (연인) 관계

He **has a** good **relationship with** his sister. 그는 여동생과 사이가 좋다.
the **relationship between** lung cancer **and** smoking 폐암과 흡연 사이의 관계
Are you in a **relationship**? 너는 사귀는 사람 있니?

484 **relative**
[rélətiv]
relatively 부 상대적으로

a person who is connected by blood or marriage
명 친척 형 상대적인, 비교상의 반 absolute 절대적인

a close **relative** / a distant **relative** 가까운 친척 / 먼 친척
What are some **relative** advantages of a big family? 대가족의 상대적인 이점은 무엇일까?

485 **bond**
[ba:nd]

something that forms a connection between people or groups
명 유대, 끈

build a strong **bond** 강한 유대를 형성하다
They have a strong **bond** as a family. 그들은 가족으로서 강한 유대를 갖고 있다.

486 **bind**
[baind]
binder 명 묶는 것, 바인더

to tie something with string or rope (bound-bound)
동 묶다, 결속시키다

bind a package with strings 끈으로 소포를 묶다
Sports can **bind** people together. 스포츠는 사람들을 함께 결속시킬 수 있다.

487 **unite**
[ju:náit]
united 형 연합한, 통합된
union 명 조합, 협회

to join together; to make people join together
동 연합하다; 통합시키다, 결속시키다

The two countries **united** against a common enemy.
그 두 나라는 공동의 적에 맞서 연합했다.
A common goal can **unite** a team. 공동의 목표는 팀을 결속시킬 수 있다.

488 **combine**
[kəmbáin]
combination 명 조합(물), 결합(물)

to mix or join things together; to become mixed or joined
동 1. 섞다, 결합하다; 섞이다 2. 단합하다, 연합하다

combine blue and yellow 파란색과 노란색을 섞다
They **combined** against a common enemy. 그들은 공동의 적에 맞서 단합했다.

489 **separate**
[sépərèit]
separation 명 분리, 헤어짐

to divide things into different parts or groups
동 1. 분리하다, 나누다; 분리되다 ((into)) 2. 헤어지다 형 [séprət] 분리된, 각기 다른

separate the students **into** two teams 학생들을 두 팀으로 분리하다
The couple decided to **separate**. 그 커플은 헤어지기로 결심했다.
That's a **separate** issue. 그것은 별개의 문제이다.

490 **divide**
[diváid]
divided 형 나누어진, 분열된
division 명 분할; 배분

to separate something into parts or groups
동 1. 나누다; 나뉘다 ((into)) 2. (몫을) 나누다, 분배하다

The teacher **divided** the class **into** two groups. 선생님은 반을 두 그룹으로 나누었다.
The task will be **divided** equally. 과제는 균등하게 분배될 것이다.

491 **apart**
[əpɑ́ːrt]

separated by a distance or period of time
부 1. (공간·시간상으로) 떨어져 2. 따로, 헤어져 3. 조각조각

The two houses are 100 meters **apart**. 그 두 집은 100미터 떨어져 있다.
They are living **apart** now. 그들은 이제 따로 살고 있다.
The vase fell and broke **apart**. 꽃병이 떨어져 산산조각이 났다.

492 **broken**
[bróukən]

damaged and separated into pieces; not working
형 1. 깨진, 부서진; 고장 난 2. 파탄 난

a **broken** window 깨진 창문
a **broken** heart 다친 마음, 실연, 상심
rebuild a **broken** friendship 깨진 우정을 회복하다

493 **involve**
[invɑ́ːlv]

to include something as a necessary part
동 1. 포함하다, 수반하다 2. 관련시키다, 연루시키다 ((in))

Rock climbing **involves** a lot of risk. 암벽 등반은 많은 위험을 수반한다.
He was **involved in** a car accident. 그는 교통사고에 연루되었다.

494 **apologize**
[əpɑ́lədʒàiz]
apology 명 사과, 사죄

to say that you are sorry for doing something wrong
동 사과하다, 사죄하다 ((to sb)) ((for sth)) = (영) apologise

Go and **apologize to** her. 가서 그녀에게 사과해라.
He **apologized to** her **for** the accident. 그는 그녀에게 그 사고에 대해 사과했다.

495 **ought**
[ɔːt]

should
동 ~해야 한다, ~하는 것이 당연하다 ((to))

You **ought to** apologize for being late. 너는 늦은 것에 대해 사과해야 한다.
They **ought to** be here by now. 그들은 지금쯤 여기 있어야 한다.

496 **otherwise**
[ʌ́ðərwàiz]

if not; or else
부 1. 그렇지 않으면 2. 그 외에는

You ought to hurry; **otherwise**, you'll be late. 너는 서둘러야 해. 그렇지 않으면 늦을 거야.
He was tired but **otherwise** in good health. 그는 피곤했지만 그 외에는 건강했다.

497 **except**
[iksépt]
exception 명 예외

not including (someone or something); apart from
전 ~을 제외하고, ~ 외에는

Everyone arrived on time **except** John. 존을 제외하고는 모두 제시간에 도착했다.
They work every day **except** Sunday. 그들은 일요일을 제외하고 매일 일한다.

498 **despite**
[dispáit]

although something happened or is true; in spite of
전 ~에도 불구하고

Despite the traffic, we arrived on time. 교통 체증에도 불구하고 우리는 제시간에 도착했다.
Despite the cold weather, he went for a walk. 추운 날씨에도 불구하고 그는 산책을 나갔다.

499 **had better**

to ought to do
~하는 것이 좋겠다, ~하는 게 좋을 거다(경고성)

You'**d better** apologize to him right now. 그에게 지금 당장 사과하는 게 좋겠다.
You **had better** not be late again. 다시는 늦지 않는 게 좋을 것이다.

500 **except for**

apart from
~을 제외하고 = except

Everything was perfect **except for** the weather. 날씨를 제외하고 모든 것이 완벽했다.
The store is open every day **except for** Sunday. 그 가게는 일요일을 제외하고 매일 연다.

Check Up

A 우리말에 맞게 빈칸에 알맞은 말을 넣으세요.

1. ~와 사이[관계]가 좋다 — have a good ________________ with
2. 가까운 친척 — a close ________________
3. 강한 유대를 형성하다 — build a strong ________________
4. 반을 두 그룹으로 나누다 — ________________ the class into two groups
5. 깨진 창문 — a ________________ window
6. 추운 날씨에도 불구하고 — ________________ the cold weather

B 우리말에 알맞은 말을 골라 문장을 완성하세요.

1. He (**related** / **involved**) the issue to everyday life. 그는 그 문제를 일상생활과 결부시켰다.
2. A common goal can (**unite** / **relate**) a team. 공동의 목표는 팀을 결속시킬 수 있다.
3. He was (**combined** / **involved**) in a car accident. 그는 교통사고에 연루되었다.
4. You'd better (**apologize** / **apologized**) to him right now. 그에게 지금 당장 사과하는 게 좋겠다.
5. They work every day (**except** / **despite**) for Sunday. 그들은 일요일을 제외하고 매일 일한다.

Build Up

A Write the correct word for each definition.

separate	bind	related	broken	except	combine

1\. 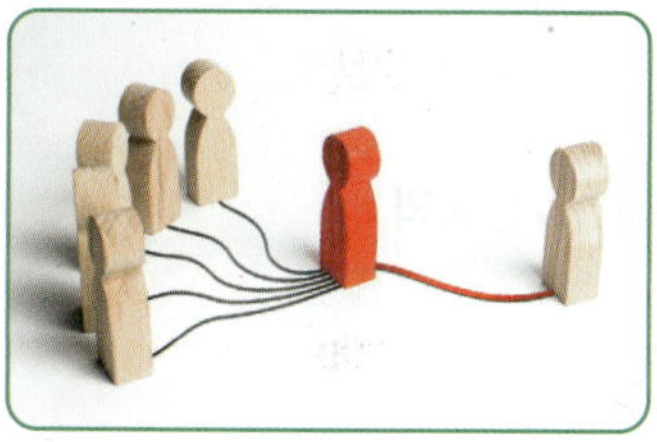

connected with something

____

2\. 

to tie something with string

____

3\. 

to mix or join things together

____

4\. 

to divide something into different parts

____

5\. 

damaged and separated into pieces

____

6\. 

not including

____

B Write the correct word or phrase next to each definition.

apologize	involve	otherwise	relate	divide	had better

1. to connect (something) with (something else) __________
2. to separate things into parts or groups __________
3. to include something as a necessary part __________
4. to say that you are sorry for doing something wrong __________
5. if not; or else __________
6. to ought to do __________

DAY 26

501 **colleague** [káliːg]
a person that you work with
명 (직장) 동료
He is my **colleague** at work. 그는 내 직장 동료이다.

502 **fellow** [félou]
a way of referring to a man or boy
명 1. (비격식) 녀석, 친구 2. 동료, 동년배 형 동료의
He's a nice **fellow**. 그는 멋진 녀석이다.
They are his **fellow** workers. 그들은 그의 직장 동료들이다.

503 **organization** [ɔ̀rgənizéiʃən]
organize 동 준비하다, 조직하다
a group of people who work together for the same purpose
명 1. 조직, 단체, 기구 2. 구조 = structure
She works for an international **organization**. 그녀는 국제 기구에서 일한다.
the **organization** of a company 회사의 구조(조직)

504 **department** [dipáːrtmənt]
a section of a large organization
명 1. (조직의 한) 부서, 부처 2. (백화점 등의) 매장
He is a new colleague in our **department**. 그는 우리 부서의 새로운 동료이다.
the **Department** of Defense 국방부
department store 백화점

505 **fault** [fɔːlt]
the responsibility for a mistake or error
명 1. 잘못, 과실 유 mistake 실수 2. 결점, 결함 *failure 실패
The accident was not my **fault**. 그 사고는 내 잘못이 아니었다.
Everyone has **faults**. 누구나 결점을 가지고 있다.

506 **crisis** [kráisis]
a situation or time that is extremely dangerous or difficult
명 위기, 고비
He is having a **crisis** at work. 그는 직장에서 위기를 겪고 있다.
face an economic **crisis** 경제 위기에 직면하다

507 **trouble** [trʌbl]
troublesome 형 골칫거리인
problems, difficulties, or worries
명 1. 곤란, 어려움 2. 병, 통증 유 problem 문제
He **got into trouble** for the mistake. 그는 그 실수 때문에 곤란한 상황에 처했다.
He **has trouble** finding a solution. 그는 해결책을 찾는 데 어려움을 겪고 있다.
have back **trouble** 허리 통증이 있다

508 **challenge** [ʧǽlindʒ]
challenging 형 도전적인, 힘든
a difficult task that tests someone's ability and skill
명 도전, 시험대 동 1. 도전하다 2. 이의를 제기하다
It was a big **challenge** for him. 그것은 그에게는 큰 도전이었다.
challenge a world record 세계 기록에 도전하다
He **challenged** the decision. 그는 그 결정에 이의를 제기했다.

509 **slave** [sleiv]

slavery 명 노예 제도

a person who is owned by another person and has to work for them

명 노예

He worked like a **slave** all day. 그는 하루 종일 노예처럼 일했다.

510 **freedom** [fríːdəm]

free 형 자유로운

the right to do what you want (without anyone stopping you)

명 자유 유 liberty 자유

A slave has no **freedom**. 노예는 자유가 없다.

freedom of expression 표현의 자유

511 **advise** [ædváiz]

advice 명 충고, 조언

advisor 명 조언자

to tell someone what you think they should do

동 충고하다, 조언하다 ((to)) 유 suggest 제안하다

The doctor **advised** him **to** exercise more. 의사는 그에게 더 많이 운동하라고 조언했다.

512 **motivate** [móutəvèit]

motive 명 동기, 이유

to make someone want to do something

동 동기를 부여하다, 자극하다 ((to)) 유 drive (~하게) 만들다, inspire 영감을 주다

The coach **motivated** him **to** try harder. 코치는 그가 더 열심히 하도록 동기를 부여했다.

He is **motivated** by success. 그는 성공에 자극받는다(동기 부여가 된다).

513 **rumor** [rúːmər]

information or a story that people talk about, but that may not be true

명 소문, 풍문

spread a **rumor** 소문을 퍼뜨리다

I heard a **rumor** that you were leaving. 나는 당신이 떠난다는 소문을 들었다.

514 **obvious** [ábviəs]

obviously 부 분명히, 명백히

easy to see or understand

형 1. (누가 봐도) 분명한, 명백한 2. 너무 뻔한 유 clear (의심의 여지 없이) 분명한

It was **obvious** that he was lying. 그가 거짓말을 하고 있음은 (누가 봐도) 분명했다.

The ending was pretty **obvious**. 결말이 좀 너무 뻔했다.

515 **stick** [stik]

to cause something to become fixed with glue, tape, etc. (stuck-stuck)

동 1. 붙이다; 붙다 2. (~에 끼여) 꼼짝하지 않다 ((in)) 명 나무 막대기, 채

He **stuck** a stamp on the envelope. 그는 봉투에 우표를 붙였다.

We were **stuck in** traffic. 우리는 교통 체증에 갇혀 있었다.

a drum **stick** 드럼 채

516 **sticky** [stíki]

sticking to a surface; tending to stick

형 1. 끈적거리는, 달라붙는 = gluey 2. 난처한, 곤란한

The floor was very **sticky**. 바닥이 매우 끈적거렸다.

a **sticky** situation 난처한 상황

517 **forward** [fɔ́:rwərd]

toward the direction that is in front of you

부 1. (위치가) 앞으로 2. (시간상) 앞으로 반 backward 뒤로 동 전달하다 ((to))

I pulled the chair **forward**. 나는 의자를 앞으로 당겼다.
Always look **forward**, not back. 항상 앞을(미래를) 보고, 뒤를 돌아보지 마세요.
Could you **forward** this email **to** John? 이 이메일을 존에게 전달해 줄 수 있나요?

518 **lean** [li:n]

to bend or move from a straight position

동 1. (몸을) 기울이다, 숙이다 2. 기대다, 의지하다 ((on))

The tower is **leaning** forward. 그 탑은 앞으로 기울어져 있다.
He **leaned** forward to see better. 그는 더 잘 보기 위해 몸을 앞으로 숙였다.
Lean on me whenever you need help. 도움이 필요할 때는 언제든지 내게 기대.

519 **stick to**

to continue doing something despite difficulties

~을 고수하다, ~을 지키다

Let's **stick to** our original plan. 우리의 원래 계획을 고수하자.
Please **stick to** the rules during the game. 게임 중에는 규칙을 지켜 주세요.

520 **look forward to**

to expect something with pleasure

~을 고대하다[기대하다]

I **look forward to** meeting you next week. 다음 주에 당신을 만나기를 고대합니다.
I'm really **looking forward to** the trip. 나는 정말 그 여행을 기대하고 있다.

Check Up

A 우리말에 맞게 빈칸에 알맞은 말을 넣으세요.

1. 백화점 ________________ store
2. 경제 위기에 직면하다 face an economic ________________
3. 해결책을 찾는 데 어려움을 겪다 have ________________ finding a solution
4. 세계 기록에 도전하다 ________________ a world record
5. 표현의 자유 ________________ of expression
6. 소문을 퍼뜨리다 spread a ________________

B 우리말에 알맞은 말을 골라 문장을 완성하세요.

1. She works for an international (**department** / **organization**). 그녀는 국제 기구에서 일한다.
2. The accident was not my (**fault** / **failure**). 그 사고는 내 잘못이 아니었다.
3. He is (**motivating** / **motivated**) by success. 그는 성공에 자극받는다(동기 부여가 된다).
4. We were (**stick to** / **stuck in**) traffic. 우리는 교통 체증에 갇혀 있었다.
5. I look (**forward** / **backward**) to meeting you. 나는 당신을 만나기를 고대합니다.

Build Up

A Write the correct word for each definition.

colleague
freedom
lean
sticky
challenge
slave

1. 

a person that you work with

____

2. 

a difficult task

____

3. 

a person who is owned by another person

____

4. 

the right to do what you want

____

5. 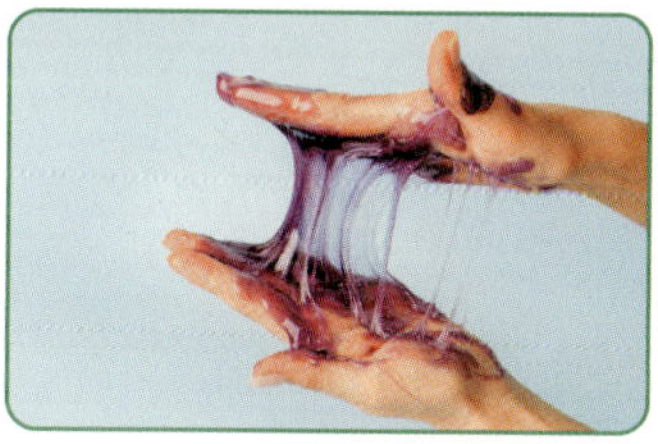

sticking to a surface

____

6. 

to bend or move from a straight position

____

B Write the correct word or phrase next to each definition.

stick to	organization	fault	obvious	forward	trouble

1. a group of people who work together for the same purpose __________
2. the responsibility for a mistake or error __________
3. problems, difficulties, or worries __________
4. easy to see or understand __________
5. toward the direction that is in front of you __________
6. to continue doing something despite difficulties __________

521 **occasion**
[əkéiʒən]
occasionally 부 가끔

an important event; a time when something happens
명 1. (특별한) 행사, 경사 2. (특정한) 경우, 때 유 event 행사

What's the **occasion**? 무슨 날이야? / 무슨 일이야?
She wears the dress on special **occasions**. 그녀는 특별한 행사 때 그 드레스를 입는다.
I've met him on several **occasions**. 나는 몇 번 그를 만났다.

522 **occur**
[əkə́ːr]
occurrence 명 발생(하는 것)

to happen or take place
동 일어나다, 발생하다

The accident **occurred** during the ceremony. 그 사고는 기념식 중에 발생했다.

523 **anniversary**
[ænəvə́ːrsəri]

a date on which an event happened in the past
명 (~주년) 기념일

They celebrated their wedding **anniversary**. 그들은 결혼기념일을 축하했다.
the 30th **anniversary** of our company 우리 회사의 창립 30주년

524 **celebration**
[sèləbréiʃən]
celebrate 동 기념하다, 축하하다

an occasion or party that celebrates a special event
명 기념 행사, 축하 행사 *congratulation 축하

The company held a **celebration** for its 50th anniversary.
그 회사는 창립 50주년 기념 행사를 개최했다.

525 **guest**
[gest]

a person who is invited to an event
명 손님, 하객, 내빈 유 visitor 방문객, 손님

make a **guest** list 초대 손님 명단을 작성하다
More than 100 **guests** were invited. 100명 이상의 하객이 초대되었다.

526 **host**
[houst]

a person who invites guests to an event
명 1. (손님을 초대한) 주인, 주최자 2. 진행자 *hostess (손님을 초대한) 여주인, 여성 진행자

John, our **host**, greeted us at the door. 우리의 호스트 존이 문 앞에서 우리를 맞이했다.
a TV game show **host** TV 게임 프로 진행자

527 **constant**
[kánstənt]

happening all the time or repeatedly
형 1. 끊임없는, 반복되는 2. 일정한, 변함없는

the **constant** noise from next door 옆집에서 나는 끊임없는 소음
move at a **constant** speed 일정한 속도로 움직이다

528 **constantly**
[kánstəntli]

all the time or very often
부 끊임없이, 거듭, 계속 = continually

They played music **constantly** during the party. 그들은 파티 내내 계속 음악을 틀었다.

529 **crazy**
[kréizi]

not sensible; very foolish

형 1. 제정신이 아닌, 미친 = mad 2. 열광하는, 광적으로 좋아하는 ((about))

Are you **crazy**? You could get hurt doing that. 너 미쳤니? 그러다 다칠 수도 있어.
That noise is driving me **crazy**. 저 소음 때문에 미치겠다.
She is **crazy about** baseball. 그녀는 야구에 미쳐(푹 빠져) 있다.

530 **careless**
[kɛ́ərlis]
care 명 조심, 주의; 돌봄

not giving enough attention to (what you are doing)

형 1. 부주의한, 조심성 없는 2. 경솔한 반 careful 조심하는

It was **careless** of me to leave the door open. 문을 열어 놓다니 내가 부주의했다.
make a **careless** remark 경솔한 발언을 하다

531 **beyond**
[bijɑ́:nd]

on the other side of something

전 1. [장소] ~ 저편에, ~ 너머 2. [시간] ~을 지나서 3. [한계] ~을 넘어서

The house is **beyond** the hill. 그 집은 언덕 너머에 있다.
The party continued **beyond** midnight. 파티는 자정을 지나서까지 계속되었다.
This task is **beyond** my ability to do. 이 일은 내 능력을 넘어서는(능력 밖의) 일이다.

532 **beneath**
[biní:θ]

under something; in a lower position than something

전 ~ 아래에, ~ 밑에 = underneath 반 above ~ 위에

There is a basement **beneath** the house. 그 집 밑에 지하실이 있다.

533 **within**
[wiðín]

during a particular period of time

전 1. [기간] ~ 이내에, ~ 안에 2. [거리·범위] ~ 내에

Finish the task **within** an hour. 그 과제를 1시간 안에 끝내세요.
It is located **within** walking distance. 그것은 걸어갈 수 있는 거리에 위치해 있다.

534 **without**
[wiðáut]

not having, using, or doing something

전 1. ~ 없이 2. (V-ing) ~하지 않고

He completed it **without** any help. 그는 아무런 도움 없이 그것을 완료했다.
He left **without** saying goodbye. 그는 작별 인사도 없이 떠났다.

535 **previous**
[prí:viəs]
previously 부 이전에

existing or happening before the present time

형 앞서의, 이전의, 바로 앞의

He is the **previous** owner of the house. 그는 이 집의 (바로) 전 주인이다.
the **previous** president 바로 직전 대통령
I met him the **previous** day. 나는 바로 전날 그를 만났다.

536 **former**
[fɔ́:rmər]

having a particular position in the past

형 (이)전의, 전임의 = ex- 명 (the former) 전자 반 the latter 후자

former President Barack Obama 버락 오바마 전 대통령
her **former** husband 그녀의 전남편
choose **the former** (둘 중에서) 전자를 택하다

537 **else**
[els]

in addition to something already mentioned
부 그 밖에, 달리, 다른

Do you need anything **else**? 그 밖에 다른 필요한 것이 있으세요?
What **else** did he say? 그가 그 외에 또 뭐라고 하던가요?

538 **instead**
[instéd]

in place of someone or something
부 대신에 ((of))

Can I have soup **instead of** salad? 샐러드 대신에 수프를 먹어도 될까요?
Lisa was sick, so I went **instead**. 리사가 아파서 내가 대신 갔다.

539 **can't wait to V / can't wait for N**

to look forward to doing something
빨리 ~을 하고 싶다, ~이 너무 기다려진다

I **can't wait to** see you. 빨리 너를 보고 싶어.
We **can't wait for** summer vacation. 우리는 여름 방학을 너무 기다리고 있어.

540 **instead of**

in place of
~ 대신에, ~이 아니라

Let's watch a movie **instead of** going out. 나가는 대신에 영화를 보자.
He took the stairs **instead of** the elevator. 그는 엘리베이터 대신 계단을 이용했다.

Check Up

A 우리말에 맞게 빈칸에 알맞은 말을 넣으세요.

1. 우리 회사의 창립 30주년 — the 30th ____________ of our company
2. 옆집에서 나는 끊임없는 소음 — the ____________ noise from next door
3. 경솔한[부주의한] 발언을 하다 — make a ____________ remark
4. 아무런 도움 없이 — ____________ any help
5. 이 집의 (바로) 전 주인 — the ____________ owner of the house
6. 그녀의 전남편 — her ____________ husband

B 우리말에 알맞은 말을 골라 문장을 완성하세요.

1. What's the (occasion / occur)? 무슨 날이야? / 무슨 일이야?
2. He is (care / crazy) about baseball. 그는 야구에 미쳐(푹 빠져) 있다.
3. It is located (without / within) walking distance. 그것은 걸어갈 수 있는 거리에 위치해 있다.
4. Can I have soup (instead / instead of) salad? 샐러드 대신에 수프를 먹어도 될까요?
5. I (can wait / can't wait) to see you. 빨리 너를 보고 싶어.

Build Up

A Write the correct word for each definition.

celebration	guest	host	beneath	occur	beyond

1. 

to happen or take place

____

2. 

an occasion or party

____

3. 

a person who invites guests to an event

____

4. 

a person who is invited to an event

____

5. 

on the other side of something

____

6. 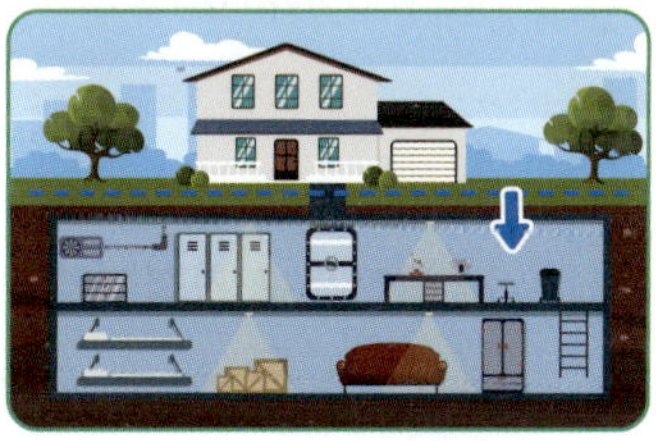

under something

____

B Write the correct word or phrase next to each definition.

anniversary	previous	crazy	careless	occasion	instead of

1. an important event; a time when something happens ______________________
2. a date on which an event happened in the past ______________________
3. not sensible; very foolish ______________________
4. not giving enough attention to (what you are doing) ______________________
5. existing or happening before the present time ______________________
6. in place of ______________________

DAY 28

541 **stuff**
[stʌf]

a group of different things, activities, or matters
명 1. 것[것들], 물건 2. (해야 할) 일[것]

What's all this **stuff**? 이것들이 다 뭐야?
They sell all kinds of camping **stuff**. 그들은 모든 종류의 캠핑 용품을 판다.
I have a lot of **stuff** to do today. 나는 오늘 해야 할 일이 많다.

542 **purchase**
[pə́ːrtʃəs]

the act of buying something
명 구입, 구매 동 구입하다, 구매하다 유 buy 사다

make a **purchase** 구매를 하다
They **purchased** lots of stuff for the party. 그들은 파티를 위해 많은 것들을 구입했다.

543 **stock**
[stɑk]

a supply of goods that is available for sale (in a store)
명 1. 재고품, 재고 2. 주식 *storage 저장, 보관; 저장소

Sorry, but the model is out of **stock**. 죄송하지만 그 모델은 재고가 없어요.
stock prices 주가

544 **available**
[əvéiləbl]

able to be used or can be bought
형 1. 이용할 수 있는, 구할 수 있는 2. (사람이) 시간이 있는

The new model is **available** online. 그 새 모델은 온라인에서 구할 수 있다.
Are you **available** this afternoon? 너 오늘 오후에 시간 있니?

545 **afford**
[əfɔ́ːrd]

to have enough money to buy or time to do something
동 (금전적·시간적으로) ~할 여유가 있다, ~할 형편이 되다 ((to))

We can't **afford to** buy a new car. 우리는 새 차를 살 여유가 없다.

546 **affordable**
[əfɔ́ːrdəbl]

cheap enough for most people to afford
형 (가격이) 알맞은, 부담 없는, 감당할 수 있는

affordable price 부담 없는(적당한) 가격
We decided to purchase a more **affordable** car. 우리는 좀 더 저렴한 차를 구입하기로 했다.

547 **reasonable**
[ríːzənəbl]

reason 명 이유; 이성; 분별

fair, practical, and sensible; not too expensive
형 1. 합리적인, 타당한 2. (가격이) 적정한, 비싸지 않은

make a **reasonable** decision 합리적인 결정을 내리다
I bought a used car at a **reasonable** price. 나는 중고차를 적정한 가격에 샀다.

548 **inexpensive**
[ìnikspénsiv]

not expensive; reasonable in price
형 비싸지 않은 유 cheap 싼

We found a relatively **inexpensive** hotel for our vacation.
우리는 휴가를 위해 비교적 비싸지 않은 호텔을 찾았다.

549 **insurance**
[inʃúərəns]
insure 동 보험에 들다

a deal where a company promises to pay you money if something bad happens
명 1. 보험 2. 보험료

Every driver should have car **insurance**. 모든 운전자는 자동차 보험을 들어야 한다.
pay **insurance** on my car 내 차에 대한 보험료를 내다

550 **loan**
[loun]

the act of borrowing money
명 대출, 대출금

apply for a **loan** to buy a house 집을 사기 위해 대출을 신청하다
repay a **loan** 대출금을 갚다(갚아 나가다)

551 **rate**
[reit]

how often something happens
명 1. 비율 2. 요금 동 평가하다; 등급을 매기다

an interest **rate** 이자율
Taxi **rates** increased last month. 지난달에 택시 요금이 올랐다.
The movie is **rated** G. 그 영화는 G(전체 관람가) 등급을 받았다. *G (General Audiences)

552 **per**
[pəːr]

for each
전 ~당, ~마다

The pay is $15 **per** hour. 급료는 시간당(시급) 15달러이다.
Rooms cost $200 **per** night. 객실 요금은 1박에 200달러이다.

553 **property**
[prápərti]

the thing or things that someone owns
명 1. 재산, 자산 2. 부동산

The library is public **property**. 도서관은 공공 재산이다.
the **property** market 부동산 시장

554 **possess**
[pəzés]
possession 명 소유, 소지

to have or own something
동 소유하다, 소지하다 *belong to ~에 속하다, ~의 소유물이다

He **possesses** lots of private property. 그는 많은 사유 재산을 소유하고 있다.

555 **reduce**
[ridjúːs]
reduction 명 축소; 할인

to make something less
동 1. 줄이다, 축소하다 2. (가격 등을) 낮추다

We need to **reduce** waste. 우리는 쓰레기를 줄여야 한다.
They decided to **reduce** prices. 그들은 가격을 인하하기로 결정했다.
The price was **reduced** by 50%. 가격이 50퍼센트 인하되었다.

556 **replace**
[ripléis]
replacement 명 대체(물)

to be used instead of something
동 1. 대체하다, 대신하다 2. 바꾸다, 교체하다 ((with))

Many jobs are being **replaced** by robots. 많은 일자리들이 로봇으로 대체되고 있다.
Kevin will **replace** her. 케빈이 그녀를 대신할 것이다.
replace an old carpet **with** a new one 낡은 카펫을 새것으로 교체하다

557 **supply**
[səplái]
supplier 명 공급자

an amount of something that is available for use
명 1. 공급(량) 2. (-s) 공급품, 용품 동 공급하다 유 provide 제공하다, 공급하다

The **supply** of water is not enough. 물 공급이 충분하지 않다.
office **supplies** 사무용품
The farm **supplies** milk to local stores. 그 농장은 지역 상점에 우유를 공급한다.

558 **demand**
[dimǽnd]
demanding 형 요구가 많은, 부담이 큰

a strong request; the need for goods or services
명 1. 요구 ((for)) 2. 수요(량) 동 요구하다

the **demand for** higher pay 임금 인상 요구
supply and **demand** 수요와 공급
The customer **demanded** a refund. 그 고객은 환불을 요구했다.

559 **use up**

to use all of something
다 쓰다, 소진하다

He **used up** all his savings. 그는 저축한 돈을 다 써 버렸다.
Don't **use up** all the hot water. 뜨거운 물을 다 쓰지 마라.

560 **run out of**

to use up; to be used up
~을 다 써버리다, ~이 다 되다[다 떨어지다]

We **ran out of** milk. 우유가 다 떨어졌다(우유를 다 써버렸다).
We are **running out of** gas. 연료(휘발유)가 거의 다 떨어져 간다.
My phone **ran out of** battery. 내 핸드폰 배터리가 다 됐다.

Check Up

A 우리말에 맞게 빈칸에 알맞은 말을 넣으세요.

1. 재고가 없는 out of ____________
2. 부담 없는(적당한) 가격 ____________ price
3. 합리적인 결정을 내리다 make a ____________ decision
4. 내 차에 대한 보험료를 내다 pay ____________ on my car
5. 공공 재산 public ____________
6. 수요와 공급 supply and ____________

B 우리말에 알맞은 말을 골라 문장을 완성하세요.

1. The new model is (available / affordable) online. 그 새 모델은 온라인에서 구할 수 있다.
2. We can't (afford / affordable) to buy a car. 우리는 차를 살 여유가 없다.
3. The pay is $15 (per / rate) hour. 급료는 시간당(시급) 15달러이다.
4. Many jobs are being (reduced / replaced) by robots. 많은 일자리들이 로봇으로 대체되고 있다.
5. He (used up / used of) all his savings. 그는 저축한 돈을 다 써 버렸다.

Build Up

A Write the correct word for each definition.

possess	afford	replace	purchase	stuff	reduce

1. 

   a group of different things

   ____

2. 

   the act of buying something

   ____

3. 

   to have enough money to buy

   ____

4. 

   to have or own something

   ____

5. 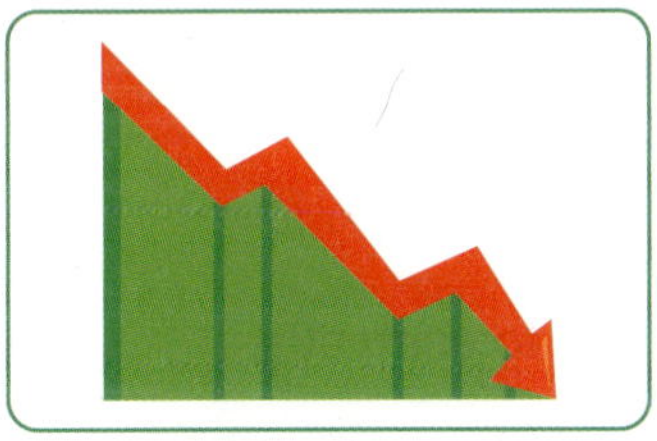

   to make something less

   ____

6. 

   to be used instead of something

   ____

B Write the correct word or phrase next to each definition.

available	reasonable	run out of	affordable	property	loan

1. able to be used or can be bought ______________________
2. cheap enough for most people to afford ______________________
3. fair, practical, and sensible; not too expensive ______________________
4. the act of borrowing money ______________________
5. the thing or things that someone owns ______________________
6. to use up; to be used up ______________________

Review Test 07 DAY 25-28

A 그림을 보고, 빈칸에 알맞은 단어를 넣으세요.

freedom	slave	colleague	stuff	broken	host

1. 

______

2. 

______

3. 

______

4. 

______

5. 

______

6. 

______

B 그림에 알맞은 문장을 골라 표시하세요.

1. 

- ☐ The two houses are close to each other.
- ☐ The two houses are apart from each other.

2. 

- ☐ The store is open every day except Sunday.
- ☐ The store is open every day this week.

3. 

- ☐ It's the 30th anniversary of the company.
- ☐ It's their 30th wedding anniversary.

4. 

- ☐ The car has broken down.
- ☐ The car is running out of gas.

C 우리말 뜻에 맞게 빈칸에 알맞은 말을 넣으세요.

rumor	relative	challenge	despite
relationship	previous	former	constant

1. have a good __________ with ~와 사이가 좋다
2. __________ advantages of a big family 대가족의 상대적인 이점
3. __________ the traffic 교통 체증에도 불구하고
4. __________ a world record 세계 기록에 도전하다
5. spread a __________ 소문을 퍼뜨리다
6. move at a __________ speed 일정한 속도로 움직이다
7. the __________ owner of the house 이 집의 (바로) 전 주인
8. __________ President Joe Biden 조 바이든 전 대통령

D 우리말 뜻에 맞게 빈칸에 알맞은 말을 넣으세요.

afford to	apologized to	involves	related to	except for	forward to

1. It is __________ climate change. 그것은 기후 변화와 관련되어 있다.
2. Rock climbing __________ a lot of risk. 암벽 등반은 많은 위험을 수반한다.
3. He __________ her for the accident. 그는 그녀에게 그 사고에 대해 사과했다.
4. Everything was perfect __________ the weather. 날씨를 제외하고 모든 것이 완벽했다.
5. We can't __________ buy a new car. 우리는 새 차를 살 여유가 없다.
6. I'm really looking __________ the trip. 나는 정말 그 여행을 기대하고 있다.

E 밑줄 친 단어와 비슷한 뜻을 가진 단어를 고르세요.

1. He <u>possesses</u> lots of private property.

   a. belongs b. affords c. has

2. The teacher <u>divided</u> the class into two groups.

   a. involved b. assigned c. separated

3. The accident <u>occurred</u> during the ceremony.

   a. took place b. took off c. went off

4. They <u>purchased</u> lots of stuff for the party.

   a. owned b. bought c. sold

F 밑줄 친 단어와 반대의 뜻을 가진 단어를 고르세요.

1. I pulled the chair <u>forward</u>.

   a. instead b. towards c. backward

2. It was <u>careless</u> of me to leave the door open.

   a. crazy b. care c. careful

3. We found a relatively <u>inexpensive</u> hotel for our vacation.

   a. affordable b. reasonable c. expensive

4. The <u>supply</u> of water is not enough.

   a. provide b. demand c. stock

G 주어진 영영풀이에 알맞은 단어를 고르세요.

1. to mix or join things together; to become mixed or joined

   a. bind　　b. combine　　c. unite

2. damaged and separated into pieces; not working

   a. apart　　b. divided　　c. broken

3. a group of people who work together for the same purpose

   a. department　　b. organization　　c. section

4. the responsibility for a mistake or error

   a. fault　　b. failure　　c. crisis

5. to continue doing something despite difficulties

   a. rely on　　b. look forward to　　c. stick to

6. an important event; a time when something happens

   a. occasion　　b. anniversary　　c. celebration

H 빈칸에 알맞은 동사 형태를 넣어 문장을 완성하세요.

1. She was ________________ a car accident. (involve in)
2. They were ________________ traffic. (stick in)
3. The price was ________________ by almost 50%. (reduce)
4. Many jobs are being ________________ by robots. (replace)

DAY 29

561 **government**
[gʌ́vərnmənt]
govern 동 통치하다, 다스리다

the group of people who officially control a country
명 정부, 정권

Countries have their own **governments**. 나라마다 고유의 정부가 있다.
The **government** has increased taxes. 정부는 세금을 인상했다.

562 **policy**
[páləsi]

a principle of action adopted by a government or business
명 정책, 방침

introduce a new **policy** 새 정책을 도입하다
You should follow the company's **policy**. 당신은 회사의 방침을 따라야 한다.

563 **economy**
[ikánəmi]

the overall economic system of a country or region
명 1. 경제, 경기 2. 절약, 아끼기

The **economy** is recovering quickly. 경제가 빠르게 회복되고 있다.
buy an **economy** pack 절약형 패키지를 사다
economy class (여객기의) 일반석, 보통석

564 **economic**
[èkənámik]
economical 형 경제적인, 절약하는

relating to the economy
형 경제의, 경제상의

Economic growth is slow. 경제 성장이 느리다.
the government's **economic** policy 정부의 경제 정책

565 **current**
[kə́:rənt]
currently 부 현재, 지금

happening or existing now
형 현재의, 지금의 유 present 현재의; recent 최근의 명 (물·공기의) 흐름, 기류, 해류

The **current** economic situation is challenging. 현재 경제 상황은 어려운 상황이다.
an air **current** / an ocean **current** 기류 / 해류

566 **announce**
[ənáuns]
announcement 명 발표

to tell people something officially
동 발표하다, 알리다

announce a new policy 새 정책을 발표하다
The results will be **announced** tomorrow. 결과는 내일 발표될 것이다.

567 **factor**
[fǽktər]

one of several things that cause a situation
명 요인, 요소, 원인

consider economic **factors** 경제적 요인들을 고려하다
Money is an important **factor** in our decision. 우리의 결정에서 돈은 중요한 요소이다.

568 **element**
[éləmənt]

a part of something
명 요소, 성분

In fact, cost was the key **element**. 사실 비용이 핵심 요소였다.
What are the **elements** of water? 물의 성분은 무엇인가요?

569 **domestic**
[dəméstik]

relating to a person's own country
형 1. 국내의 반 international 국제의 2. 가정의, 가사의

The **domestic** market has grown rapidly. 국내 시장이 빠르게 성장했다.
domestic flights 국내선 항공편
domestic chores 집안일, 가사일

570 **trade**
[treid]
trader 명 상인, 거래자

the activity of buying, selling, or exchanging goods
명 무역, 교역 동 무역하다, 거래하다, 교환하다 ((with/for))

international **trade** / domestic **trade** 국제 무역 / 국내 무역
The company **trades with** Europe. 그 회사는 유럽과 거래하고 있다.
Let's **trade** my bike **for** yours. 내 자전거와 네 자전거를 바꾸자.

571 **profit**
[práfit]
profitable 형 수익성이 있는

the money that you make in business
명 (금전적인) 이익, 수익 반 loss 손실, 손해

The company made a huge **profit** last year. 그 회사는 작년에 막대한 이익을 냈다.

572 **benefit**
[bénəfit]
beneficial 형 유익한, 이로운

a good or helpful result or effect
명 혜택, 이득 유 advantage 유리한 점, 이점 동 득이 되다; 득을 보다

Employees will enjoy various **benefits**. 직원들은 다양한 혜택을 누리게 될 것이다.
This program will **benefit** all of you. 이 프로그램은 여러분 모두에게 득이 될 것이다.

573 **continuous**
[kəntínjuəs]
continue 동 계속되다; 계속하다
continuously 부 끊임없이

continuing to happen; not stopping
형 1. 계속되는, 지속적인 2. 끊임없는 유 constant 일정한, 반복되는

continuous economic growth 지속적인 경제 성장
There was a **continuous** line of cars. 끊임없는 자동차의 행렬이 이어졌다.

574 **manage**
[mǽnidʒ]
management 명 관리
manager 명 운영자, 관리자

to succeed in doing something, especially something difficult
동 1. (어떻게든) 해내다 2. 경영하다, 관리하다

We couldn't **manage** it without you. 네가 없었다면 우리는 해내지 못했을 거야.
manage a new department 새 부서를 관리하다

575 **calculate**
[kǽlkjulèit]
calculation 명 계산; 추산
calculator 명 계산기

to find out an amount or cost by using numbers
동 1. 계산하다 2. 추산하다

Let's **calculate** the total cost. 총 비용을 계산해 보자.
calculate the value of the painting 그 그림의 가치를 추산하다

576 **estimate**
[éstəmèit]

to guess or calculate the cost, size, etc. of something
동 추정하다, 어림잡다 ((at)) 명 [éstəmət] 추정(치)

The cost is **estimated at** $900. 비용은 900달러로 추정된다.
a rough **estimate** 대략의 추정치

577 **productive**
[prədʌ́ktiv]

produce 동 생산하다
product 명 생산품, 제품
producer 명 생산자

producing a large amount of goods
형 (대량으로) 생산하는, 생산적인 반 unproductive 비생산적인

a highly **productive** factory 매우 생산성 높은 공장
The meeting was very **productive**. 그 회의는 아주 생산적이었다.

578 **guarantee**
[gærəntíː]

to promise that something is true or will happen
동 1. 보장하다 2. 품질 보증을 하다 명 보증, 보증서

I **guarantee** you will love it. 네가 그것을 좋아할 거라고 나는 장담한다.
The TV is **guaranteed** for twelve months. 이 TV는 12개월 동안 품질 보증이 된다.
a three-year **guarantee** 3년간의 보증(서)

579 **continue V-ing / continue to V**

to keep doing something
계속해서 ~하다, ~하기를 계속하다

She **continued** work**ing** despite the noise. 소음에도 불구하고 그녀는 계속 일했다.
She **continued to** work after a cup of coffee. 커피 한 잔 후에 그녀는 일을 계속했다.

580 **keep (on) V-ing**

to continue doing something
계속해서 ~하다, 줄곧 ~하다

You have to **keep** try**ing**. 너는 계속 시도해야[노력해야] 해.
He **kept on** practic**ing** even after he failed. 그는 실패 후에도 계속 연습했다.

Check Up

A 우리말에 맞게 빈칸에 알맞은 말을 넣으세요.

1. 새 정책을 도입하다 introduce a new ________________
2. 현재 경제 상황 the ________________ economic situation
3. 경제적 요인들을 고려하다 consider economic ________________
4. 국내선 항공편 ________________ flights
5. 지속적인 경제 성장 ________________ economic growth
6. 3년간의 보증(서) a three-year ________________

B 우리말에 알맞은 말을 골라 문장을 완성하세요.

1. The (**economy** / **economic**) is recovering quickly. 경제가 빠르게 회복되고 있다.
2. Employees will enjoy various (**profits** / **benefits**). 직원들은 다양한 혜택을 누리게 될 것이다.
3. We couldn't (**manage** / **managed**) it without you. 네가 없었다면 우리는 해내지 못했을 거야.
4. The TV is (**guarantee** / **guaranteed**) for twelve months. 이 TV는 12개월 동안 보장된다.
5. She continued (**work** / **working**) despite the noise. 소음에도 불구하고 그녀는 계속 일했다.

Build Up

A **Write the correct word for each definition.**

calculate | domestic | announce | estimate | productive | trade

1. 

to tell people something officially

____

2. 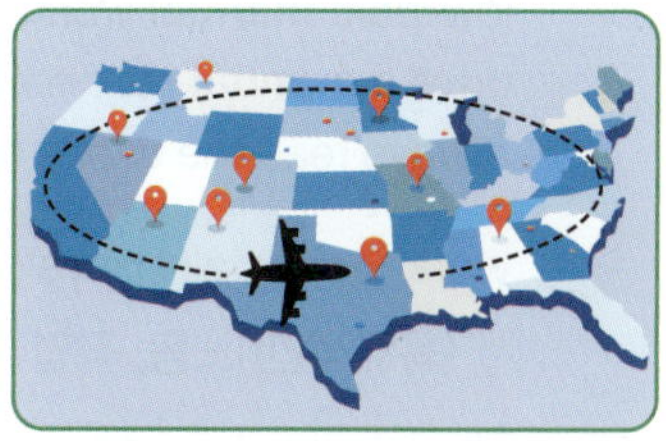

relating to a person's own country

____

3. 

the activity of buying or selling goods

____

4. 

to find out an amount by using numbers

____

5. 

to guess or calculate

____

6. 

producing a large amount of goods

____

B **Write the correct word or phrase next to each definition.**

keep (on) V-ing | guarantee | government | profit | benefit | current

1. the group of people who officially control a country ______________________
2. happening or existing now ______________________
3. the money that you make in business ______________________
4. a good or helpful result or effect ______________________
5. to promise that something is true or will happen ______________________
6. to continue doing something ______________________

581 **manual**
[mǽnjuəl]
manually 부 수동으로

using your hands or physical strength
형 1. 손으로 하는, 육체 노동의 2. 수동의 반 automatic 자동의 명 (제품) 설명서

low-paid **manual** workers 저임금 육체 노동자들
drive a **manual** car 수동 자동차를 운전하다
Always read the user's **manual** first. 항상 사용자 설명서를 먼저 읽어라.

582 **labor**
[léibər]

work, especially physical work
명 (육체적인) 노동, 작업

The job requires manual **labor**. 그 일은 육체 노동을 필요로 한다.

583 **shift**
[ʃift]

to move or change something
동 옮기다, 이동하다, 바꾸다 ((to)) 명 1. (입장 등의) 변화 ((in)) 2. 교대 (근무)

The company **shifted** its focus **to** online. 그 회사는 온라인으로 초점을 바꾸었다.
a **shift in** policy 정책의 변화[전환]
a night **shift** 야간 근무

584 **strategy**
[strǽtədʒi]
strategic 형 전략적인

a plan that you use to achieve something
명 전략, 계획

set up a new marketing **strategy** 새로운 마케팅 전략을 세우다

585 **mission**
[míʃən]
missionary 명 (외국에 파견되는) 선교사

a specific task or duty assigned to a person or group
명 1. 임무 2. 사명, 목적 3. 사절단 *duty 의무 *task 과제

carry out a **mission** successfully 임무를 성공적으로 수행하다
the **mission** of a school 학교의 사명
a trade **mission** 무역 사절단

586 **accomplish**
[əkámpliʃ]
accomplishment 명 성취, 업적

to succeed in doing or completing something
동 이루다, 성취하다, 완수하다 = achieve

accomplish a task 과제를 완료하다
They shouted, "Mission **accomplished**!" 그들은 "임무 완수(했음)!"라고 외쳤다.

587 **formal**
[fɔ́ːrməl]
form 명 형태, 형식

made or done officially; suitable for official occasions
형 1. 공식적인, 정식의 = official 2. 격식을 차린

receive a **formal** invitation 공식 초대장을 받다
wear **formal** dress 정장을 입다
The dinner was very **formal**. 그 만찬은 아주 격식을 차린 자리였다.

588 **informal**
[infɔ́ːrməl]

relaxed and friendly
형 1. 격식에 얽매이지 않는, 비공식적인 2. 평상복의 = casual

have an **informal** meeting 비공식적인 회의를 갖다
wear **informal** clothes 편안한 옷[평상복]을 입다

589 **quit**
[kwit]

to leave your job, school, etc. (quit–quit)
동 1. (직장 등을) 그만두다 = leave 2. (하던 일을) 그만하다 = stop

He **quit** the company. 그는 회사를 그만두었다.
He has **quit** smoking. 그는 담배를 끊었다.

590 **abandon**
[əbǽndən]

to leave someone, especially someone you are responsible for
동 1. 버리다, 버리고 떠나다 2. 포기하다, 단념하다

Many pets are **abandoned** by their owners. 많은 애완동물들이 주인에게서 버려진다.
He **abandoned** his plans to travel. 그는 그의 여행 계획을 포기했다.

591 **fortune**
[fɔ́ːrʧən]

a very large amount of money or property
명 1. 부, 재산, 거금 2. 운 반 misfortune 불운, 불행

He **made a fortune** after becoming a YouTuber. 그는 유튜버가 된 후 큰돈을 벌었다.
Fortune smiled on him. 행운이 그에게 미소를 보냈다(그에게 행운이 따랐다).

592 **fortunately**
[fɔ́ːrʧənətli]
fortunate 형 운이 좋은

by good luck; luckily
부 운 좋게, 다행히도 반 unfortunately 불행하게도

Fortunately, I passed the exam. 다행히도 나는 그 시험에 합격했다.
Fortunately, no one was hurt. 다행히 아무도 다치지 않았다.

593 **several**
[sévərəl]

more than two but not very many
형 몇몇의, 서넛의, 대여섯의

I have met him **several** times. 나는 그를 몇 번 본 적이 있다.
wait for **several** days 며칠 동안 기다리다

594 **dozen**
[dʌzn]

a group of twelve of the same thing
명 12개짜리 한 묶음, 다스

Give me a **dozen**, please. 한 다스(12개) 주세요.
half a **dozen** eggs 계란 6개

595 **expand**
[ikspǽnd]
expansion 명 확대, 확장

to make something larger or greater; to become larger or greater
동 (범위·한도를) 확대하다, 확장시키다; 커지다, 확장되다

They have **expanded** their business into Asia. 그들은 사업을 아시아로 확장시켰다.
The K-pop market is **expanding**. 케이팝 시장이 확장되고 있다.

596 **extend**
[iksténd]
extension 명 확장; 연장

to make something longer or bigger
동 1. 더 길게[크게] 만들다 2. (기한 등을) 연장하다

The city plans to **extend** the road. 시는 그 도로를 연장할 계획이다.
The teacher **extended** the due date. 선생님은 (제출) 마감일을 연장했다.

597 **industry**
[índəstri]
industrial 형 산업의, 공업의

a group of businesses that provide a particular product
명 1. 산업, 공업 2. (특정 분야의) ~업
The computer **industry** is expanding greatly. 컴퓨터 산업이 크게 확장되고 있다.
work in the service **industry** 서비스업에 종사하다

598 **manufacture**
[mænjufǽktʃər]
manufacturer 명 제조자, 제조사

to produce goods in large numbers
동 (대량으로) 제조하다, 생산하다 명 제조, (대량) 생산
The factory **manufactures** cars. 그 공장은 자동차를 생산한다.
the **manufacture** of cars 자동차 제조

599 **get some rest**

to take a break or relax
좀 쉬다, 휴식을 취하다
Why don't you **get some rest**? 좀 쉬는 게 어때요?
The doctor advised him to **get some rest**. 의사는 그에게 좀 쉴 것을 권했다.

600 **wrap up**

to finish or complete
1. 마무리하다 2. 싸다, 포장하다
Let's **wrap** it **up**. 이제 마무리합시다.
Don't forget to **wrap up** the present. 선물 포장하는 것을 잊지 마.

Check Up

A 우리말에 맞게 빈칸에 알맞은 말을 넣으세요.

1. 정책의 변화[전환] — a ________________ in policy
2. 새로운 마케팅 전략을 세우다 — set up a new marketing ________________
3. 임무를 성공적으로 수행하다 — carry out a ________________ successfully
4. 과제를 완료하다 — ________________ a task
5. 며칠 동안 기다리다 — wait for ________________ days
6. 서비스업에 종사하다 — work in the service ________________

B 우리말에 알맞은 말을 골라 문장을 완성하세요.

1. The job requires manual (**labor** / **workers**). 그 일은 육체 노동을 필요로 한다.
2. The dinner was very (**formal** / **informal**). 그 만찬은 아주 격식을 차린 자리였다.
3. The K-pop market is (**extending** / **expanding**). 케이팝 시장이 확장되고 있다.
4. The teacher (**extended** / **expanded**) the due date. 선생님은 (제출) 마감일을 연장했다.
5. Many pets (**abandoned** / **are abandoned**) by their owners. 많은 애완동물들이 주인에게서 버려진다.

Build Up

A Write the correct word for each definition.

informal	formal	dozen	fortune	extend	expand

1. 

suitable for official occasions

______

2. 

relaxed and friendly

______

3. 

a very large amount of money

______

4. 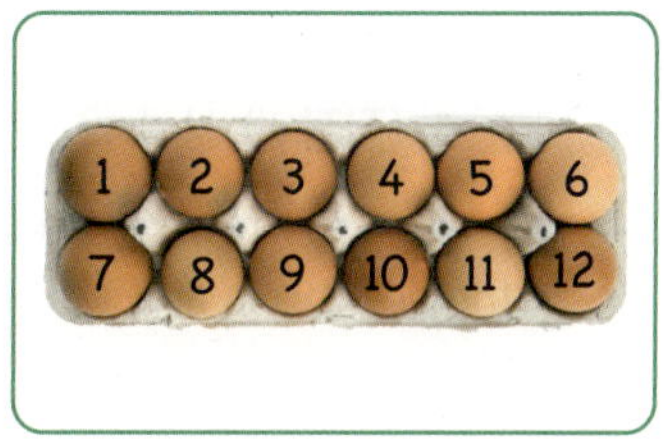

a group of twelve of the same thing

______

5. 

to make something larger or greater

______

6. 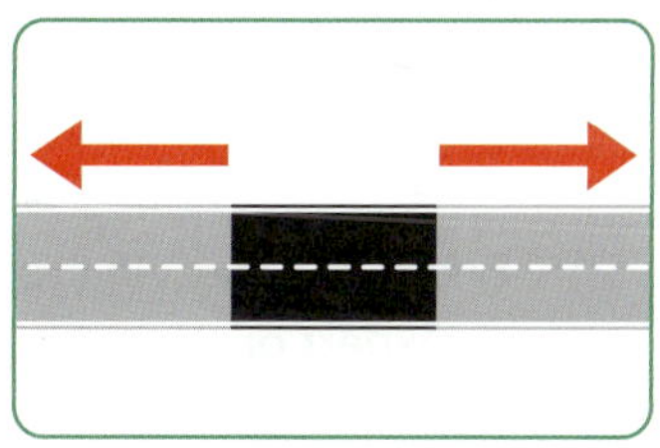

to make something longer or bigger

______

B Write the correct word or phrase next to each definition.

abandon	manual	quit	manufacture	wrap up	accomplish

1. using your hands or physical strength ______
2. to succeed in doing or completing something ______
3. to leave your job, school, etc. ______
4. to leave someone, especially someone you are responsible for ______
5. to produce goods in large numbers ______
6. to finish or complete ______

601 **employy**

[implɔ́i]

employment 명 고용
employer 명 고용주
employee 명 피고용인, 직원

to give someone a job to do for payment

동 고용하다 유 hire (단기간) 빌리다, 고용하다

The company **employs** 250 staff. 그 회사는 250명의 직원을 고용하고 있다.
They **employed** a lawyer. 그들은 변호사를 고용했다.

602 **apply**

[əplái]

application 명 지원(서); 응용 프로그램 (= app)
applicant 명 지원자

to make a formal request, usually in writing

동 1. 지원하다, 신청하다 ((for)) 2. 적용되다 ((to)) 3. 바르다

She decided to **apply for** the job. 그녀는 그 일자리에 지원하기로 결심했다.
The rules **apply to** all employees. 그 규칙은 모든 직원에게 적용된다.
apply sunscreen 자외선 차단제를 바르다

603 **boss**

[bɔːs]

bossy 형 두목 행세를 하는

the person who is in charge of you at work

명 1. (직장의) 상사 2. (큰 조직의) 장, 사장

I talked to my **boss** about it. 나는 그것에 관해 내 상사와 이야기했다.
the new **boss** at IBM IBM의 신임 사장

604 **secretary**

[sékrətèri]

a person who works in an office and assists another person

명 비서

Kelly is employed as a **secretary**. 켈리는 비서로 고용되었다(고용되어 있다).

605 **expert**

[ékspəːrt]

a person who is very knowledgeable or skilled in a particular area

명 전문가 ((in/on)) 유 master 거장, 달인 형 전문가의, 전문적인

She is an **expert in** this field. 그녀는 이 분야의 전문가이다.
an **expert on** AI AI(인공 지능)에 대한 전문가
seek an **expert** opinion 전문가의 의견을 구하다

606 **profession**

[prəféʃən]

professional 형 전문직의, 프로의

a job that needs a high level of education and training

명 (전문적인) 직업, 전문직 유 occupation 직업

He is a doctor by **profession**. 그는 직업이 의사이다.
enter the medical **profession** 의료계에 들어가다(의사가 되다)

607 **command**

[kəmǽnd]

commander 명 지휘관, 사령관

to order someone (officially) to do something

동 명령하다, 지휘하다 ((to)) 명 명령, 지휘

He **commanded** them **to** be quiet. 그는 그들에게 조용히 할 것을 명령했다.
follow the captain's **commands** 선장[주장]의 명령을 따르다

608 **order**

[ɔ́ːrdər]

to tell someone to do something

동 1. 명령하다 ((to)) 2. 주문하다 명 1. 명령 2. 주문 3. 순서

He **ordered** everyone **to** leave. 그는 모두에게 떠날 것을 명령했다.
We **ordered** pizza for dinner. 우리는 저녁으로 피자를 주문했다.
Can I take your **order**? 주문을 받아도 될까요?
List the files in alphabetical **order**. 파일들을 알파벳 순으로 정리해라.

609 **advertise**
[ǽdvərtàiz]

advertisement 명 광고 (= ad)
advertiser 명 광고주

to tell the public about a product or service
동 (신문 등에) 광고하다, 알리다

They plan to **advertise** their new product on TV. 그들은 그들의 신제품을 TV에 광고할 계획이다.
a poster **advertising** the concert 그 콘서트를 알리는 포스터

610 **promote**
[prəmóut]

promotion 명 판촉, 홍보; 승진

to help sell a product, service, etc.
동 1. (제품 등을) 홍보[판촉]하다 2. 촉진하다 3. 승진시키다 ((to))

He is in London to **promote** his new album. 그는 새 앨범을 홍보하기 위해 런던에 있다.
promote economic growth 경제 성장을 촉진하다
She was **promoted to** manager. 그녀는 매니저로 승진했다.

611 **commerce**
[kámə:rs]

the activity of buying and selling, especially on a large scale
명 상업, 무역 유 trade 무역

The city is the global center of **commerce**. 그 도시는 세계 상업의 중심지이다.

612 **commercial**
[kəmə́:rʃəl]

relating to buying and selling things
형 상업의, 상업적인 명 (TV·라디오의) 광고 (방송)

The movie was a huge **commercial** success. 그 영화는 엄청난 상업적 성공을 거뒀다.
see a TV **commercial** TV 광고를 보다

613 **magazine**
[mæ̀gəzí:n]

a thin book published every week or month
명 잡지

a weekly **magazine** 주간지
She was interviewed in a **magazine**. 그녀는 한 잡지에서 인터뷰를 했다.

614 **article**
[á:rtikl]

a piece of writing in a newspaper or magazine
명 (신문·잡지 등의) 글, 기사

read an interesting **article** 흥미로운 기사를 읽다
a magazine **article** on fashion trends 패션 트렌드에 관한 잡지 기사

615 **publish**
[pʌ́bliʃ]

publisher 명 출판사
publication 명 출판(물)

to produce (a book, magazine, etc.) for sale
동 1. 출판하다, 발행하다 2. 공표하다, 발표하다 유 issue 발행하다; 발표하다

The magazine is **published** monthly. 그 잡지는 매월 발행된다.
The report will be **published** on the Internet. 그 보고서는 인터넷으로 발표될 것이다.

616 **release**
[rilí:s]

to let (someone or something) go free
동 1. 풀어 주다, 석방하다 ((from)) 2. 공개[발표]하다 명 석방; 발표, 개봉, 출시

He was **released from** prison. 그는 감옥에서 석방되었다.
release a new smartphone 새 스마트폰을 출시하다
The movie's **release** is next week. 그 영화의 개봉은 다음 주이다.

617 **boom**
[buːm]

a sudden increase in trade and economic activity
명 1. (사업·경제의) 붐, 호황 ((in)) 2. (갑작스런) 인기, 붐 반 slump 불황; 슬럼프

a **boom in** car sales 자동차 판매의 호황
the disco **boom** of the 1970s 1970년대의 디스코 붐

618 **boost**
[buːst]

to increase or improve something
동 1. 밀어 올리다 2. 북돋우다 = boost up 명 격려, 부양책

boost the economy 경기를 부양하다
He **boosted** her **up**. 그는 그녀를 격려했다.
a major **boost** to the economy 주요 경기 부양책

619 **in order to**

for the purpose of doing something
~하기 위하여

He worked hard **in order to** save money. 그는 돈을 모으기 위해 열심히 일했다.
I exercise regularly **in order to** stay healthy. 나는 건강을 유지하기 위해 규칙적으로 운동한다.

620 **out of order**

not working; broken
고장이 난

The copy machine is **out of order**. 복사기가 고장 났다.
The elevator was **out of order**, so I used the stairs. 엘리베이터가 고장 나서 나는 계단을 이용했다.

Check Up

A 우리말에 맞게 빈칸에 알맞은 말을 넣으세요.

1. 선장의 명령을 따르다 — follow the captain's ____________
2. 전문가의 의견을 구하다 — seek an ____________ opinion
3. 그 콘서트를 알리는[광고하는] 포스터 — a poster ____________ the concert
4. 그의 새 앨범을 홍보하다 — ____________ his new album
5. 새 스마트폰을 출시하다 — ____________ a new smartphone
6. 자동차 판매의 호황 — a ____________ in car sales

B 우리말에 알맞은 말을 골라 문장을 완성하세요.

1. Kelly is (**applied / employed**) as a secretary. 켈리는 비서로 고용되었다(고용되어 있다).
2. He is a doctor by (**expert / profession**). 그는 직업이 의사이다.
3. We (**ordered / commanded**) pizza for dinner. 우리는 저녁으로 피자를 주문했다.
4. The magazine (**published / is published**) monthly. 그 잡지는 매월 발행된다.
5. The copy machine is out of (**broken / order**). 복사기가 고장 났다.

Build Up

A Write the correct word for each definition.

apply	order	magazine	article	promote	advertise

1. 

to make a formal request

____

2. 

to tell someone to do something

____

3. 

to tell the public about a product

____

4. 

to help sell a product or service

____

5. 

a thin book published every week or month

____

6. 

a piece of writing in a newspaper or magazine

____

B Write the correct word or phrase next to each definition.

boost	commercial	secretary	in order to	release	command

1. a person who works in an office and assists another person _______________
2. to order someone (officially) to do something _______________
3. to increase or improve something _______________
4. relating to buying and selling things _______________
5. to let (someone or something) go free _______________
6. for the purpose of doing something _______________

621 **exhibit**
[igzíbit]
exhibition 명 전시회

to show something in a public place
동 전시하다 = display 명 전시, 전시회

Many paintings are **exhibited** in the gallery. 그 미술관에는 많은 그림들이 전시되어 있다.
see the Picasso **exhibit** 피카소 전시회를 보다

622 **precious**
[préʃəs]

worth a lot of money; having great value
형 귀중한, 값비싼, 소중한 = valuable; priceless

exhibit **precious** paintings by local artists 지역 화가들의 귀중한 그림들을 전시하다
precious memories 소중한 추억

623 **worth**
[wəːrθ]
worthy 형 ~할 만한 (가치가 있는)

having a particular value, especially in money
형 ~의 가치가 있는, ~할 가치가 있는 반 worthless 가치 없는 명 가치, 값어치

This painting is **worth** $100,000. 이 그림은 10만 달러의 가치가 있다.
The book is **worth** reading. 그 책은 읽을 가치가 있다.
purchase 100 dollars' **worth** of flowers 100달러어치의 꽃을 구입하다

624 **value**
[vǽljuː]
valuable 형 귀중한, 값비싼

how much something is worth in money
명 1. (금전적) 가치, 가격 2. 가치, 유용성 ((of))

go up in **value** 가치가 오르다
understand the **value of** traditional music 전통 음악의 가치를 이해하다

625 **talented**
[tǽləntid]
talent 명 재능; 재능 있는 사람(들), 예능인

having a natural ability to do something well
형 (타고난) 재능이 있는 ((in/at)) = gifted

She is a very **talented** musician. 그녀는 아주 재능 있는 음악가이다.
She is **talented in** music. 그녀는 음악에 소질이 있다.

626 **genius**
[dʒíːnjəs]

a person who is unusually intelligent or artistic
명 1. 천재, 천재성 2. 특별한 재능 ((for))

Einstein was a **genius**. 아인슈타인은 천재였다.
He had a **genius for** solving puzzles. 그는 퍼즐을 푸는 데 재능이 있었다.

627 **decade**
[dékeid]

a period of 10 years
명 10년

The museum was built a **decade** ago. 그 박물관은 10년 전에 지어졌다.
His works have been loved for **decades**. 그의 작품은 수십 년 동안 사랑받아 왔다.

628 **century**
[séntʃəri]

a period of 100 years
명 100년, 세기

many **centuries** ago 몇백 년 전, 수 세기 전
The picture was painted in the 16th **century**. 그 그림은 16세기에 그려졌다.
the early 20th **century** 20세기 초

629 **general** [dʒénərəl]

generally 부 일반적으로; 대개, 보통

not detailed, but including the most basic information

형 1. 전반적인 2. 일반적인, 일반의 반 particular 특정한

What's your **general** impression of the place? 그 장소에 대한 전반적인 인상은 어떤가요?
In **general**, teenagers love hip-hop. 일반적으로 십대들은 힙합을 좋아한다.

630 **concept** [kánsept]

an idea or a principle

명 개념 ((of))

the basic **concepts of** art 예술의 기본 개념
The **concept of** beauty has changed over time. 미의 개념은 시간이 지남에 따라(시대에 따라) 변해 왔다.

631 **steal** [sti:l]

to take something that belongs to someone else (stole-stolen)

동 훔치다, 도둑질하다

steal money from the store 가게에서 돈을 훔치다
The priceless painting was **stolen**. 그 귀중한 그림이 도난당했다.

632 **thief** [θi:f]

a person who steals things

명 도둑, 절도범 *복수형 thieves

The **thief** stole several valuable works of art. 그 도둑은 여러 개의 귀중한 미술품들을 훔쳤다.

633 **commit** [kəmít]

to do something wrong or illegal

동 (죄·과실 등을) 범하다, 저지르다

commit a mistake 실수를 범하다
commit a crime 범죄를 저지르다

634 **crime** [kraim]

criminal 형 범죄의 명 범죄자

activities that involve breaking the law

명 범죄

He committed many **crimes**. 그는 많은 범죄를 저질렀다.
The **crime** rate is rising. 범죄율이 증가하고 있다.

635 **investigate** [invéstəgèit]

investigation 명 조사, 수사
investigator 명 조사관, 수사관

to try to find out the truth about something, such as a crime

동 조사하다, 수사하다

investigate a crime scene 범죄 현장을 조사하다
The police are **investigating** the case. 경찰이 그 사건을 수사하고 있다.

636 **inspect** [inspékt]

inspection 명 점검, 검사
inspector 명 조사관, 감독관

to look at something carefully to find out more about it

동 점검하다, 검사하다 = examine

The police **inspected** the scene. 경찰이 현장을 점검했다.
inspect a building for safety 안전을 위해 건물을 검사하다

637 **appropriate** [əpróupriət]

suitable or proper for a particular time, situation, or purpose

형 적절한, 적합한, 알맞은 ((for)) 반 inappropriate 부적절한

take **appropriate** action 적절한 조치를 취하다

The movie is **appropriate for** children over 13. 이 영화는 13세 이상의 어린이에게 적합하다.

638 **moral** [mɔ́:rəl]

morality 명 도덕(성)

relating to principles of right and wrong in behavior

형 1. 도덕상의, 윤리의 2. 도덕적인 반 immoral 비도덕적인

He has high **moral** standards. 그는 높은 도덕적 기준을 가지고 있다.

a very **moral** man 아주 도덕적인 사람

639 **go through**

to experience a difficult or unpleasant situation

1. (어려운 일을) 겪다, 통과하다 2. (꼼꼼히) 검토하다

He **went through** many difficulties at work. 그는 직장에서 많은 어려움을 겪었다.

You need to **go through** the details. 너는 세부사항을 잘 검토해야 한다.

640 **can't help V-ing**

to be unable to control or stop

~하지 않을 수 없다

I **can't help** fall**ing** in love with you. 나는 당신과 사랑에 빠지지 않을 수 없어요.

We **couldn't help** laugh**ing** at his jokes. 우리는 그의 농담에 웃지 않을 수 없었다.

Check Up

A 우리말에 맞게 빈칸에 알맞은 말을 넣으세요.

1. 귀중한 그림들을 전시하다 exhibit ________________ paintings
2. 전통 음악의 가치 the ________________ of traditional music
3. 아주 재능 있는 음악가 a very ________________ musician
4. 예술의 기본 개념 the basic ________________ of art
5. 범죄를 저지르다 ________________ a crime
6. 적절한 조치를 취하다 take ________________ action

B 우리말에 알맞은 말을 골라 문장을 완성하세요.

1. Many paintings (**exhibited** / **are exhibited**) in the gallery. 그 미술관에는 많은 그림들이 전시되어 있다.
2. This painting is (**worth** / **value**) $100,000. 이 그림은 10만 달러의 가치가 있다.
3. In (**general** / **generally**), teenagers love hip-hop. 일반적으로 십대들은 힙합을 아주 좋아한다.
4. The police are (**investigating** / **inspecting**) the case. 경찰이 그 사건을 수사하고 있다.
5. I can't help (**fall** / **falling**) in love with you. 나는 당신과 사랑에 빠지지 않을 수 없어요.

Build Up

A Write the correct word for each definition.

decade	century	investigate	precious	thief	exhibit

1. 

to show something in a public place

____

2. 

worth a lot of money

____

3. 

a period of 10 years

____

4. 

a period of 100 years

____

5. 

a person who steals things

____

6. 

to try to find out the truth about something

____

B Write the correct word or phrase next to each definition.

go through	genius	inspect	moral	steal	crime

1. a person who is unusually intelligent or artistic ______________
2. to take something that belongs to someone else ______________
3. activities that involve breaking the law ______________
4. to look at something carefully to find out more about it ______________
5. relating to principles of right and wrong in behavior ______________
6. to experience a difficult or unpleasant situation ______________

Review Test 08 DAY 29-32

A 그림을 보고, 빈칸에 알맞은 단어를 넣으세요.

calculate	extend	announce	investigate	article	decade

1. 

____

2. 

____

3. 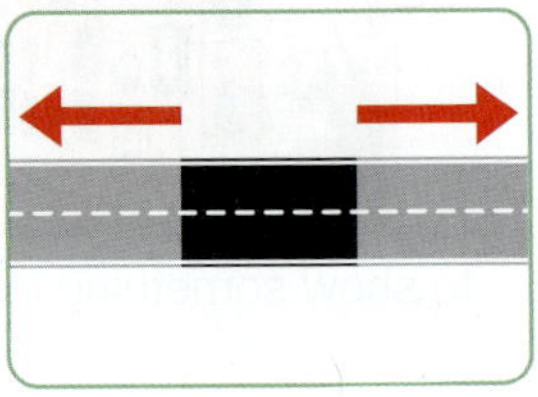

____

4. 

____

5. 

____

6. 

____

B 그림에 알맞은 문장을 골라 표시하세요.

1. 

☐ They have been waiting for several hours.

☐ There is a continuous line of people.

2. 

☐ They are watching a TV commercial.

☐ The new product was a huge commercial success.

3. 

☐ There are a dozen eggs.

☐ There are half a dozen eggs.

4. 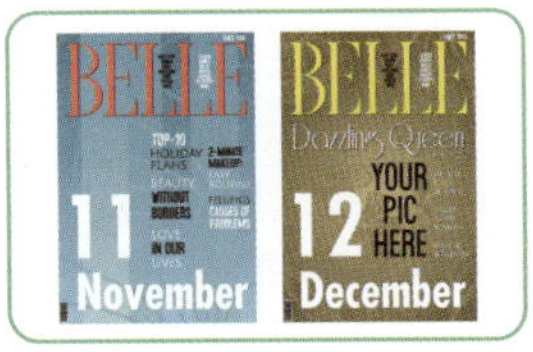

☐ The magazine is published monthly.

☐ The magazine is published weekly.

C 우리말 뜻에 맞게 빈칸에 알맞은 말을 넣으세요.

policy	mission	advertise	productive
release	commit	extend	continuous

1. introduce a new ____________ 새 정책을 도입하다
2. ____________ economic growth 지속적인 경제 성장
3. a highly ____________ factory 매우 생산성 높은 공장
4. carry out a ____________ successfully 임무를 성공적으로 수행하다
5. ____________ the road 그 도로를 연장하다
6. ____________ their new product on TV 그들의 신제품을 TV에 광고하다
7. ____________ a new smartphone 새 스마트폰을 출시하다
8. ____________ a crime 범죄를 저지르다

D 우리말 뜻에 맞게 빈칸에 알맞은 말을 넣으세요.

continued	in order to	estimated	apply for	worth	fortune

1. The cost is ____________ at $900. 비용은 900달러로 추정된다.
2. She ____________ working despite the noise. 소음에도 불구하고 그녀는 계속 일했다.
3. He worked hard ____________ save money. 그는 돈을 모으기 위해 열심히 일했다.
4. He made a ____________ after becoming a YouTuber. 그는 유튜버가 된 후 큰돈을 벌었다.
5. She decided to ____________ the job. 그녀는 그 일자리에 지원하기로 결심했다.
6. The book is ____________ reading. 그 책은 읽을 가치가 있다.

E 밑줄 친 단어와 비슷한 뜻을 가진 단어를 고르세요.

1. They <u>accomplished</u> the task.

   a. assigned b. applied c. achieved

2. He <u>commanded</u> them to be quiet.

   a. promoted b. ordered c. celebrated

3. The copy machine is <u>out of order</u>.

   a. working b. operating c. broken

4. Many paintings are <u>exhibited</u> in the gallery.

   a. visited b. displayed c. demonstrated

F 밑줄 친 단어와 반대의 뜻을 가진 단어를 고르세요

1. The <u>domestic</u> market has grown rapidly.

   a. local b. national c. international

2. The company made a huge <u>profit</u> last year.

   a. benefit b. lost c. loss

3. He learned to drive a <u>manual</u> car.

   a. automatic b. physical c. robotic

4. The dinner was very <u>formal</u>.

   a. official b. general c. informal

G 주어진 영영풀이에 알맞은 단어를 고르세요.

1. the group of people who officially control a country

   a. organization　　b. government　　c. economy

2. happening or existing now

   a. recent　　b. current　　c. currently

3. a person who is very knowledgeable or skilled in a particular area

   a. secretary　　b. profession　　c. expert

4. a period of 100 years

   a. decade　　b. country　　c. century

5. to take something that belongs to someone else

   a. thief　　b. steal　　c. stolen

6. to experience a difficult or unpleasant situation

   a. keep on　　b. carry out　　c. go through

H 빈칸에 알맞은 동사 형태를 넣어 문장을 완성하세요.

1. The K-pop market is ______________________. (expand)
2. He ______________________ practicing even after he failed. (keep on)
3. Kelly is ______________________ as a secretary. (employ)
4. Many pets are ______________________ by their owners. (abandon)

ANSWER KEY

DAY 01

Check Up .... p. 8

Ⓐ 1. potential 2. mature 3. actual
4. private / personal 5. privacy
6. responsible

Ⓑ 1. personality 2. actually 3. frankly
4. in person 5. personal

Build Up .... p. 9

A 1. physical 2. mental 3. mature
4. mate 5. crowd 6. gather

B 1. personality 2. potential 3. actually
4. private 5. responsible
6. as a matter of fact

DAY 02

Check Up .... p. 12

Ⓐ 1. attract 2. appeal 3. behave
4. proper 5. extreme 6. severe

Ⓑ 1. rapidly 2. gradual 3. affects
4. effect 5. impressed

Build Up .... p. 13

A 1. figure 2. impress 3. extreme
4. affect 5. beg 6. gradually

B 1. appearance 2. attract 3. appeal
4. properly 5. influence 6. figure out

DAY 03

Check Up .... p. 16

Ⓐ 1. feature 2. typical 3. disabled
4. truth 5. attempt 6. tend to

Ⓑ 1. characteristic 2. hesitate 3. confident
4. encourage 5. climbing

Build Up .... p. 17

A 1. feature 2. bald 3. unique
4. hesitant 5. confident 6. courage

B 1. characteristic 2. bold 3. capable
4. encourage 5. tend to 6. give up

DAY 04

Check Up .... p. 20

Ⓐ 1. positive 2. strict 3. diligent
4. sincere 5. intelligent 6. intelligence

Ⓑ 1. generous 2. differs 3. difference
4. vary 5. equals

Build Up .... p. 21

A 1. generous 2. violent 3. panic
4. identical 5. outstanding 6. intelligence

B 1. negative 2. strict 3. indeed
4. equal 5. be different from 6. be similar to

DAY 01-04

Review Test 01 pp. 22-25

A 1. figure 2. mental 3. physical
4. variety 5. courage 6. outstanding

B 1. She is suffering from a severe headache.
2. He looks very confident.
3. The museum attracts many visitors.
4. The houses are similar to each other.

C 1. gather 2. appeal 3. responsible
4. attempt 5. tend to 6. artificial intelligence
7. disabled 8. with confidence

D 1. appearance 2. impressed 3. in person
4. properly 5. figure out 6. give up

E 1. b 2. b 3. c 4. b

F 1. a 2. c 3. c 4. b

G 1. a 2. b 3. b 4. c 5. b 6. c

H 1. affected 2. influenced 3. solving
4. differs

DAY 05

Check Up .... p. 28

Ⓐ 1. detect 2. emergency 3. escape
4. arrange / organize 5. organize 6. stare

Ⓑ 1. detected 2. invisible 3. organized
4. disgusted 5. realized

Build Up .... p. 29

A 1. detector 2. emergency 3. stain
4. glance 5. disgusting 6. recognize

B 1. invisible 2. escape 3. remain
4. maintain 5. realize 6. keep an eye on

DAY 06

Check Up .... p. 32

Ⓐ 1. routine 2. skip 3. lack
4. plenty 5. instance 6. in case

Ⓑ 1. asleep 2. case 3. was exhausted
4. odd 5. even

Build Up .... p. 33

A 1. awake 2. asleep 3. shave
4. rush 5. extraordinary 6. exhausted

B 1. simple 2. routine 3. lack
4. odd 5. drag 6. stay up late

DAY 07

Check Up .... p. 36

Ⓐ 1. chores 2. task 3. tap
4. knock 5. leaking 6. complete

Ⓑ 1. Fasten 2. broken 3. repaired
4. broke down 5. cleaning

Build Up .... p. 37

A 1. chore 2. lawn 3. firmly
4. lift 5. tap 6. repair

B 1. household 2. task 3. leak
4. shut 5. break 6. pause

DAY 08

Check Up .... p. 40

Ⓐ 1. hunger 2. flavors 3. supper / dinner
4. raw 5. slice 6. pass down

Ⓑ 1. digest 2. poured 3. crushed
4. eat out 5. passed down

Build Up .... p. 41

A 1. hunger 2. thirst 3. tender
4. tough 5. spill 6. stir

B 1. swallow 2. digest 3. pour
4. chop 5. steam 6. eat out

DAY 05-08

Review Test 02 pp. 42-45

A 1. detector 2. exhausted 3. lawn
4. leak 5. pour 6. ladder

B 1. There's a lot of dirt on the floor.
2. Milk spilled onto the table.
3. The building is being repaired.
4. She is fastening her seatbelt.

C 1. detect 2. escape 3. routine 4. in case
5. plenty of 6. chores 7. break 8. slice

D 1. emergency 2. maintain 3. lack of
4. disgusting 5. realized 6. stayed up

E 1. c 2. b 3. c 4. c

F 1. b 2. c 3. c 4. a

G 1. b 2. a 3. c 4. a 5. c 6. a

H 1. detected 2. staring 3. broke down
4. passed down

DAY 09

Check Up .... p. 48

Ⓐ 1. mood 2. pure 3. pride
4. expose 5. attitude 6. interest

Ⓑ 1. amazed 2. entertaining 3. pride
4. proud 5. rather

Build Up .... p. 49

A 1. amazed 2. entertain 3. pure
4. proud 5. prefer 6. position

B 1. emotional 2. amaze 3. amuse 4. expose
5. attitude 6. have (an) interest in

DAY 10

Check Up .... p. 52

Ⓐ 1. recharge 2. concern 3. confused
4. depressed 5. fright 6. get over

Ⓑ 1. fascinated 2. anxious 3. concerned
4. disappointed 5. frustrated

Build Up .... p. 53

A 1. refresh 2. recharge 3. anxious
4. confused 5. satisfy 6. frighten

B 1. fascinate 2. concern 3. confuse
4. disappoint 5. annoy 6. get over

DAY 11

Check Up .... p. 56

Ⓐ 1. comment 2. aware 3. considerable
4. steady 5. comfort 6. awkward

Ⓑ 1. opinion 2. conscious 3. reminds
4. unlike 5. considering

Build Up .... p. 57

A 1. opinion 2. aware 3. recall
4. consider 5. steady 6. comfort

B 1. thought 2. quite 3. considerable
4. stable 5. awkward 6. remind A of B

DAY 12

Check Up .... p. 60

Ⓐ 1. belief 2. regard 3. vision
4. visual 5. decision 6. jealous

Ⓑ 1. trust 2. regardless 3. decided
4. appreciate 5. supposed

Build Up .... p. 61

A 1. believe 2. decide 3. regret
4. moment 5. grateful 6. admire

B 1. faith 2. regardless 3. decide to
4. be supposed to 5. appreciate 6. assume

DAY 09-12

Review Test 03 pp. 62-65

A 1. amused 2. position 3. consider
4. anxious 5. recall 6. admire

B 1. The fireworks amazed the children.
2. She has an interest in science.
3. The chair looks pretty unstable.
4. The phone battery is recharging.

C 1. mood 2. pure 3. interest 4. depressed
5. get over 6. steady 7. regardless of
8. decision

D 1. proud of 2. prefer, to 3. confused, with
4. rather 5. reminds, of 6. supposed to

E 1. b 2. a 3. c 4. c

F 1. b 2. c 3. c 4. b

G 1. c 2. c 3. a 4. b 5. b 6. c

H 1. fascinated 2. frustrated 3. frightened
4. considering

DAY 13

Check Up .... p. 68

Ⓐ 1. communication 2. remark / comment 3. accent 4. proverb 5. definite 6. gesture

Ⓑ 1. communicate 2. pronunciation 3. define 4. unlikely 5. willing

Build Up .... p. 69

A 1. communication 2. vocabulary 3. gesture 4. significant 5. envelope 6. stamp

B 1. mention 2. pronounce 3. phrase 4. proverb 5. definite 6. be likely to

DAY 14

Check Up .... p. 72

Ⓐ 1. blame 2. admission 3. recommend / suggest 4. proposal 5. contract 6. make up

Ⓑ 1. punished 2. refused 3. admitted 4. opposed 5. resist

Build Up .... p. 73

A 1. praise 2. punish 3. complain 4. accept 5. reject 6. contract

B 1. blame 2. deny 3. oppose 4. propose 5. signature 6. put off

DAY 15

Check Up .... p. 76

Ⓐ 1. discussion 2. claim 3. demonstrate 4. criticize 5. translator 6. specific

Ⓑ 1. debated 2. arguing 3. interpreter 4. content 5. insisted

Build Up .... p. 77

A 1. discuss 2. argue 3. context 4. translate 5. translator 6. particular

B 1. debate 2. criticize 3. content 4. interpret 5. specific 6. bet

DAY 16

Check Up .... p. 80

Ⓐ 1. session 2. confirm 3. urgent 4. eager 5. force 6. generation, generation

Ⓑ 1. accused 2. urged 3. inspired 4. convinced 5. was forced

Build Up .... p. 81

A 1. determine 2. approve 3. conflict 4. urge 5. desire 6. force

B 1. committee 2. conclude 3. eager 4. drive 5. persuade 6. generation

DAY 13-16

Review Test 04 pp. 82-85

A 1. envelope 2. contract 3. signature 4. argue 5. approve 6. translator

B 1. She is unlikely to arrive early.
2. Only members are admitted to the club.
3. They are accusing him of lying.
4. He is eager to become a singer.

C 1. accent 2. significant 3. blame 4. make up 5. confirm 6. conflict 7. urgent 8. accused of

D 1. willing to 2. blamed, for 3. put off 4. content with 5. insisted on 6. convinced, to

E 1. a 2. c 3. b 4. c

F 1. a 2. b 3. a 4. c

G 1. c 2. b 3. b 4. a 5. c 6. c

H 1. was praised 2. translated 3. were forced 4. inspired

DAY 17

Check Up .... p. 88

A 1. due 2. birth 3. breath 4. breast
5. absolute 6. according to

B 1. recent 2. breed 3. developing
4. Either 5. neither

Build Up .... p. 89

A 1. pregnant 2. due 3. newborn
4. feed 5. develop 6. survive

B 1. birth 2. breathe 3. chest
4. breed 5. absolute 6. due to

DAY 18

Check Up .... p. 92

A 1. vital 2. deaf 3. cancer
4. prevent 5. poison 6. die of

B 1. injured 2. wounded 3. damage
4. blinded 5. prevents

Build Up .... p. 93

A 1. medical 2. injury 3. scratch
4. scream 5. operate 6. recover

B 1. vital 2. damage 3. the flu
4. suffer 5. overcome 6. pass away

DAY 19

Check Up .... p. 96

A 1. principle 2. assign 3. cope 4. prime
5. enroll 6. sign up / register

B 1. principal 2. junior 3. register
4. space 5. on purpose

Build Up .... p. 97

A 1. principal 2. lecture 3. instruct
4. object 5. aim 6. structure

B 1. principle 2. cope 3. primary 4. purpose
5. sign up for 6. on purpose

DAY 20

Check Up .... p. 100

A 1. concentrate / focus 2. examine 3. refer
4. achieve 5. barely 6. in advance

B 1. interrupted 2. deserve 3. intend
4. intention 5. proved

Build Up .... p. 101

A 1. emphasize 2. disturb 3. examine
4. progress 5. achieve 6. intense

B 1. concentrate 2. hardly 3. intentional
4. prove 5. indicate 6. intend to

DAY 17-20

Review Test 05 pp. 102-105

A 1. due 2. survive 3. recover
4. lecture 5. object 6. progress

B 1. The woman is pregnant.
2. I like neither coffee nor tea.
3. The rain prevented them from going out.
4. They are operating on a patient.

C 1. due to 2. newborn 3. according to
4. vital 5. damage 6. cancer 7. achieve
8. cope with

D 1. blind 2. suffers from 3. aim to
4. deserve to 5. on purpose 6. intend to

E 1. a 2. c 3. a 4. b

F 1. b 2. a 3. c 4. b

G 1. a 2. c 3. c 4. c 5. a 6. a

H 1. fed 2. developed 3. instructed
4. advanced

DAY 21

Check Up .... p. 108

Ⓐ 1. costume 2. naked 3. suitable
4. amount 5. quantities 6. prefer

Ⓑ 1. quality 2. bare 3. a bit
4. pretended 5. rather

Build Up .... p. 109

A 1. closet 2. drawer 3. cotton
4. costume 5. bare 6. plain

B 1. quantity 2. naked 3. fancy
4. alter 5. ignore 6. prefer A to B

DAY 22

Check Up .... p. 112

Ⓐ 1. hold 2. ceremony 3. compete
4. slide 5. row 6. lost

Ⓑ 1. leaped 2. beat 3. defeated
4. rewarded 5. held

Build Up .... p. 113

A 1. ceremony 2. athlete 3. compete
4. row 5. slippery 6. award

B 1. sweat 2. competition 3. aloud
4. loss 5. reward 6. take place

DAY 23

Check Up .... p. 116

Ⓐ 1. abroad / overseas 2. sails 3. deck
4. national 5. transport 6. baggage

Ⓑ 1. International 2. destination 3. took off
4. ease 5. made

Build Up .... p. 117

A 1. abroad 2. harbor 3. compass
4. wrap 5. passenger 6. transport

B 1. sail 2. needle 3. section
4. destination 5. tension 6. take off

DAY 24

Check Up .... p. 120

Ⓐ 1. society 2. aid 3. appointment
4. donate 5. funds 6. adapt to

Ⓑ 1. identity 2. devoted 3. is devoted
4. depends 5. adopted

Build Up .... p. 121

A 1. identity 2. diverse 3. majority
4. appointment 5. donate 6. obtain

B 1. aid 2. necessary 3. appoint
4. contribute 5. charity 6. depend on

DAY 21-24

Review Test 06 pp. 122-125

A 1. bare 2. cotton 3. athlete
4. award 5. passenger 6. identity

B 1. The closet is full of clothes.
2. They are wearing stage costumes.
3. The opening ceremony is being held now.
4. The surface of the road looks slippery.

C 1. amount of 2. hold 3. compete
4. slippery 5. lost 6. appointment
7. donate 8. funds

D 1. naked 2. suitable for 3. pretended to
4. depend on 5. rather, than
6. contributed, to

E 1. a 2. b 3. b 4. c

F 1. a 2. b 3. b 4. c

G 1. a 2. b 3. b 4. c 5. a 6. c

H 1. be held 2. altered 3. made it
4. prefers

DAY 25

Check Up p. 128

Ⓐ 1. relationship 2. relative 3. bond
4. divide / separate 5. broken 6. despite

Ⓑ 1. related 2. unite 3. involved
4. apologize 5. except

Build Up p. 129

A 1. related 2. bind 3. combine
4. separate 5. broken 6. except

B 1. relate 2. divide 3. involve
4. apologize 5. otherwise 6. had better

DAY 26

Check Up p. 132

Ⓐ 1. department 2. crisis 3. trouble
4. challenge 5. freedom 6. rumor

Ⓑ 1. organization 2. fault 3. motivated
4. stuck in 5. forward

Build Up p. 133

A 1. colleague 2. challenge 3. slave
4. freedom 5. sticky 6. lean

B 1. organization 2. fault 3. trouble
4. obvious 5. forward 6. stick to

DAY 27

Check Up p. 136

Ⓐ 1. anniversary 2. constant 3. careless
4. without 5. previous 6. former

Ⓑ 1. occasion 2. crazy 3. within
4. instead of 5. can't wait

Build Up p. 137

A 1. occur 2. celebration 3. host
4. guest 5. beyond 6. beneath

B 1. occasion 2. anniversary 3. crazy
4. careless 5. previous 6. instead of

DAY 28

Check Up p. 140

Ⓐ 1. stock 2. affordable 3. reasonable
4. insurance 5. property 6. demand

Ⓑ 1. available 2. afford 3. per
4. replaced 5. used up

Build Up p. 141

A 1. stuff 2. purchase 3. afford
4. possess 5. reduce 6. replace

B 1. available 2. affordable 3. reasonable
4. loan 5. property 6. run out of

DAY 25-28

Review Test 07 pp. 142-145

A 1. colleague 2. slave 3. freedom
4. host 5. stuff 6. broken

B 1. The two houses are apart from each other.
2. The store is open every day except Sunday.
3. It's their 30th wedding anniversary.
4. The car is running out of gas.

C 1. relationship 2. relative 3. despite
4. challenge 5. rumor 6. constant
7. previous 8. former

D 1. related to 2. involves 3. apologized to
4. except for 5. afford to 6. forward to

E 1. c 2. c 3. a 4. b

F 1. c 2. c 3. c 4. b

G 1. b 2. c 3. b 4. a 5. c 6. a

H 1. involved in 2. stuck in 3. reduced
4. replaced

DAY 29

Check Up .... p. 148

Ⓐ 1. policy 2. current 3. factors
4. domestic 5. continuous 6. guarantee

Ⓑ 1. economy 2. benefits 3. manage
4. guaranteed 5. working

Build Up .... p. 149

A 1. announce 2. domestic 3. trade
4. calculate 5. estimate 6. productive

B 1. government 2. current 3. profit
4. benefit 5. guarantee 6. keep (on) V-ing

DAY 30

Check Up .... p. 152

Ⓐ 1. shift 2. strategy 3. mission
4. accomplish 5. several 6. industry

Ⓑ 1. labor 2. formal 3. expanding
4. extended 5. are abandoned

Build Up .... p. 153

A 1. formal 2. informal 3. fortune
4. dozen 5. expand 6. extend

B 1. manual 2. accomplish 3. quit
4. abandon 5. manufacture 6. wrap up

DAY 31

Check Up .... p. 156

Ⓐ 1. commands / orders 2. expert
3. advertising 4. promote 5. release
6. boom

Ⓑ 1. employed 2. profession 3. ordered
4. is published 5. order

Build Up .... p. 157

A 1. apply 2. order 3. advertise
4. promote 5. magazine 6. article

B 1. secretary 2. command 3. boost
4. commercial 5. release 6. in order to

DAY 32

Check Up .... p. 160

Ⓐ 1. precious 2. value 3. talented
4. concepts 5. commit 6. appropriate

Ⓑ 1. are exhibited 2. worth 3. general
4. investigating 5. falling

Build Up .... p. 161

A 1. exhibit 2. precious 3. decade
4. century 5. thief 6. investigate

B 1. genius 2. steal 3. crime
4. inspect 5. moral 6. go through

DAY 29-32

Review Test 08 pp. 162-165

A 1. announce 2. calculate 3. extend
4. article 5. decade 6. investigate

B 1. There is a continuous line of people.
2. They are watching a TV commercial.
3. There are half a dozen eggs.
4. The magazine is published monthly.

C 1. policy 2. continuous 3. productive
4. mission 5. extend 6. advertise
7. release 8. commit

D 1. estimated 2. continued 3. in order to
4. fortune 5. apply for 6. worth

E 1. c 2. b 3. c 4. b

F 1. c 2. c 3. a 4. c

G 1. b 2. b 3. c 4. c 5. b 6. c

H 1. expanding 2. kept on 3. employed
4. abandoned

INDEX

D

Q

R

S

T

U

V

W

A*List VOCA

숙어·구문 표현 연습장

중학 필수

A*List VOCA

숙어·구문 표현 연습장

중학 필수

DAY 01

1. **사적인 질문**을 드려도 될까요?

   May I ask you ___a___ ______ ______?

2. 그녀는 아주 사랑스러운 **성격을 가졌다**(성격이 사랑스럽다).

   She ___has___ ______ very lovely ______.

3. 그는 잘생겼지만 **개성이 별로 없다**.

   He's handsome, but he ___has___ ______ ______.

4. 운동은 **정신 건강**에 좋다.

   Exercise is good for ______ ______.

5. 그 선수는 강한 **체력을 가지고 있다**(체력이 강하다).

   The player ___has___ great ______ ______.

6. 그는 작가**로서** 큰 **잠재력을 가지고 있다**.

   He ______ great ______ ______ a writer.

7. 그녀는 나이**에 비해** 아주 **어른스럽다**.

   She ___is___ very ______ ______ her age.

8. 그는 전체 프로젝트**를 책임지고 있었다**.

   He ___was___ ______ ______ the entire project.

9. 너는 그 사람을 **직접** 만난 적이 있니?

   Have you ever met him ______ ______?

10. **사실** 나는 어제 그를 만났다.

    ___As___ ______ ______ ______ ______, I met him yesterday.

1. a personal question 사적인 질문 (하나) 2. have a lovely personality 사랑스러운 성격을 가지고 있다(성격이 사랑스럽다)
3. have little personality 개성이 별로 없다 4. mental health 정신 건강
5. have (great) physical strength (강한) 체력을 가지고 있다(체력이 강하다) 6. have potential as ~로서 잠재력을 가지고 있다
7. be mature for one's age 나이에 비해 어른스럽다[성숙하다] 8. be responsible for ~에 대해 책임이 있다, ~을 책임지고 있다
9. in person 본인이 직접, 몸소, 실물로 10. as a matter of fact 사실, 사실은

DAY 02

1. 그의 연설은 많은 **주목을 끌었다.**

His speech ______________ a lot of ______________.

2. 그 영화는 10대들**의 흥미를 끌었다**(10대들에게 어필했다).

The movie ______________ ______________ teenagers.

3. 그녀는 도와달라**고 간청했다.**

She ___made___ ___an___ ______________ ______________ help.

4. 시장은 그들에게 도움**을 간청했다.**

The mayor ______________ them ______________ help.

5. **얌전하게 굴어라!**

______________ yourself!

6. 그 환자는 **빠르게 회복했다.**

The patient ___made___ ______________ ______________ ______________.

7. 그 건물은 화재**로** 큰 **피해를 입었다.**

The building ___was___ badly ______________ ______________ the fire.

8. 그녀는 **극심한 스트레스를 받고** 있다.

She is ___under___ ______________ ______________.

9. 누가 그랬는지 **알아냈**니?

Did you ______________ ______________ who did it?

10. 흡연은 건강**에** 나쁜 **영향을 미친다.**

Smoking ___has___ ______________ bad ______________ ______________ your health.

1. attract attention 주목을 끌다, 관심을 끌다 2. appeal to ~의 흥미를 끌다, ~에게 어필하다
3. make an appeal for ~을 간청하다[호소하다] 4. beg A for B A에게 B를 간청하다[애원하다/구걸하다]
5. behave oneself 예의 바르게 행동하다, 얌전하게 굴다 6. make a rapid recovery 빠르게 회복하다
7. be affected by ~의 영향을 받다, ~로 피해를 입다, ~로 충격을 받다 8. be under extreme stress 극심한 스트레스를 받다
9. figure out 알아내다, 이해하다, 계산하다 10. have an effect on ~에 영향을 미치다

DAY 03

1. 새 스마트폰**의 주요 특징[기능]**은 무엇인가요?

What's ___the___ _______ _______ _______ the new smartphone?

2. 오늘은 **전형적인** 영국 **날씨**이다.

It's _______ British _______ today.

3. 그는 세 가지 언어를 **구사할 수 있다**.

He ___is___ _______ _______ ___speaking___ three languages.

4. **주저하지** 말고 무엇이든 질문하세요.

Don't _______ _______ ask any questions.

5. 그는 **자신 있게** 대답했다.

He answered _______ _______.

6. 나는 그에게 사실을 말할 **용기가** 없었다.

I didn't ___have___ _______ _______ _______ tell him the truth.

7. 나는 언젠가 에베레스트 산 등반**을 시도할** 것이다.

I'll _______ _______ climb Mt. Everest someday.

8. 너는 쉽게 포기하**는 경향이 있다**.

You _______ _______ give up easily.

9. 성공할 때까지 절대 **포기하지** 마라.

Never _______ _______ until you succeed.

10. 나는 그 산을 **오르는 데 성공했다**.

I _______ _______ ___climbing___ the mountain.

1. the main feature of ~의 주요 특징[특색/기능] 2. typical weather 전형적인[일반적인] 날씨
3. be capable of V-ing ~을 할 수 있다, ~할 능력이 있다 4. hesitate to ~하기를 주저하다[망설이다]
5. with confidence 자신 있게, 자신감을 가지고 6. have the courage to ~할 용기가 있다
7. attempt to ~하기를 시도하다 8. tend to ~하는 경향이 있다, ~하기 쉽다
9. give up 포기하다, 그만두다 10. succeed in V-ing ~에[하는 데] 성공하다

DAY 04

1. 그 책은 아이들**에게 나쁜[부정적인] 영향을 미쳤다**.

The book ___had___ ______ ______ ______ ___on___ children.

2. 그는 돈**을 잘 쓴다**(아끼지 않는다).

He ___is___ ______ ______ his money.

3. 우리 할머니는 항상 내**게 너그러우셨다**.

My grandma ___was___ always ______ ______ me.

4. 부디 저희의 **진심 어린 사과**를 받아 주십시오.

Please accept our ______ ______.

5. 그녀는 **겁에 질려 있었다**.

She ___was___ ______ ______ ______.

6. 그는 그의 형**과는** 많은 점에서 **다르다**.

He ______ ______ his brother in many ways.

7. 시장에는 **다양한** 과일이 있다.

There is ___a___ ___wide___ ______ ______ fruits in the market.

8. 그녀의 드레스는 내 것**과** 거의 **같다**.

Her dress ___is___ almost ______ ______ mine.

9. 그의 의견은 내 의견**과 다르다**.

His opinion ___is___ ______ ______ mine.

10. 그들의 집은 서로 **비슷하다**.

Their houses ______ ______ ______ each other.

1. have a negative effect on ~에 부정적인[나쁜] 영향을 미치다 2. be generous with ~에 후하다, ~에 대해 관대하다[너그럽다]
3. be generous to (someone) (사람)에 대해 너그럽다[아량이 있다] 4. sincere apology 진심 어린 사과
5. be in a panic 패닉 상태에 있다, 겁에 질리다, 허둥거리다 6. differ from ~와 다르다
7. a wide variety of 다양한 8. be identical to ~와 동일하다, ~와 같다
9. be different from ~와 다르다 10. be similar to ~와 비슷하다

DAY 05

1. 연기가 감지되면 즉시 **연기 감지기**가 울린다.

   The ______ ______ goes off as soon as smoke is detected.

2. 그 화재는 5킬로미터 떨어진 곳**에서도 보였다**.

   The fire __was__ ______ ______ 5 kilometers away.

3. **비상시에는** 이 번호로 전화하세요.

   __In__ ______ ______, call this number.

4. 그들은 재빨리 비상 상황**에서 탈출했다**.

   They quickly ______ ______ the emergency.

5. 우리는 깜짝 **파티를 준비했다**.

   We ______ ______ surprise ______.

6. 그 행사는 파티 기획자**에 의해 준비되었다**.

   The event __was__ ______ ______ a party planner.

7. 그녀는 그녀의 시계**를 흘끗 보았다**.

   She ______ ______ her watch.

8. 그녀는 **역겨움에** 코를 막았다.

   She covered her nose ______ ______.

9. 왜 나를 그렇게 **빤히 쳐다보니**?

   Why are you ______ ______ me like that?

10. 제 가방 좀 **지켜봐** 주실래요?

    Can you ______ ______ ______ __on__ my bag?

1. smoke detector 연기 감지기 2. be visible from ~에서부터 보이다
3. in an emergency 비상시에 4. escape from ~에서 탈출하다
5. arrange a party 파티를 준비하다 6. be organized by ~에 의해 준비되다[조직되다]
7. glance at ~을 흘끗 보다 8. in disgust 역겨워서, 역겨움에
9. stare at ~을 응시하다[빤히 쳐다보다] 10. keep an eye on ~을 지켜보다[주시하다/눈여겨보다]

DAY 06

1. 너의 **아침 루틴**은 무엇이니?

What's your ______________ ______________?

2. 그는 보통 오후 11시쯤 **잠이 든다**.

He usually ______________ ______________ around 11:00 PM.

3. 그는 샤워를 하고 **면도를 했다**.

He showered and ______________ ______________ ______________.

4. 그는 버스를 타**기 위해 서둘러**야 했다.

He had to ______________ ______________ catch the bus.

5. 나는 **수면 부족**으로 피곤하다.

I'm tired from ______________ ______________ ______________ ____sleep____.

6. **예를 들면**, 너는 음악가가 될 수 있다.

______________ ______________, you can be a musician.

7. 1, 3, 5는 **홀수**이다.

1, 3, and 5 are ______________ ______________.

8. 4는 **짝수**이다.

4 is ____an____ ______________ ______________.

9. 나는 숙제를 끝내기 위해 **늦게까지 깨어 있었다**.

I ______________ ______________ ______________ to finish my homework.

10. 비가 올 **경우를 대비해** 우산을 가지고 가라.

Take an umbrella ______________ ______________ ______________ it rains.

1. morning routine 아침 루틴(일과) 2. fall asleep 잠이 들다
3. have a shave 면도를 하다 4. rush to ~하기 위해 서두르다, 서둘러서 ~하다
5. a lack of sleep 수면 부족 6. for instance 예를 들면, 예를 들어 = for example
7. an odd number 홀수 8. an even number 짝수
9. stay up (late) (늦게까지) 깨어 있다, 잠을 안 자다 10. just in case ~할 경우에 대비하여, 혹시 모르니까

DAY 07

1. 그녀는 항상 일요일에 **집안일을 한다**.

   She always ________ ________ on Sundays.

2. 우리는 일주일에 두 번 **잔디를 깎는다**.

   We ___mow___ ________ ________ twice a week.

3. 그녀는 문**을 노크하**고 기다렸다.

   She ________ ________ the door and waited.

4. **(여러분의) 안전벨트를 매** 주세요.

   ________ ________ ________, please.

5. **좀 쉬었다** 합시다.

   Let's ________ ________ ________.

6. 그것은 **수리 중이다**.

   It ___is___ ________ ________.

7. 비가 **쉬지 않고** 내렸다.

   The rain fell ________ ________.

8. 문 앞에서 그녀는 **잠시 멈췄다**.

   At the doorway, she ________ ________.

9. 내 차가 고속도로에서 **고장이 났다**.

   My car ________ ________ on the highway.

10. 나는 집을 **청소하느라 바쁘다**.

    I ___am___ ________ ________ the house.

1. do chores 집안일(잡다한 일)을 하다 2. mow the lawn 잔디를 깎다
3. knock on the door 문을 노크하다 4. fasten one's seatbelt 안전벨트를 매다
5. take a break 잠시 쉬다[휴식을 취하다] 6. be under repair 수리 중이다
7. without pause 쉬지 않고, 쉴 새 없이 8. pause briefly 잠시 멈추다
9. break down (기계 등이) 고장 나다 10. be busy V-ing ~하느라 바쁘다

DAY 08

1. 그들은 변화**를 갈망하고 있다**.

They ______________ ______________ change.

2. 이 수프는 **풍부한 맛이 난다**.

The soup ______has______ ______________ ______________ ______________.

3. 그는 직장에서 **힘든 시간을 보냈다**.

He ______had______ ______________ ______________ ______________ at work.

4. 너는 **생선회**를 먹니?

Do you eat ______________ ______________?

5. 그녀는 유리컵**에** 우유를 **따랐다**.

She ______________ the milk ______________ a glass.

6. **엎질러진 우유에 울어 봤자** 소용없다(이미 엎질러진 물이다).

It's no use ______crying______ ______________ ______________ ______________.

7. 당근을 잘게 **다지세요**.

______________ the carrots ______________ into small pieces.

8. 피자 **한 조각**이 있다.

There is ______________ ______________ ______________ pizza.

9. 우리는 주말에 종종 **외식을 한다**.

We often ______________ ______________ on weekends.

10. 엄마는 내게 가족 요리법**을 물려주셨다**.

My mom ______________ ______________ family recipes to me.

1. hunger for ~을 갈망하다 2. have a rich flavor 풍부한 맛이 나다, 맛이 풍부하다
3. have a tough time 힘든 시간을 보내다 4. raw fish 날생선, 생선회
5. pour A into B A를 B에 따르다 6. cry over spilled milk 엎질러진 우유를 두고 울다(이미 끝난 일을 두고 한탄하다)
7. chop up 잘게 썰다, 다지다 8. a slice of ~ 한 조각
9. eat out 외식하다 10. pass down ~을 물려주다, ~을 전해 주다

DAY 09

1. 그들은 불꽃놀이**에 감탄했다**.

They ___were___ ________ ________ the fireworks.

2. 우리는 모두 그의 재미있는 춤**에 즐거워했다**.

We ___were___ all ________ ________ his funny dance.

3. 나는 내 일**에 자부심을 가지고 있다**.

I ________ ________ ___in___ my work.

4. 나는 나 자신**이 자랑스럽다[자랑스러움을 느낀다]**.

I ________ ________ ___of___ myself.

5. 그녀는 절친에게 **자신의 비밀을 털어놓았다**.

She ________ ________ ________ to her best friend.

6. 나는 여름**보다** 겨울을 **더 좋아한다[선호한다]**.

I ________ winter ________ summer.

7. 그는 삶에 대해 **긍정적인 태도를 가지고 있다**.

He ___has___ ________ ________ ________ toward life.

8. 나는 춤추**고 싶은 기분이다**.

I'm ___in___ ________ ________ ________ dancing.

9. 그녀는 과학**에 관심이 있다**.

She ___has___ ________ ________ ________ science.

10. 곧 그녀는 학업**에 흥미를 잃었다**.

Soon, she ________ ________ ________ her studies.

1. be amazed by ~에 감탄하다[놀라다] 2. be amused by ~을 즐거워하다[재미있어하다]
3. take pride in ~에 자부심을 갖다, ~을 자랑스러워하다 4. feel proud of ~이 자랑스럽다, ~에 자랑스러움을 느끼다
5. reveal one's secret ~의 비밀을 밝히다[드러내다] 6. prefer A to B B보다 A를 더 좋아하다[선호하다]
7. have a positive attitude 긍정적인 태도를 가지다 8. be in the mood for[to] ~하고 싶다, ~할 기분이다
9. have (an) interest in ~에 관심이 있다 10. lose interest in ~에 흥미를 잃다

DAY 10

1. 나는 그의 목소리**에 마음을 빼앗겼다[매료되었다]**.

   I ___was___ ______ ______ his voice.

2. 그녀는 **재충전을 하**기 위해 여행을 갔다.

   She took a trip to ______ ______ ______.

3. 나는 기후 변화**에 대해 걱정한다**.

   I ___am___ ______ ______ climate change.

4. 나는 그를 그의 형**과 혼동했다**.

   I ______ him ______ his brother.

5. 나는 다음에 무엇을 해야 할지 **혼란스럽다**.

   I'm ______ ______ what to do next.

6. 그는 시험 결과**에 만족했다**.

   He ___was___ ______ ______ his exam results.

7. 우리는 그 음식**에 실망했다**.

   We ___are___ ______ ______ the food.

8. 그녀는 그 결과**에 좌절감을 느꼈다**.

   She ___felt___ ______ ______ the results.

9. 그녀는 결코 그 충격**을 극복하지**(충격에서 벗어나지) 못했다.

   She never ______ ______ the shock.

10. 그들은 그 문제**에 대해 관심이 없다**.

    They ___are___ ___not___ ______ ______ the issue.

1. be fascinated by ~에 마음을 빼앗기다[매료되다] 2. recharge one's batteries (원기 회복을 위해) 재충전을 하다
3. be concerned about ~에 대해 걱정하다 4. confuse A with B A를 B와 혼동하다[착각하다]
5. be confused about ~에 대해 혼란스러움을 느끼다 6. be satisfied with ~에 만족하다
7. be disappointed with ~에 실망하다 8. feel frustrated with ~에 좌절감을 느끼다
9. get over (곤란을) 극복하다, (병 등에서) 회복하다 10. be concerned with ~에 관심이 있다, ~와 관련되다

DAY 11

1. 나는 그 문제**에 대해 다른 견해를 갖고 있다**.

I ___have___ ______ ______ ______ ___on___ the issue.

2. 그는 그 영화**에 대해 논평했다**.

He ___made___ ______ ______ ___about___ the movie.

3. 그들은 밖의 소음**을 의식하고 있었다**.

They ___were___ ______ ______ the noise outside.

4. 계란을 사**야 한다고** 내게 **상기시켜 줘**.

______ me ______ buy some eggs.

5. 그녀는 늦게 도착**할 것 같다**.

She ___is___ ______ ______ arrive late.

6. 그는 전문가**로 여겨진다**.

He ___is___ ______ an expert.

7. 그 모델은 **꾸준히 잘 팔린다**(스테디셀러이다).

The model is ______ ______ ______.

8. 당신에게 **위안이 되는 음식**(소울푸드)은 무엇입니까?

What's your ______ ______?

9. 그녀의 미소는 내게 그녀의 어머니**를 떠올리게 한다[생각나게 한다]**.

Her smile ______ me ______ her mother.

10. 우리는 그 규칙**을** 잘 **알고 있다**.

We ___are___ well ______ ______ the rules.

1. have a different opinion on ~에 대해 다른 견해를 가지다 2. make a comment about[on] ~에 대해 논평하다[의견을 말하다]
3. be conscious of ~을 의식하다[인식하고 있다] 4. remind A to A에게 ~할 것을 상기시키다
5. be likely to ~할 것 같다 6. be considered ~로 여겨지다[간주되다]
7. a steady seller 꾸준히 잘 팔리는 것, 스테디셀러 8. comfort food 위안이 되는 음식, 소울푸드
9. remind A of B A에게 B를 떠올리게 하다[생각나게 하다] 10. be aware of ~을 알고 있다, ~을 눈치채고 있다

DAY 12

1. 그는 성공**에 대한** 확고한 **믿음을 가지고 있다**.

He ___has___ ______ firm ______ ______ success.

2. 나는 그**를** 굉장히 **신뢰한다**.

I ___have___ great ______ ______ him.

3. 그녀는 신**에 대한 믿음을 잃었다**(신앙심을 잃었다).

She ______ ______ ______ ___in___ God.

4. 그녀는 그를 멘토**로 여긴다**.

She ______ him ______ a mentor.

5. 그녀는 **좋은 시력을 갖고 있다**(시력이 좋다).

She ___has___ ______ ______.

6. 마침내 나는 **결정을 내렸다**.

Finally, I ______ ______ ______.

7. 그는 그 도시를 떠난 것**에 대해 후회가 없다**.

He ______ ______ ______ ___about___ leaving the city.

8. 그는 나의 성공**을 시기했다[질투했다]**.

He ___was___ ______ ______ my success.

9. 나는 오늘 그를 만나**기로 되어 있다**.

I ___am___ ______ ______ meet him today.

10. 그녀는 진실을 말하**기로 결심했다**.

She ______ ______ tell the truth.

1. have a belief in ~에 대한 믿음을 가지다 2. have faith in ~을 믿고 있다[신뢰하다]
3. lose one's faith in ~에 대한 믿음을 잃다 4. regard A as B A를 B로 간주하다[여기다]
5. have good vision 좋은 시력을[비전을] 가지다 6. make a decision 결정을 내리다, 결정하다
7. have no regrets (about) (~에 대해) 후회가 없다[후회하지 않는다] 8. be jealous of ~을 시기하다[질투하다]
9. be supposed to ~하기로 되어 있다, ~해야 한다 10. decide to ~하기로 결심하다[결정하다]

DAY 13

1. 그는 훌륭한 **의사소통 능력**을 가지고 있다.

   He has good ________ ________.

2. 그는 그 웹사이트의 새 디자인**에 대해 언급했다**.

   He ________ ________ the new design of the website.

3. 그녀는 강한 **영국 억양을 가지고 있다**.

   She ___has___ a strong ________ ________.

4. 그 새 디자인은 단순함**에 역점을 두었다**.

   The new design ________ ________ ________ ___on___ simplicity.

5. **(학교) 학기**는 다음 주에 시작된다.

   The ________ ________ starts next week.

6. 그들은 기후 변화에 대한 **중요한 발견을 했다**.

   They ___made___ ________ ________ ________ about climate change.

7. 그는 다정한 **제스처를 취했다**.

   He ________ ________ friendly ________.

8. 그녀는 봉투에 **우표를 붙였다**.

   She ________ ________ ________ on the envelope.

9. 그녀는 일찍 도착**할 것 같지 않다**.

   She ________ ________ ________ arrive early.

10. 저는 **기꺼이** 당신을 도와드리**겠습니다**.

    I'm ________ ________ help you.

1. communication skills 의사소통 능력[기술] 2. remark on ~에 대해 언급하다
3. have a British accent 영국식 억양을 가지고 있다 4. put an accent on ~에 역점을 두다
5. school term (학교) 학기 6. make a significant discovery 중요한 발견을 하다
7. make a gesture 제스처를 취하다 8. put a stamp 우표를 붙이다
9. be unlikely to ~할 것 같지 않다 10. be willing to 기꺼이 ~하다, ~할 의향이 있다

DAY 14

1. 그녀는 선생님**에게 칭찬받았다**.

She ___was___ ______ ______ her teacher.

2. 그는 경기에 진 것을 불운 **탓으로 돌렸다**.

He ______ his bad luck ______ losing the game.

3. 그녀는 규칙을 어겨**서 벌을 받았다**.

She ___was___ ______ ______ breaking the rules.

4. 그들은 형편없는 서비스**에 대해 항의했다[불평했다]**.

They ______ ______ the poor service.

5. 그녀는 **그의 초대를 받아들이지** 않았다.

She didn't ______ ___his___ ______.

6. 그는 그녀의 생일에 그녀**에게 청혼했다**.

He ______ ______ her on her birthday.

7. 당신은 먼저 **계약서에 서명해**야 한다.

You need to ______ ______ ______ first.

8. 여기에 **서명해** 주세요.

Please ______ ___your___ ______ here.

9. 그는 계약서에 **서명하는 것을 미루었다**.

He ______ ______ ___signing___ the contract.

10. 나는 그 제안을 거절하기로 **결심했다**.

I ______ ______ ___my___ ______ to refuse the proposal.

1. be praised by ~에게 칭찬을[칭송을] 받다 2. blame A for B B를 A의 탓으로 돌리다
3. be punished for ~로 인해 처벌받다 4. complain about ~에 대해 불평하다[항의하다]
5. accept one's invitation ~의 초대를 받아들이다 6. propose to ~에게 청혼하다
7. sign a contract 계약서에 서명하다, 계약을 하다 8. put one's signature 서명하다
9. put off (V-ing) (~하는 것을) 미루다, 연기하다 10. make up one's mind 결심하다, 마음을 정하다

DAY 15

1. 우리는 그 제안**에 대해 논의할** 것이다.

   We'll ___have___ ________ ________ ________ the proposal.

2. 그들은 항상 돈 문제로 서로 **다툰다**.

   They're always ________ ________ each other about money.

3. 그들은 전쟁 **반대 시위를 했다**.

   They ________ ________ a war.

4. 그녀는 그의 행동**에 대해서** 그를 **비난했다**.

   She ________ him ________ his behavior.

5. **문맥에서** 의미를 추측해 보세요.

   Guess the meaning ________ ________ ________.

6. 그녀의 책들은 28개 언어**로 번역되었다**.

   Her books ___have___ ___been___ ________ ________ 28 languages.

7. 아이들**에게 특별히 주의를 기울여** 주세요.

   Please ___pay___ ________ ________ ________ the children.

8. 그들은 **구체적인 지침을 제공했다**.

   They ___provided___ ________ ________.

9. 그녀는 자신의 일**에 만족한다**.

   She ___is___ ________ ________ her job.

10. 그는 우리와 함께 가**겠다고 우겼다[주장했다]**.

    He ________ ________ coming with us.

1. have a discussion about ~에 대해 논의하다 2. argue with ~와 다투다[언쟁을 벌이다]
3. demonstrate against ~에 반대하는 시위[데모]를 하다 4. criticize A for B B에 대해서 A를 비난하다[비판하다]
5. from the context 문맥에서 6. be translated into ~로 번역되다 7. pay particular attention to ~에 특별히 주의를 기울이다[신경 쓰다/주목하다] 8. provide specific guidelines 구체적인 지침을 제공하다
9. be content with ~에 만족하다 10. insist on ~을 고집하다[주장하다]

DAY 16

1. 출발하기 전에 **당신의 예약을 확인해** 주세요.

Please ______ ______ ______ before you leave.

2. 나는 흡연**을 찬성하지** 않는다.

I don't ______ ______ smoking.

3. 이 두 아이디어는 서로 **상충한다[충돌한다]**.

These two ideas ______ ______ each other.

4. 그는 도둑질을 한 **혐의로 고발되었다**.

He __was__ ______ ______ stealing.

5. 그는 성공**을 갈망한다**.

He __is__ ______ ______ success.

6. 성공에 대한 그의 갈망이 그를 열심히 일하**게 만든다**.

His desire for success ______ him ______ work hard.

7. 그 제안을 받아들이**도록** 그를 **설득해** 봐라.

Try to ______ him ______ accept the proposal.

8. 이 이야기들은 **대대로** 전해져 내려온다.

The stories are passed down __from__ ______ __to__ ______.

9. 그들은 그에게 문서에 서명하**도록 강요했다**[**억지로** 서명하**게 했다**].

They ______ him ______ sign the document.

10. 그는 그 문서에 서명할 **수밖에 없었다**.

He __was__ ______ ______ sign the document.

1. confirm one's reservation 예약을 확인하다[확정하다] 2. approve of ~을 찬성하다
3. conflict with ~와 상충하다[충돌하다] 4. be accused of ~로 고발되다[고소되다] 5. be eager for ~을 갈망하다
6. drive A to A를 ~하게 만들다 7. persuade A to A를 ~하도록 설득하다
8. from generation to generation 세대에서 세대로, 대대로 9. force (someone) to do (something) ~에게 …하기를 강요하다[억지로 ~하게 하다] 10. be forced to ~하도록 강요받다, 억지로 ~하게 되다, ~할 수밖에 없다

DAY 17

1. **최근 몇 년 동안** 많은 변화가 있었다.

   There have been many changes ______ ______ ______.

2. 제 아내가 **임신을 했어요**.

   My wife ______ ______.

3. 그녀는 지난주에 아들**을 낳았다**.

   She ______ ______ to ______ a baby boy last week.

4. 그녀는 **숨을 한 번** 깊이 **들이쉬었다**(심호흡을 했다).

   She took ______ ______ deep ______.

5. 그 새 소프트웨어는 삼성**에 의해 개발되었다**.

   The new software was ______ ______ ______ Samsung.

6. 그 왕은 **절대(적인) 권력**을 가졌다.

   The king had ______ ______.

7. 당신은 차**나** 커피 **중에서** 선택할 수 있다.

   You can choose ______ tea ______ coffee.

8. 나는 커피**도** 차**도** 좋아하지 **않는다**.

   I like ______ coffee ______ tea.

9. 폭풍우**로 인해** 비행기가 취소되었다.

   ______ ______ the storm, the flight was canceled.

10. 일기 예보**에 따르면** 오늘 눈이 올 것이다.

    ______ ______ the weather report, it will snow today.

1. in recent years 최근 몇 년 동안 2. be pregnant 임신하다
3. give birth to 출산하다, (아이)를 낳다 4. take a (deep) breath (깊은) 숨을 쉬다, (깊이) 숨을 들이쉬다, (심)호흡을 하다
5. be developed by ~에 의해 개발되다 6. absolute power 절대(적인) 권력
7. either A or B A이거나 B 둘 중 하나 8. neither A nor B A도 아니고 B도 아닌
9. due to ~ 때문에, ~로 인해 10. according to ~에 따르면, ~에 따라서

DAY 18

1. 그는 병원에서 **(의료) 치료**를 받았다.

He received ______________ ______________ in the hospital.

2. 그는 다리**에** 심한 **부상을 입었다**.

He ___had___ ______________ serious ______________ ______________ his leg.

3. 그는 전쟁 중에 다리**에** 심한 **부상을 입었다**.

He ___was___ badly ______________ ______________ his leg during the war.

4. 그 불은 그 건물에 **심한 손상을 초래했다**.

The fire ___caused___ ______________ ______________ to the building.

5. 그는 지난달에 **암으로 사망했다**.

He ______________ ______________ ______________ last month.

6. 나는 지난주에 **독감에 걸렸다**.

I ______________ ______________ ______________ last week.

7. 그녀는 종종 스트레스**에 시달린다**.

She often ______________ ______________ stress.

8. 그는 아직 수술**에서 회복 중**이다.

He is still ______________ ______________ his operation.

9. 그는 불길이 퍼지**는 것을 막았다**.

He ______________ the fire ______________ spreading.

10. 우리 할머니는 작년에 **돌아가셨다**.

My grandmother ______________ ______________ last year.

1. medical treatment 의료 치료 2. have an injury to ~에 부상을 입다
3. be wounded in ~에 부상을 입다 4. cause (severe) damage (심한) 손상을 초래하다[입히다]
5. die of cancer 암으로 사망하다[죽다] 6. have the flu 독감에 걸리다
7. suffer from ~에 시달리다, ~을 겪다 8. recover from ~에서 회복하다
9. prevent A from V-ing A가 ~하는 것을 막다 10. pass away 사망하다, 돌아가시다

DAY 19

1. 리포트 쓰기**의 원칙**은 명확해야 한다는 것이다.

The ______ ______ ______ writing reports is to be clear.

2. 그녀는 미국 역사에 대해 **강의했다**.

She gave ______ ______ ______ on American history.

3. 선생님은 우리에게 **과제를 부과했다**.

The teacher ______ ______ ______ to us.

4. 변화**에 대처하**기가 어려웠다.

It was hard to ______ ______ the changes.

5. 많은 사람들이 **황금(주요) 시간대의 TV 프로그램**을 본다.

Many people watch a ______ show ______ on ______ ______ ______.

6. 당신의 방문**(의) 목적**은 무엇입니까?

What is the ______ ______ ______ your visit?

7. 나는 글쓰기 강좌**에 등록했다**.

I ______ in ______ a writing course.

8. 나는 이번 주에 수강 **신청을 해**야 한다.

I have to ______ for ______ classes this week.

9. 그녀는 여름 캠프**를 신청했다**.

She ______ ______ ______ the summer camp.

10. 누군가 **고의로** 불을 질렀다.

Someone set the fire ______ ______.

1. the principle of ~의 원칙 2. give a lecture 강의를[강연을] 하다
3. assign a task 과제를 부과하다 4. cope with ~에 대처하다[대응하다]
5. a show on prime-time television 황금(주요) 시간대의 TV 프로그램 6. the purpose of ~의 목적
7. enroll in ~에 등록하다 8. register for (classes) (수강) 신청을 하다, (~에) 등록하다
9. sign up for ~을 신청하다, ~에 가입하다[등록하다] 10. on purpose 고의로, 일부러

DAY 20

1. 나는 공부**에 집중할** 수가 없다.

   I can't ____________ ____________ my studies.

2. 그 경기는 비**로 중단되었다**.

   The game ____was____ ____________ ____________ rain.

3. 안내 책자**를 참고하세요**.

   Please ____________ ____________ the guidebook.

4. 그는 수학에서 **빠른 진전을 보이고** 있다.

   He is ____making____ ____________ ____________ in math.

5. 나는 **내 목표를 이루기[달성하기]** 위해 열심히 노력했다.

   I worked hard to ____________ ____________ ____________.

6. 그는 칭찬받**아 마땅하다**.

   He ____________ ____________ be praised.

7. 나는 누구에게도 해를 끼칠 **의도가 없었다**.

   I ____had____ ____________ ____________ ____________ harming anyone.

8. 그 작업은 불가능한 **것으로 판명되었다**.

   The task ____________ ____________ ____be____ impossible.

9. 좋은 자리를 원한다면 **미리** 예약하세요.

   Book ____________ ____________ if you want good seats.

10. 네 공부를 방해**할 생각[의도]은** 없었어.

   I didn't ____________ ____________ disturb your studying.

1. concentrate on ~에 집중하다 2. be interrupted by ~로 인해 방해받다[중단되다]
3. refer to ~을 참고하다[나타내다/언급하다] 4. make rapid progress 빠른 진전을 보이다, 빠르게 향상되다
5. achieve one's goal 목표를 이루다[달성하다] 6. deserve to ~을 받을 만하다[자격이 있다], ~해야 마땅하다
7. have no intention of ~할 의도가 없다 8. prove to be ~임이 판명되다[드러나다]
9. in advance 미리, 사전에 10. intend to ~하려고 의도하다, ~할 작정이다

DAY 21

1. 그 수건들은 백 퍼센트 **순면**이다.

The towels are 100% ______ ______.

2. 아이들은 **핼러윈 의상**을 입고 있었다.

The children were dressed in ______ ______.

3. 그들은 **대량으로** 상품을 생산한다.

They produce goods ___in___ ______ ______.

4. 그는 **맨발로** 돌아다녔다.

He walked around ___in___ ______ ______.

5. 이 드레스는 그 파티**에 어울린다**.

This dress ___is___ ______ ______ the party.

6. 그들은 **엄청난 양의** 음식을 먹었다.

They ate ___a___ ___huge___ ______ ______ food.

7. 그는 **약간의** 빵만을 먹었다.

He ate only ___a___ ______ ______ bread.

8. 그녀는 파티에서 행복**한 척했다**.

She ______ ______ be happy at the party.

9. 나는 양**보다** 질을 **선호한다**.

I ______ quality ______ quantity.

10. 나는 TV를 보**느니 차라리** 책을 읽**고 싶다**.

I ___would___ ______ read books ______ watch TV.

1. pure cotton 순면 2. Halloween costumes 핼러윈 의상
3. in large quantities 대량으로 4. in bare feet 맨발로
5. be suitable for ~에 적합하다[어울리다/알맞다] 6. a huge amount of 엄청난 양의
7. a bit of 약간의, 조금의 8. pretend to ~인 척하다 9. prefer A to B B보다 A를 더 좋아하다[선호하다]
10. would rather A (than B) (B하느니) 차라리 A하고 싶다, (B보다) A하는 게 낫다

DAY 22

1. 그 도시는 내년에 **올림픽을 개최할** 것이다.

The city will ______________ ______________ ______________ next year.

2. **개막식**은 오전 9시에 열릴 것이다.

The ______________ ______________ will be held at 9:00 AM.

3. 그들은 올림픽 메달**을 놓고 경쟁할** 것이다.

They will ______________ ______________ Olympic medals.

4. 200명 이상의 선수들이 그 마라톤**에 참가할** 것이다.

More than 200 athletes will ______________ ______________ the marathon.

5. 사람들이 **일렬로 줄을 섰다.**

People ___lined___ ___up___ ______________ ______________ ______________.

6. **길을 잃지** 않도록 조심해라.

Be careful not to ______________ ______________.

7. 그들은 1천만 달러의 **손실을 봤다.**

They ___made___ ______________ ______________ of 10 million dollars.

8. 그는 최우수 선수로 **상을 받았다.**

He ___won___ ______________ ______________ for best player.

9. 다음 올림픽은 로스앤젤레스에서 **열릴** 것이다.

The next Olympics will ______________ ______________ in Los Angeles.

10. 그 사고가 언제 **일어났**습니까?

When did the accident ______________ ______________?

1. hold the Olympics 올림픽을 개최하다 2. opening ceremony 개막식
3. compete for ~을 위해 경쟁하다[겨루다] 4. compete in ~에 참가하다[출전하다]
5. line up in a row 일렬로 줄을 서다 6. get lost 길을 잃다, 어찌할 바를 모르다
7. make a loss 손실[손해]을 보다 8. win an award 상을 받다
9. be held (행사 등이) 열리다, 개최되다 10. take place (사건 등이) 일어나다, (행사 등이) 열리다

DAY 23

1. 그녀는 내년에 **해외에서 공부할** 것이다.

   She will ______________ ______________ next year.

2. **나침반의 바늘**은 항상 북쪽을 가리킨다.

   The ______________ ______________ always points north.

3. 그녀는 선물 상자에 **리본을 묶었다**.

   She ______________ ______________ ______________ around the gift box.

4. 오늘은 **국경일**이다.

   It's a ______________ ______________ today.

5. 그들은 인천**국제공항**에 도착했다.

   They arrived at Incheon ______________ ______________.

6. **수화물 찾는 곳**은 1층에 있다.

   ______________ ______________ is on the first floor.

7. 그녀는 집에 도착하자 **편안함을 느꼈다**.

   She ___felt___ ______________ ______________ once she arrived home.

8. 비행기가 부드럽게 **이륙했다**.

   The airplane ______________ ______________ smoothly.

9. 들어오기 전에 신발**을 벗어** 주세요.

   Please ______________ ______________ your shoes before you come in.

10. 여러 번의 시도 끝에 마침내 나는 **해냈다**.

    After many tries, I finally ______________ ______________.

1. study abroad[overseas] 해외에서 공부하다, 유학하다 2. compass needle 나침반의 바늘
3. tie a ribbon 리본을 묶다 4. national holiday 국경일
5. international airport 국제 공항 6. baggage claim 수화물 찾는 곳
7. feel at ease 편안하게 느끼다, 안심하다 8. take off (비행기 등이) 이륙하다, 날아오르다
9. take off (옷 등을) 벗다 10. make it 성공하다, 해내다; (늦지 않게) 도착하다

DAY 24

1. 우리는 **다문화 사회**에 살고 있다.

We live in a ______________ ______________.

2. **신분증**을 보여 주시겠어요?

Can I see your ______________ ______________?

3. 나는 치과 **예약을 했다**(치과 의사와 약속을 잡았다).

I ______________ ______________ ______________ with a dentist.

4. 그는 지역 동물 보호소**에** 100달러를 **기부했다**.

He ______________ $100 ______________ the local animal shelter.

5. 그녀는 다른 사람들을 돕는 **데 자신의 삶을 바쳤다**.

She ______________ her life ______________ helping others.

6. 너는 언제든 내**게 기대**도 돼.

You can ______________ ______________ me at any time.

7. 그들은 보호소에서 **강아지를 입양했다**.

They ______________ ______________ ______________ from the shelter.

8. 그녀는 가족**에게 헌신적이다**.

She is ______________ ______________ her family.

9. 우리 형과 나는 서로 **의지한다**.

My brother and I ______________ ______________ each other.

10. 우리가 가느냐 마느냐는 날씨**에 달려 있다**.

Whether we go or not ______________ ______________ the weather.

1. multicultural society 다문화 사회 2. identity card 신분증
3. make an appointment 예약을 하다 4. donate (money) to (돈을) ~에 기부하다
5. devote one's life to ~하는 데 생을 바치다 6. rely on ~에 기대다[의지하다]
7. adopt a puppy 강아지를 입양하다 8. be devoted to ~에게 헌신적이다
9. depend on ~에 의지하다[의존하다] 10. depend on ~에 달려 있다

DAY 25

1. 그는 그 문제를 일상생활**과 결부시켰다.**

He ______________ the issue ______________ everyday life.

2. 그것은 기후 변화**와 관련되어 있다.**

It ____is____ ______________ ______________ climate change.

3. 대가족**의 상대적인 이점**은 무엇일까?

What are some ______________ ______________ ____of____ a big family?

4. 그들은 가족으로서 **강한 유대를 갖고 있다.**

They ____have____ ______________ ______________ ______________ as a family.

5. 선생님은 반을 두 그룹**으로 나누었다.**

The teacher ______________ the class ______________ two groups.

6. 그는 교통사고**에 연루되었다.**

He ____was____ ______________ ______________ a car accident.

7. 그는 그녀**에게** 그 사고**에 대해 사과했다.**

He ______________ ____to____ her ______________ the accident.

8. **교통 체증에도 불구하고** 우리는 제시간에 도착했다.

______________ ____the____ ____traffic____, we arrived on time.

9. 그에게 지금 당장 사과하는 **게 좋겠다.**

____You'd / You had____ ______________ apologize to him right now.

10. 날씨**를 제외하고** 모든 것이 완벽했다.

Everything was perfect ______________ ______________ the weather.

1. relate A to B A를 B와 연관 짓다[결부시키다] 2. be related to ~와 관련이[관계가] 있다
3. a relative advantage of ~의 상대적인 이점 4. have a strong bond 강한 유대감을 갖다, 사이가 끈끈하다
5. divide A into B A를 B로 나누다 6. be involved in ~에 연루되다[관련되다]
7. apologize to A for B A에게 B에 대해 사과하다 8. despite the traffic 교통 체증에도 불구하고
9. had better ~하는 것이 좋겠다, ~하는 게 좋을 거다(경고성) 10. except for ~을 제외하고

DAY 26

1. 그녀는 **국제 기구**에서 일한다.

   She works for ___an___ ______ ______.

2. 그는 직장에서 **위기를 겪고** 있다.

   He is ___having___ ______ ______ at work.

3. 그는 그 실수 **때문에 곤란한 상황에 처했다**.

   He ___got___ ___into___ ______ ______ the mistake.

4. 그것은 그에게는 **큰 도전**이었다.

   It was ______ ______ ______ for him.

5. 의사는 그에게 더 많이 운동하**라고 조언했다**.

   The doctor ______ him ______ exercise more.

6. 코치는 그가 더 열심히 하**도록 동기를 부여했다**.

   The coach ______ him ______ try harder.

7. **소문을 퍼뜨리**는 것은 좋지 않다.

   It's not nice to ______ ______ ______.

8. 우리는 교통 체증**에 갇혀 있었다**.

   We ___were___ ______ ______ traffic.

9. 우리의 원래 계획**을 고수하**자.

   Let's ______ ______ our original plan.

10. 다음 주에 당신을 만나기**를 고대합니다**.

    I ______ ______ ______ meeting you next week.

1. international organization 국제 기구 2. have a crisis 위기를 겪다
3. get into trouble for ~ 때문에 곤란한 상황에 처하다[혼이 나다] 4. a big challenge 큰 도전[과제]
5. advise A to A에게 ~할 것을 조언하다 6. motivate A to A가 ~하도록 동기를 부여하다
7. spread a rumor 소문을 퍼뜨리다 8. be stuck in ~에 끼여 꼼짝하지 못하다, ~에 갇히다
9. stick to ~을 고수하다, ~을 지키다 10. look forward to ~을 고대하다[기대하다]

DAY 27

1. 그녀는 **특별한 행사 때[경우에]** 그 드레스를 입는다.

   She wears the dress ___on___ ______ ______.

2. 그들은 **결혼기념일**을 축하했다.

   They celebrated their ______ ______.

3. 그 회사는 창립 50주년 **기념 행사를 개최했다**.

   The company ___held___ ______ ______ for its 50th anniversary.

4. 그녀는 야구**에 미쳐[푹 빠져] 있다**.

   She ___is___ ______ ______ baseball.

5. 그는 그 문제에 대해 **경솔한 발언을 했다**.

   He ___made___ ______ ______ ______ about the issue.

6. 그 과제를 **1시간 안에** 끝내세요.

   Finish the task ______ ______ ______.

7. 나는 **바로 전날** 그를 만났다.

   I met him ___the___ ______ ______.

8. 그는 그녀의 **전남편**이다.

   He is her ______ ______.

9. **빨리** 너를 **보고 싶어**.

   I ___can't___ ______ ______ ___see___ you.

10. 그는 엘리베이터 **대신** 계단을 이용했다.

    He took the stairs ______ ______ the elevator.

1. on special occasions 특별한 행사 때[경우에/일이 있을 때] 2. wedding anniversary 결혼기념일
3. hold a celebration 기념 행사를 개최하다[열다] 4. be crazy about ~에 미치다[푹 빠지다/열광하다]
5. make a careless remark 경솔한[부주의한] 발언을 하다 6. within an hour 1시간 안에[내에]
7. the previous day 바로 전날 8. former husband 전남편 (= ex-husband)
9. can't wait to V 빨리 ~을 하고 싶다, ~이 너무 기다려진다 10. instead of ~ 대신에

DAY 28

1. 죄송하지만 그 모델은 **재고가 없어요**.

Sorry, but the model is ______________ ______________ ______________.

2. 그 새 모델은 **온라인에서 구할 수 있다**.

The new model is ______________ ______________.

3. 우리는 새 차를 살 **여유가 없다[형편이 안 된다]**.

We ____can't____ ______________ ______________ buy a new car.

4. 나는 중고차를 **적정한[합리적인] 가격에** 샀다.

I bought a used car ______________ ______________ ______________ ______________.

5. 급료는 **시간당**(시급) 15달러이다.

The pay is $15 ______________ ______________.

6. 도서관은 **공공 재산**이다.

The library is ______________ ______________.

7. 우리는 **쓰레기를 줄여**야 한다.

We need to ______________ ______________.

8. 많은 일자리들이 로봇**으로 대체되고** 있다.

Many jobs are ____being____ ______________ ______________ robots.

9. 그는 저축한 돈을 **다 써버렸다**.

He ______________ ______________ all his savings.

10. 우리는 연료(휘발유)**가 거의 다 떨어져 간다**.

We are ______________ ______________ ______________ gas.

1. out of stock 재고가 없는, 품절된 2. available online 온라인에서 구(매)할 수 있는
3. can't afford to (금전적으로) ~할 여유가 없다[형편이 안 된다] 4. at a reasonable price 적정한[합리적인] 가격에
5. per hour 시간당 6. public property 공공 재산
7. reduce waste 쓰레기를 줄이다 8. be replaced by ~에 의해 대체되다, ~로 교체되다
9. use up 다 쓰다, 소진하다 10. run out of ~을 다 써버리다, ~이 다 되다[다 떨어지다]

DAY 29

1. **경제 성장**이 느리다.

   ________ ________ is slow.

2. **현재 경제 상황**은 어려운 상황이다.

   The ________ economic ________ is challenging.

3. 정부는 **새 정책을 발표했다**.

   The government ________ ________ ________ ________.

4. 우리는 **경제적 요인들**을 고려해야 한다.

   We should consider ________ ________.

5. **국내 시장**이 빠르게 성장했다.

   The ________ ________ has grown rapidly.

6. 그 회사는 작년에 **막대한 이익을 냈다**.

   The company made ________ ________ ________ last year.

7. 직원들은 **다양한 혜택들**을 누리게 될 것이다.

   Employees will enjoy ________ ________.

8. 비용은 900달러**로 추정된다**.

   The cost is ________ ________ $900.

9. 소음에도 불구하고 그녀는 **계속 일했다**.

   She continued ________ despite the noise.

10. 너는 **계속 시도해**야 해.

    You have to keep ________.

1. economic growth 경제 성장 2. current economic situation 현(재의) 경제 상황
3. announce a new policy 새 정책을 발표하다 4. economic factors 경제적 요인들
5. domestic market 국내 시장 6. make a huge profit 막대한 이익[수익]을 내다
7. various benefits 다양한 혜택들 8. be estimated at ~로 추정되다[추산되다]
9. continue V-ing 계속해서 ~하다 10. keep (on) V-ing 계속해서 ~하다, 줄곧 ~하다

DAY 30

1. 그 일은 **육체 노동**을 필요로 한다.

   The job requires ______ ______.

2. 우리는 **새로운 마케팅 전략**을 세워야 한다.

   We need to set up ___a___ ___new___ ______ ______.

3. 그들은 **그 임무를** 성공적으로 **수행했다**.

   They ______ ______ ___the___ ______ successfully.

4. 마침내 우리는 **그 과제를 완료[완수]했다**.

   At last, we ______ ___the___ ______.

5. 많은 애완동물들이 주인**에게서 버려진다**.

   Many pets ___are___ ______ ______ their owners.

6. 그는 유튜버가 된 후 **큰돈을 벌었다**.

   He ___made___ ______ ______ after becoming a YouTuber.

7. 그들은 **(그들의) 사업을** 아시아로 **확장시켰다**.

   They have ______ ___their___ ______ into Asia.

8. 시는 **그 도로를 연장할** 계획이다.

   The city plans to ______ ______ ______.

9. (당신은) **좀 쉬는** 게 어때요?

   Why don't you ___get___ ______ ______?

10. 이제 **마무리**합시다.

    Let's ______ ___it___ ______.

1. manual labor 육체 노동 2. a new marketing strategy 새로운 마케팅 전략
3. carry out a mission (어떤) 임무를 수행하다 4. accomplish a task (어떤) 과제를 완료하다[완수하다]
5. be abandoned by ~에게서 버려지다[버림받다] 6. make a fortune 큰돈을 벌다, 재산을 모으다, 부자가 되다
7. expand one's business (~의) 사업을 확장하다 8. extend a road (어떤) 도로를 연장하다
9. get some rest 좀 쉬다, 휴식을 취하다 10. wrap up 마무리하다; 싸다[포장하다]

DAY 31

1. 그들은 **변호사를 고용했다**.

They ________ ____a____ ________.

2. 그녀는 그 일자리**에 지원하**기로 결심했다.

She decided to ________ ________ the job.

3. 그 규칙은 모든 직원**에게 적용된다**.

The rules ________ ________ all employees.

4. 우리는 저녁으로 **피자를 주문했다**.

We ________ ________ for dinner.

5. 그들은 그들의 신제품을 **TV에 광고할** 계획이다.

They plan to ________ their new product ________ ________.

6. 그 영화는 엄청난 **상업적 성공**을 거뒀다.

The movie was ________ huge ________ ________.

7. 그는 감옥**에서 석방되었다**.

He ____was____ ________ ________ prison.

8. 삼성은 다음 달에 **새 스마트폰을 출시할** 것이다.

Samsung will ________ ________ ________ ________ next month.

9. 그는 돈을 모으**기 위해** 열심히 일했다.

He worked hard ________ ________ ________ save money.

10. 복사기가 **고장 났다**.

The copy machine is ________ ________ ________.

1. employ a lawyer 변호사를 고용하다 2. apply for ~에 지원하다, ~을 신청하다
3. apply to ~에 적용되다 4. order pizza 피자를 주문하다
5. advertise A on TV A를 TV에 광고하다 6. a commercial success 상업적 성공
7. be released from ~에서 풀려나다[석방되다] 8. release a new smartphone 새 스마트폰을 출시하다
9. in order to ~하기 위하여 10. out of order 고장이 난

DAY 32

1. 그 미술관에는 많은 그림들이 **전시되어 있다.**

   Many paintings ________ ________ in the gallery.

2. 그 책은 **읽을 가치가 있다.**

   The book ____is____ ________ ________.

3. 전통 음악**의 가치**를 이해하는 것은 중요하다.

   It's important to understand ____the____ ________ ________ traditional music.

4. 그의 작품은 **수십 년 동안** 사랑받아 왔다.

   His works have been loved ________ ________.

5. 그 그림은 **16세기에** 그려졌다.

   The picture was painted ____in____ ________ ________ ________.

6. **일반적으로[보통]** 십대들은 힙합을 좋아한다.

   ________ ________, teenagers love hip-hop.

7. 그 귀중한 그림이 **도난당했다.**

   The priceless painting ________ ________.

8. 그는 많은 **범죄를 저질렀다.**

   He ________ many ________.

9. 그는 직장에서 많은 어려움**을 겪었다.**

   He ________ ________ many difficulties at work.

10. 나는 당신과 사랑에 **빠지지 않을 수 없어요.**

    I ____can't____ ________ ________ in love with you.

1. be exhibited 전시되다 2. be worth V-ing ~할 가치가 있다, ~할 만하다
3. the value of ~의 가치 4. for decades 수십 년 동안
5. in the 16th century 16세기에 6. in general 보통, 대개, 일반적으로
7. be stolen 도난당하다, 도둑맞다 8. commit a crime 범죄를 저지르다
9. go through (어려운 일을) 겪다, 통과하다 10. can't help V-ing ~하지 않을 수 없다

MEMO

MEMO

MEMO

DAY 17

No.	Word	Definition	Write	Meaning
321	**recent**	happening not long ago	recent	형 최근의
322	**recently**	not long ago		부 최근에
323	**pregnant**	having a baby developing inside the body		형 (사람·포유 동물이) 임신한
324	**due**	expected to happen		형 1. ~하기로 되어 있는[예정된] 2. ~로 인한, ~ 때문에 ((to))
325	**birth**	the time when a baby is born; the process of being born		명 1. 탄생, 출생 2. 출산
326	**newborn**	recently born		형 갓 태어난 명 신생아
327	**breath**	the air that you take into your lungs and send out again		명 1. 호흡 2. 입김, 숨
328	**breathe**	to take air into your lungs and send it out again		동 숨을 쉬다, 호흡하다
329	**breed**	to produce young animals		동 1. (동물이) 새끼를 낳다, 번식하다 2. 사육하다, 번식시키다
330	**feed**	to give food to a person or an animal		동 밥을 먹이다, 먹이를 주다
331	**chest**	the front part of your body between your neck and waist		명 가슴, 흉부
332	**breast**	one of the two soft, round parts on a woman's chest		명 1. 가슴, 유방 2. (새·동물의) 가슴살
333	**develop**	to gradually grow or become bigger		동 1. 성장[발달]하다; 성장[발달]시키다 2. 개발하다
334	**survive**	to continue to live or exist		동 1. 살아남다, 생존하다 2. (위기 등을) 견뎌 내다
335	**absolute**	complete and total		형 1. 완벽한, 완전한 2. 절대적인, 무제한의
336	**absolutely**	completely; totally		부 1. 전적으로, 완전히 2. 전혀 (~ 않다)
337	**either**	one or the other of two (things or people)		대 (둘 중) 어느 하나 부 1. [부정문] ~도 또한 2. ~거나, ~든 ((or))
338	**neither**	not one or the other of two (things or people)		대 (둘 중) 어느 것도 ~ 아니다 부 1. [부정문] ~도 또한 2. ~도 …도 아니다 ((nor))
339	**due to**	because of		~ 때문에, ~로 인해
340	**according to**	as reported by someone or something		~에 따르면, ~에 따라서

DAY 18

341 **medical** related to the treatment of disease or injury

342 **vital** extremely important; essential

343 **injury** a wound or damage to someone's body (in an accident or attack)

344 **injured** having an injury

345 **wound** an injury, especially one (that is) made by a knife or bullet

346 **damage** harm or injury

347 **blind** not able to see

348 **deaf** unable to hear or unable to hear very well

349 **cancer** a serious disease

350 **flu** an illness like a very bad cold that causes pains and fever

351 **prevent** to stop someone doing something; to stop something from happening

352 **poison** a substance that can kill you if you eat or drink it

353 **scratch** to rub your skin with your nails

354 **scream** to give a loud, high cry

355 **suffer** to experience physical or mental pain

356 **operate** to use and control a machine or make it work

357 **recover** to get well again after being sick, hurt, etc.

358 **overcome** to succeed in dealing with a problem

359 **prevent A from V-ing** to stop[keep] A from doing something

360 **pass away / die of** to die

committee	명 위원회
	명 1. (특정한 활동을 하는) 기간, 시간 2. (의회 등의) 회기, 회의
	동 1. (공식적으로) 결정하다, 확정하다 2. 파악하다, 밝히다
	동 확인하다, 확정하다
	동 1. 승인하다 2. 찬성하다 ((of))
	동 1. 결론을 내리다 2. 끝내다; 끝나다 ((with))
	명 갈등, 충돌 동 상충하다, 충돌하다 ((with))
	동 1. 비난하다 2. 고발하다, 고소하다 ((of))
	동 (강력히) 권고하다, 촉구하다 ((to)) 명 (강한) 충동, 욕구 ((to))
	형 긴급한, 다급한
	명 욕구, 갈망 ((for/to)) 동 원하다 ((to))
	형 갈망[열망]하는, 간절히 바라는 ((for/to))
	동 1. (~하게) 만들다, 몰아가다 ((to)) 2. 운전하다
	동 억지로 ~을 시키다, 강요하다 ((to)) 명 1. 힘 2. 무력, 폭력
	동 1. (~하도록) 설득하다 ((to)) 2. 납득시키다
	동 1. 납득시키다, 확신시키다 2. 설득하다 ((to))
	동 1. 고무하다, 격려하다 2. 영감을 주다
	명 세대(비슷한 연령층), 대(代)
	~에게 …하기를 강요하다
	~할 수밖에 없다

DAY 16

301	**committee**	a group of people who are chosen to do a particular job	medical	형 의학의, 의료의
302	**session**	a period of time used for a particular activity		형 1. 필수적인, 극히 중요한 2. 생명의, 생명 유지에 필요한
303	**determine**	to officially decide something		명 (사고로 인한) 부상, 상해 ((to))
304	**confirm**	to say or show that something is true or correct		형 1. 부상을 당한, 다친 2. (the injured) 부상자들
305	**approve**	to allow or officially agree to something		명 (칼·총과 같은 흉기로 인한) 상처, 부상 동 상처[부상]를 입히다 ((in))
306	**conclude**	to decide something (after studying all the information about it)		명 손상, 피해, 훼손 동 손상을 입히다, 피해를 주다
307	**conflict**	a serious disagreement or argument		형 1. 눈이 먼, 맹인의 2. (the blind) 맹인들 동 눈이 멀게 만들다
308	**accuse**	to say that someone has done something wrong		형 1. 귀가 먹은, 청각 장애가 있는 2. (the deaf) 청각 장애인들
309	**urge**	to strongly suggest (someone) to do something		명 암
310	**urgent**	very important and needing to be dealt with immediately		명 (흔히 the flu) 독감
311	**desire**	a strong wish to have or do something		동 1. 막다, 방해하다 ((from)) 2. 예방하다, 방지하다
312	**eager**	wanting to do or have something very much		명 독, 독약 동 독을 넣다, 독살하다
313	**drive**	to force someone to act in a particular way		동 긁다, 할퀴다 명 긁힌 자국
314	**force**	to make someone do something (that they do not want to do)		동 비명을 지르다, 소리치다 명 비명
315	**persuade**	to make someone do or believe something		동 1. (질병 등에) 시달리다, 고통받다 ((from)) 2. (부상·고통 등을) 겪다
316	**convince**	to make someone believe that something is true		동 1. (기계를) 가동[조작]하다; 가동[작동]되다 2. 수술하다 ((on))
317	**inspire**	to make someone feel that they want to do something		동 회복되다; 회복하다, 되찾다 ((from))
318	**generation**	all the people who were born at about the same time		동 1. 극복하다, 이겨 내다 2. [수동형으로] ~에 압도당하다 ((with/by))
319	**force** (someone) **to do** (something)	to make (someone) do (something) against their will		A가 ~하는 것을 막다
320	**be forced to**	to have no choice but to do		사망하다, 돌아가시다 / ~로 죽다

DAY 19

361	**principle**	a rule or belief that influences your behavior
362	**principal**	most important; head teacher; chief
363	**junior**	low or lower in rank; younger in age
364	**senior**	having a higher position or rank; older in age
365	**lecture**	a talk to a group of people about a subject
366	**instruct**	to teach or educate
367	**assign**	to give someone a particular job or responsibility
368	**cope**	to deal successfully with something difficult
369	**prime**	main; most important; excellent
370	**primary**	main; most important; most basic
371	**purpose**	the reason why something is done or used
372	**aim**	a goal or purpose that you try to achieve
373	**object**	a thing that you can see or touch
374	**structure**	the way that parts of something are arranged
375	**enroll**	to officially arrange to join a school or course
376	**register**	to record your name on an official list
377	**space**	an empty area that is free to be used
378	**blank**	empty; with no writing, pictures, or sound
379	**sign up for**	to enroll in or register for something
380	**on purpose**	purposely; intentionally

discuss	동 논의하다, 토론하다 ((with))
______	명 논의, 토의, 토론 ((about))
______	동 토론하다, 논쟁하다 명 토론, 논쟁
______	동 1. 언쟁을 하다, 말다툼을 하다 ((with)) 2. 주장하다
______	동 주장하다, 우기다, 고집하다
______	동 1. 주장하다 2. 요구하다, 청구하다 명 1. 주장 2. 청구 ((for))
______	동 1. 증명하다 2. (사용법을) 설명하다, 보여 주다 3. 시위[데모]를 하다
______	동 1. 비난[비판]하다 ((for)) 2. 비평하다
______	명 1. (글의) 문맥 2. (어떤 일의) 정황, 맥락
______	명 1. 속에 든 것들, 내용물 2. 목차 형 만족하는
______	동 번역하다, 통역하다 ((into))
______	명 1. 번역가, 통역가 2. 번역기
______	동 1. 통역하다 2. 해석하다, 이해하다 ((as))
______	명 통역사
______	형 특정한, 특별한
______	형 1. 특정한 2. 구체적인, 명확한
______	동 1. (내기 등에) 돈을 걸다 2. 장담하다 명 내기, 내기 돈
______	부 약간, 다소, 조금
______	~에 만족하다
______	~을 고집하다, ~을 주장하다

DAY 15

281	**discuss**	to talk about something with someone	principle	명 1. (개인의) 신념, 원칙 2. (기본이 되는) 원리, 원칙
282	**discussion**	the act of discussing something		형 주요한, 주된 명 교장, (단체의) 장
283	**debate**	to discuss a subject formally		형 손아래의, 후배의 ((to)) 명 1. 손아랫사람, 후배 2. (고등학교) 2학년, (4년제 대학) 3학년
284	**argue**	to speak angrily to someone (because you disagree with them)		형 손위의, 선배의 ((to)) 명 1. 연장자, 선배 2. (고교·대학의) 상급생
285	**insist**	to say firmly that something is true		명 강의, 강연 동 강의하다 ((on))
286	**claim**	to say that something is true, even though it has not been proved		동 1. 가르치다 2. 지시하다
287	**demonstrate**	to show or prove something clearly		동 (일 등을) 맡기다, 부과하다, 배정하다 ((to))
288	**criticize**	to say that someone or something is bad		동 대처하다, 대응하다 ((with))
289	**context**	the parts of a text that help to understand its meaning		형 1. 주된, 주요한 2. 최고의, 최상의
290	**content**	the things that are contained in something		형 1. 주된, 주요한 2. 최초의, 초기의
291	**translate**	to change written or spoken words into another language		명 1. 목적, 의도 ((of)) 2. (-s) 용도
292	**translator**	a person who translates from one language into another		명 1. 목적, 목표 ((of)) 2. 겨냥, 조준 동 1. 목표로 하다 ((to)) 2. 겨냥하다 ((at))
293	**interpret**	to translate spoken words from one language into another		명 1. 물건, 물체 2. 목적 ((of)) 동 반대하다 ((to))
294	**interpreter**	someone who changes spoken words from one language into another		명 1. (사물 등의) 구조 ((of)) 2. 구조물, 건축물
295	**particular**	special or single		동 (강좌·학교 등에) 등록하다; 등록시키다 ((in))
296	**specific**	connected with one particular thing only		동 등록하다 ((for)); (출생 등을) 신고하다 명 등록부, 명부
297	**bet**	to risk money on the result of a race or game		명 1. (비어 있는) 공간, 자리 2. 우주
298	**slightly**	a little; a bit		형 빈, 공백의 명 빈칸, 공란
299	**be content with**	to be happy with; to be satisfied with		~을 신청하다, ~에 가입하다[등록하다]
300	**insist on**	to keep doing something, even if it annoys other people		고의로, 일부러

DAY 20

No.	Word	Definition		Meaning
381	**emphasize**	to say something in a strong way	praise	동 칭찬하다 명 칭찬, 찬사, 찬양 ((for))
382	**concentrate**	to give all your attention to something		동 비난하다, ~을 탓하다 ((for)) 명 책임, 탓 ((on))
383	**interrupt**	to stop someone while they are talking or doing something		동 처벌하다, 벌주다 ((for))
384	**disturb**	to interrupt what someone is doing		동 불평하다, 항의하다 ((about sth)) ((to sb))
385	**examine**	to look at something carefully		동 1. (기꺼이) 받아들이다 2. (동의하여) 수락하다, 인정하다
386	**refer**	to mention or speak about something		동 (요청·부탁 등을) 거절하다, 거부하다
387	**progress**	the process of getting better (at doing something)		동 (주장·요구·제안 등을) 거부하다, 받아들이지 않다
388	**advance**	progress or the forward movement of something		동 1. 부인하다 2. 거부하다, 허락하지 않다
389	**achieve**	to succeed in reaching a goal, especially by working hard		동 1. 인정하다, 시인하다 2. (입장 등을) 허락하다
390	**deserve**	to have earned something by good or bad actions		명 1. 시인, 인정 ((of)) 2. 가입, 입장, 입학 3. 입장료
391	**hardly**	almost not, or only a very small amount		동 (계획·정책 등에) 반대하다
392	**barely**	only just		동 1. 저항하다, 대항하다 2. (열·손상 등에) 강하다 3. 참다, 견디다
393	**intense**	extreme or very strong		동 1. 제안하다 2. 추천하다 3. 시사하다, 암시하다
394	**intend**	to have a plan or purpose		동 1. 추천하다 2. 권(장)하다
395	**intention**	what you intend or plan to do; your aim		동 1. 제안하다 2. 청혼하다 ((to))
396	**intentional**	planned or intended		명 1. 제안, 제의 2. 청혼, 프러포즈
397	**prove**	to show that something is true by providing facts, etc.		명 계약(서) 동 계약하다 ((with))
398	**indicate**	to show that something is true or exists		명 1. 서명 2. 특징
399	**in advance**	ahead of time		미루다, 연기하다
400	**intend to**	to mean to; to plan to		결심하다, 마음을 정하다

DAY 14

No.	Word	Definition	Answer	Meaning
261	**praise**	to say that someone or something is very good	emphasize	동 강조하다
262	**blame**	to say that a person or thing is responsible for (something bad)		동 집중하다 ((on))
263	**punish**	to make someone suffer (because they have done something wrong)		동 1. (말·행동 등을) 방해하다, 가로막다 2. 중단시키다
264	**complain**	to say that you are unhappy or not satisfied (about something)		동 1. (일·수면 등을) 방해하다 2. 불안하게 하다 3. 어지럽히다
265	**accept**	to take or receive something that is offered		동 1. 조사하다, 검토하다 2. 검사하다, 진찰하다 3. 시험을 실시하다 ((on/in))
266	**refuse**	to say that you will not do or accept something		동 1. 참고[참조]하다 2. 지시하다, 나타내다 3. 언급하다 ((to))
267	**reject**	to refuse to accept something		명 진전, 진보 동 진행되다, 진척되다
268	**deny**	to say that something is not true		명 1. 진전, 발전 2. (군대의) 전진 동 1. (기술 등이) 진보하다 2. 전진하다
269	**admit**	to agree unwillingly that something is true		동 이루다, 달성하다, 성취하다
270	**admission**	the act of agreeing that something is true		동 ~을 받을 만하다, ~할 자격이 있다, ~해야 마땅하다 ((to))
271	**oppose**	to disagree with a plan or activity and try to stop it		부 거의 ~ 아니다[없다], 거의 ~하지 않다
272	**resist**	to refuse to accept or be changed by something		부 1. 간신히, 가까스로 2. 거의 ~ 않다
273	**suggest**	to tell someone your ideas about what they should do		형 1. 극심한, 강렬한 2. 치열한
274	**recommend**	to tell someone that something is good or useful		동 의도하다, (~하려고) 생각하다 ((to))
275	**propose**	to suggest a plan or action		명 의사, 의도, 목적 ((of))
276	**proposal**	a formal suggestion or plan		형 의도적인, 고의로 한
277	**contract**	an official agreement		동 1. 증명하다, 입증하다 2. (~임이) 드러나다, 판명되다
278	**signature**	a person's name written in that person's handwriting		동 1. 나타내다, 보여 주다 2. 가리키다
279	**put off (V-ing)**	to delay doing something		미리, 사전에
280	**make up one's mind**	to decide to		~하려고 의도하다, ~할 작정이다

DAY 21

401	**closet**	a small room or space in a wall used for storing things
402	**drawer**	a container like a box that is part of a piece of furniture
403	**cotton**	cloth or thread (that is) made from the cotton plant
404	**costume**	a set of clothes worn to show a particular character, time period, or style
405	**quality**	how good or bad something is
406	**quantity**	the amount or number of something
407	**bare**	not covered by clothes
408	**naked**	not wearing any clothes
409	**sew**	to use a needle and thread to make or repair clothes
410	**suitable**	acceptable or right for someone or something
411	**plain**	simple and not complicated
412	**fancy**	complicated or having a lot of decoration
413	**amount**	a quantity of something such as time or money
414	**bit**	a small amount or piece of something
415	**alter**	to change or to make someone or something change
416	**mend**	to fix or repair something
417	**ignore**	to intentionally pay no attention to something
418	**pretend**	to behave as if something is true
419	**prefer A to B**	to like A more than B
420	**would rather A (than B)**	to prefer A to B

Answer	Meaning
communicate	동 1. 의사소통을 하다, 연락하다 2. 전하다, 전달하다
______	명 1. 의사소통 2. 전달, 보도 3. 통신
______	동 (간단히) 언급하다, 거론하다 명 언급, 거론
______	동 언급하다, 발언하다, 논평하다 ((on)) 명 발언, 언급
______	명 어휘, 어휘력
______	명 1. 말투, 억양 2. (단어의) 강세 3. 강조, 역점 ((on))
______	동 발음하다
______	명 발음
______	명 구; 문구, 구절
______	명 속담, 격언
______	명 1. 용어 2. 학기 3. (일정한) 기간, 기한
______	부 1. 또렷하게 2. 명확히, 알기 쉽게
______	동 1. (단어의 뜻을) 정의하다 2. 규정하다, 분명히 밝히다
______	형 명확한, 확실한
______	형 중요한, 의미 있는
______	명 1. 몸짓, 제스처 2. (감정·의사의) 표현, 표시 동 제스처를 하다 ((to))
______	명 (편지) 봉투
______	명 1. 우표 2. 도장, 스탬프
______	~할 것 같다 / ~할 것 같지 않다
______	기꺼이 ~하다, ~할 의향이 있다

DAY 13

241	**communicate**	to exchange information or have a conversation with others
242	**communication**	the act of communicating with other people
243	**mention**	to speak or write about something (or someone) briefly
244	**remark**	to say or write a comment about something (or someone)
245	**vocabulary**	all the words in a particular language
246	**accent**	the way that someone speaks, showing where he or she comes from
247	**pronounce**	to make the sound of a letter or word
248	**pronunciation**	how words are pronounced
249	**phrase**	a group of words that are often used together
250	**proverb**	a famous phrase or sentence that gives you advice
251	**term**	a word or phrase that is used to mean a particular thing
252	**clearly**	in a clear manner
253	**define**	to say exactly what something means
254	**definite**	sure or certain
255	**significant**	important or noticeable
256	**gesture**	a movement you make with your body (to show a feeling or message)
257	**envelope**	a flat paper container used for sending letters in
258	**stamp**	a small piece of paper (that) you stick on an envelope
259	**be likely to / be unlikely to**	to probably will / to probably won't
260	**be willing to**	to be prepared or open to do something

closet

closet	명 벽장, (붙박이) 옷장
	명 서랍
	명 1. 솜, 면직물 2. 목화
	명 (특정 지역이나 시대의) 의상, 복장
	명 질, 품질 ((of))
	명 (세거나 잴 수 있는) 양, 수량, 분량 ((of))
	형 맨살을 드러낸
	형 (완전히) 벌거벗은, 아무것도 걸치지 않은
	동 바느질하다, 꿰매다
	형 적절한, 적합한, 알맞은 ((for))
	형 1. 꾸미지 않은, 평범한 2. 분명한 명 평지, 평원
	형 1. 화려한, 장식이 많은 2. 값비싼, 고급의
	명 1. (시간·물질 등의) 양 2. (돈의) 액수, 총액 ((of))
	명 한 조각 부 1. (a bit) 조금, 약간 2. (a bit) 잠시
	동 1. 바꾸다, 변경하다; 바뀌다 2. (옷을) 고치다
	동 1. 수리하다, 고치다 2. (옷 등을) 수선하다, 꿰매다
	동 1. 무시하다 2. (사람을) 못 본 척하다
	동 1. ~인 척하다 ((to)) 2. ~라고 가장하다[상상하다]
	B보다 A를 더 좋아하다[선호하다]
	(B하느니) 차라리 A하고 싶다, (B보다) A하는 게 낫다

DAY 22

421	**hold**	to organize an event
422	**ceremony**	a formal event
423	**athlete**	a person who competes in sports
424	**sweat**	the liquid that is on your skin when you are hot
425	**compete**	to try to win a competition
426	**competition**	the activity of competing or the contest itself
427	**bounce**	to move up or away after hitting a surface
428	**leap**	to jump high or far
429	**slide**	to move smoothly along a surface
430	**slippery**	difficult to stand or move on (because something is smooth or wet)
431	**row**	a straight line of people or things
432	**aloud**	in a voice that other people can hear
433	**beat**	to hit (someone or something) repeatedly, usually very hard
434	**defeat**	to win against someone (in a war or competition)
435	**lost**	unable to find your way
436	**loss**	the state of no longer having something
437	**award**	a prize given to someone (for something they have achieved)
438	**reward**	a deserved outcome or result
439	**be held**	to take place
440	**take place**	to happen, to occur; to be held

believe	동 1. 믿다 2. (~라고) 생각하다[여기다]
	명 믿음, 신념 ((in))
	명 1. 믿음, 신뢰 2. 신념 3. 신앙(심) ((in))
	명 신뢰, 신임 동 1. 신뢰하다 2. (무엇이 옳다고) 믿다
	동 1. (~로) 여기다, 간주하다 ((as)) 2. 평가하다 명 고려, 관심 ((to))
	부 상관없이, 개의치 않고 ((of))
	명 1. 시력 2. 전망, 비전, 통찰력
	형 (눈으로) 보는, 시각의, 시각적인
	동 1. 추측하다, 생각하다 2. 가정하다
	동 추정하다, 가정하다
	동 결정하다, 결심하다 ((to))
	명 결정, 판단
	동 후회하다 명 후회, 유감
	명 1. 잠깐, 잠시 2. (특정한) 순간, 시점
	형 감사하는, 고맙게 여기는 ((for))
	형 질투하는, 시기하는, 시샘하는 ((of))
	동 1. 존경하다 2. 감탄하며 바라보다
	동 1. (진가를) 알아보다, 인정하다 2. 감사하다
	~하기로 되어 있다, ~해야 한다
	~하기로 결심하다[결정하다]

DAY 12

No.	Word	Definition	Answer	Korean
221	**believe**	to accept something as true	hold	동 1. (행사 등을) 열다, 개최하다 2. 잡다, 들다, 안다 3. 버티다, 유지하다
222	**belief**	a strong feeling (that) something is true or real		명 의식, 예식
223	**faith**	a strong belief or trust (in someone or something)		명 운동선수
224	**trust**	the belief (that) someone or something is good or honest		명 땀 동 땀을 흘리다
225	**regard**	to think about someone or something in a particular way		동 1. 경쟁하다, 겨루다 ((for/with/against)) 2. (경기 등에) 참가하다 ((in))
226	**regardless**	without being affected by something		명 1. 경쟁 2. 대회, 시합
227	**vision**	the ability to see		동 (공 등이) 튀다, 튀어 오르다
228	**visual**	relating to seeing		동 (높이) 뛰어오르다, 뛰어넘다 명 높이뛰기, 도약
229	**suppose**	to think (that) something is true or possible		동 미끄러지다, 미끄러지듯이 움직이다 명 미끄럼틀
230	**assume**	to think (that) something is true, although you have no proof		형 미끄러운, 미끈거리는
231	**decide**	to make a choice to do something		명 1. (죽 늘어선) 열, 줄 2. (극장 등의 좌석) 줄 동 노를 젓다
232	**decision**	a choice you make about something		부 1. 소리 내어 2. 큰 소리로, 크게
233	**regret**	to feel sorry about something you have done		동 1. (세게 계속) 때리다, 두드리다 2. 이기다 3. (심장이) 뛰다
234	**moment**	a very short period of time		동 패배시키다, 물리치다, 이기다 명 패배
235	**grateful**	feeling or showing thanks		형 1. 길을 잃은 2. 잃어버린, 분실된
236	**jealous**	feeling unhappy because you want something that someone else has		명 1. 분실, 상실 2. (금전적) 손실 3. 패배
237	**admire**	to respect someone		명 상 동 (상 등을) 수여하다, 주다
238	**appreciate**	to recognize the worth of something		명 보상 동 보상하다, 보답하다
239	**be supposed to**	to be expected to do something		(행사 등이) 열리다, 개최되다
240	**decide to**	to make a decision		(사건 등이) 일어나다; (행사 등이) 열리다

DAY 23

441	**abroad**	in or to a foreign country	thought	명 생각, 의견
442	**overseas**	in or to a foreign country that is across the sea		명 의견, 견해 ((about/on/of))
443	**harbor**	an area of water near the coast where ships are kept		명 논평, 의견 동 논평하다, 견해를 밝히다 ((about/on))
444	**sail**	to travel in a ship or boat		명 이론, 학설
445	**compass**	a device that is used to find direction		부 꽤, 제법 형 예쁜
446	**needle**	a small, thin piece of steel		부 상당히, 꽤, 매우
447	**deck**	the top outside floor of a ship or boat		형 1. 알고 있는, 인식하고 있는 2. 알아차린 ((of))
448	**section**	one of the parts that something is divided into		형 1. 의식하는, 알고 있는 ((of)) 2. 의식이 있는
449	**wrap**	to cover something or someone with paper, cloth, etc.		동 상기시키다, 생각나게 하다 ((remind A of B))
450	**tie**	to fasten something with string, rope, etc.		동 1. 기억해 내다, 상기하다 2. 생각나게 하다
451	**national**	relating to one particular nation; related to a whole nation		전 1. ~와 다른 2. ~답지 않은 3. ~와 달리
452	**international**	relating to more than one nation		형 1. ~할 것 같은 ((to)) 2. 있을 법한, 그럴듯한
453	**passenger**	a person who rides in a vehicle, such as a bus, boat, or plane		동 1. 잘 생각하다, 숙고하다 2. ~로 여기다[생각하다] 3. 고려하다
454	**destination**	the place that someone or something is going to		형 상당한, 많은
455	**transport**	to carry (someone or something) from one place to another		형 1. 꾸준한 2. 변함없는, 고정적인
456	**baggage**	all the cases and bags that you take with you (when you travel)		형 1. 안정된, 안정적인 2. 견고한
457	**ease**	the state of being comfortable		명 1. 안락, 편안함 2. 위로, 위안 동 위로하다, 위안하다
458	**tension**	a feeling that you are nervous, worried, and not relaxed		형 1. 어색한, 불편한 2. 곤란한
459	**take off**	to leave the ground and begin to fly		A에게 B를 떠올리게 하다[생각나게 하다]
460	**make it**	to be successful at something		~을 알고 있다, ~을 눈치채고 있다

DAY 11

201	**thought**	something that you think of
202	**opinion**	your thoughts or ideas about something
203	**comment**	something that you say or write to give your opinion
204	**theory**	an idea or set of ideas that are suggested to explain something
205	**pretty**	to some extent
206	**quite**	to a great degree
207	**aware**	knowing or realizing something; conscious of something
208	**conscious**	noticing or realizing something
209	**remind**	to help someone remember something
210	**recall**	to remember something
211	**unlike**	different from someone or something
212	**likely**	probably going to happen; expected
213	**consider**	to think about something carefully
214	**considerable**	large in size, amount, or degree
215	**steady**	happening at a gradual, regular rate
216	**stable**	firmly fixed; not likely to move, change, or fail
217	**comfort**	the state of being relaxed and free from pain
218	**awkward**	making you feel embarrassed
219	**remind A of B**	to make A think of B
220	**be aware of**	to be conscious of

abroad	부 해외에(서), 해외로, 외국으로
______	부 해외에[로], 외국에[으로] 형 해외의, 외국의
______	명 항구, 항만
______	동 항해하다 명 (배의) 돛
______	명 1. 나침반 2. (제도용) 컴퍼스
______	명 1. (바느질용) 바늘 2. (주사) 바늘 3. (계기의) 바늘
______	명 1. (배의) 갑판 2. (이층 버스의) 층
______	명 부분, 구획
______	동 1. 싸다, 포장하다 2. 두르다
______	동 묶다, 매다 명 넥타이
______	형 1. 국가의, 전국적인 2. 국립의
______	형 국제적인, 국가 간의
______	명 승객, 여객
______	명 1. 목적지 2. (물품의) 도착지
______	동 수송[운송]하다, 실어 나르다
______	명 (여행용) 짐, 수화물
______	명 쉬움, 편안함 동 (고통 등을) 완화하다; 편해지다
______	명 1. (심리적) 긴장 2. (관계 등의) 긴장 상태
______	1. 이륙하다 2. (옷 등을) 벗다
______	1. 성공하다, 해내다 2. (늦지 않게) 도착하다

DAY 24

461	**society**	a large group of people who live in the same country or area
462	**identity**	who someone is
463	**diverse**	very different from each other
464	**majority**	most of the people or things in a group
465	**aid**	money or food that is sent to help a country (or group of people)
466	**necessary**	needed in order to do something; essential
467	**appoint**	to officially choose someone for a position
468	**appointment**	a formal arrangement to meet or visit someone
469	**donate**	to give money or goods to a person or organization
470	**contribute**	to give something to help someone or something
471	**fund**	an amount of money that is collected for a purpose
472	**charity**	an organization for helping people in need
473	**obtain**	to get something, especially by making an effort
474	**devote**	to use time or energy for a particular purpose or person
475	**depend**	to be decided by; to change according to
476	**rely**	to depend on
477	**adopt**	to take someone else's child into your family
478	**adapt**	to change something to make it suitable for a new situation
479	**be devoted to**	to devote yourself to someone or something
480	**depend on**	to rely on someone or something

fascinate	동 마음을 사로잡다, 매혹하다, 매료시키다
______	형 마음을 빼앗긴, 매료된
______	동 생기를 되찾게 하다, 상쾌하게 하다
______	동 1. (전기를) 재충전하다 2. (휴식으로) 재충전하다
______	형 걱정하는, 근심하는, 불안해하는 ((about))
______	명 걱정, 불안(감) ((about))
______	명 1. 우려, 걱정 ((about/for)) 2. 관심사 동 1. 걱정시키다 2. 관련이 있다
______	형 1. 걱정하는, 염려하는 ((about/for)) 2. 관련이 있는, 관심이 있는 ((with))
______	동 1. 혼란스럽게 하다 2. 혼동하다 ((confuse A with B))
______	형 혼란스러운, 헷갈리는 ((about))
______	동 우울하게 하다
______	형 1. 우울한, 의기소침한 2. 불경기의
______	명 (섬뜩하게) 놀람, 공포
______	동 깜짝 놀라게 하다, 겁먹게 하다
______	동 만족시키다, (요구 등을) 충족시키다 ((with))
______	동 실망시키다; [수동형으로] 실망하다 ((with/at/about))
______	동 짜증 나게 하다, 귀찮게 하다
______	동 좌절감을 주다, 좌절시키다
______	1. (곤란을) 극복하다 2. (병 등에서) 회복하다
______	1. ~에 관심이 있다 2. ~와 관련되다

DAY 10

181	**fascinate**	to attract or interest someone very much	society	명 1. 사회 2. 협회, 단체
182	**fascinated**	extremely interested	________	명 1. 신원, 신분 2. 정체성, 독자성
183	**refresh**	to make someone feel less tired or less hot	________	형 다양한, 여러 가지의
184	**recharge**	to fill a battery with electricity	________	명 대부분, 대다수, 다수
185	**anxious**	feeling worried or nervous	________	명 1. 원조, 지원 2. 도움
186	**anxiety**	the feeling of being very worried	________	형 필요한, 필수적인 ((for))
187	**concern**	a feeling of worry, usually shared by many people	________	동 1. 임명하다, 지명하다 ((as)) 2. (시간·장소 등을) 정하다
188	**concerned**	worried about something	________	명 1. (공식적인) 약속, (진찰 등의) 예약 2. 임명, 지명
189	**confuse**	to make someone uncertain (or unable to understand)	________	동 1. 기부하다, 기증하다 2. 헌혈하다; (장기를) 기증하다 ((to))
190	**confused**	unable to understand or think clearly	________	동 1. 기부[기증]하다 2. 기여하다; (~의) 원인이 되다 ((to))
191	**depress**	to make someone feel sad or unhappy	________	명 기금, 자금
192	**depressed**	very sad and unhappy	________	명 1. 자선 단체, 구호 단체 2. 자선
193	**fright**	a sudden feeling of shock and fear	________	동 (노력 끝에) 얻다, 획득하다
194	**frighten**	to make someone feel afraid	________	동 (시간·노력 등을) 바치다, 쏟다 ((to))
195	**satisfy**	to make someone pleased by doing what they want	________	동 1. (~에) 달려 있다 2. 의존하다, 의지하다 ((on, upon))
196	**disappoint**	to make someone feel unhappy; to let down	________	동 1. (~에) 기대다, 의지하다 2. 믿다 ((on, upon))
197	**annoy**	to make someone slightly angry	________	동 1. 입양하다 2. 채택하다
198	**frustrate**	to make someone feel angry, disappointed, or discouraged	________	동 적응하다, 익숙해지다 ((to))
199	**get over**	to overcome	________	~에게 헌신적이다
200	**be concerned with**	to be interested in; to relate to	________	~에 의지[의존]하다, ~에 달려 있다

DAY 25

481	**relate**	to connect (something) with (something else)
482	**related**	connected with something or someone
483	**relationship**	the way in which two things are connected
484	**relative**	a person who is connected by blood or marriage
485	**bond**	something that forms a connection between people or groups
486	**bind**	to tie something with string or rope
487	**unite**	to join together; to make people join together
488	**combine**	to mix or join things together; to become mixed or joined
489	**separate**	to divide things into different parts or groups
490	**divide**	to separate something into parts or groups
491	**apart**	separated by a distance or period of time
492	**broken**	damaged and separated into pieces; not working
493	**involve**	to include something as a necessary part
494	**apologize**	to say that you are sorry for doing something wrong
495	**ought**	should
496	**otherwise**	if not; or else
497	**except**	not including (someone or something); apart from
498	**despite**	although something happened or is true; in spite of
499	**had better**	to ought to do
500	**except for**	apart from

Answer	Meaning
emotional	형 1. 감정의, 정서의 2. 감정적인
________	명 1. (일시적인) 기분 2. 분위기
________	동 (대단히) 놀라게 하다, 경탄하게 하다
________	형 놀란, 경탄한
________	동 즐겁게 하다, 재미있게 하다
________	형 즐거워하는, 재미있어 하는
________	동 즐겁게 해 주다
________	형 재미있는, 즐거움을 주는
________	형 1. 순수한 2. 맑은, 깨끗한
________	명 1. 관심, 흥미 ((in)) 2. 관심사 동 관심을 끌다
________	명 1. 자랑스러움, 자부심 2. 자존심; 자만심
________	형 1. 자랑스러워하는, 자랑스러운 ((of)) 2. 거만한, 오만한
________	동 1. 드러내다, 노출시키다 2. 폭로하다 ((to))
________	동 (비밀 등을) 드러내 보이다, 밝히다 ((to))
________	동 (…보다) ~을 더 좋아하다, 선호하다 ((to))
________	부 1. 꽤, 약간, 상당히 2. 오히려, 차라리
________	명 태도, 자세
________	명 1. (자리 잡고 있는) 위치 2. (몸의) 자세 3. 입장, 처지 4. 직책
________	~하고 싶다, ~할 기분이다
________	~에 관심이 있다 / ~에 흥미를 잃다

DAY 09

161	**emotional**	relating to emotions
162	**mood**	the way you feel at a particular time
163	**amaze**	to surprise someone very much
164	**amazed**	very surprised
165	**amuse**	to make someone laugh or smile
166	**amused**	showing that you think something is funny
167	**entertain**	to amuse people
168	**entertaining**	interesting and amusing
169	**pure**	not mixed with anything else
170	**interest**	the feeling of wanting to know more about something
171	**pride**	a feeling that you are proud of something
172	**proud**	feeling very pleased about something you have done; feeling pride
173	**expose**	to show something that is usually hidden or covered
174	**reveal**	to make something known to someone
175	**prefer**	to like one thing better than another
176	**rather**	to some degree
177	**attitude**	the way that you think and feel about something
178	**position**	the place where someone or something is located
179	**be in the mood for[to]**	to feel like
180	**have (an) interest in / lose interest in**	to be interested in / to no longer be interested in

relate	동 1. 관련시키다, 결부시키다 2. 이해하다, 공감하다 ((to))
	형 1. 관련된 2. 친척의 ((to))
	명 1. (사람·집단 사이의) 관계 ((with/between)) 2. (연인) 관계
	명 친척 형 상대적인, 비교상의
	명 유대, 끈
	동 묶다, 결속시키다
	동 연합하다; 통합시키다, 결속시키다
	동 1. 섞다, 결합하다; 섞이다 2. 단합하다, 연합하다
	동 1. 분리하다, 나누다; 분리되다 ((into)) 2. 헤어지다 형 분리된, 각기 다른
	동 1. 나누다; 나뉘다 ((into)) 2. (몫을) 나누다, 분배하다
	부 1. (공간·시간상으로) 떨어져 2. 따로, 헤어져 3. 조각조각
	형 1. 깨진, 부서진; 고장 난 2. 파탄 난
	동 1. 포함하다, 수반하다 2. 관련시키다, 연루시키다 ((in))
	동 사과하다, 사죄하다 ((to sb)) ((for sth))
	동 ~해야 한다, ~하는 것이 당연하다 ((to))
	부 1. 그렇지 않으면 2. 그 외에는
	전 ~을 제외하고, ~ 외에는
	전 ~에도 불구하고
	~하는 것이 좋겠다, ~하는 게 좋을 거다(경고성)
	~을 제외하고

DAY 26

No.	Word	Definition		Meaning
501	**colleague**	a person that you work with	hunger	명 1. 배고픔, 굶주림 2. (~에 대한) 갈구 동 굶주리다, 갈망하다 ((for))
502	**fellow**	a way of referring to a man or boy		명 1. 목마름, 갈증 2. 갈망 ((for))
503	**organization**	a group of people who work together for the same purpose		명 저녁 식사, 가벼운 만찬
504	**department**	a section of a large organization		명 1. 맛, 풍미 2. 조미료, 향신료
505	**fault**	the responsibility for a mistake or error		동 (음식 등을) 삼키다 명 제비
506	**crisis**	a situation or time that is extremely dangerous or difficult		동 1. (음식을) 소화하다; 소화되다 2. 이해하다
507	**trouble**	problems, difficulties, or worries		형 1. (음식이) 연한 2. 다정한, 상냥한
508	**challenge**	a difficult task that tests someone's ability and skill		형 1. (고기가) 질긴 2. 강인한, 거친 3. 힘든, 어려운
509	**slave**	a person who is owned by another person and has to work for them		형 1. 익히지 않은, 날것의 2. 가공하지 않은
510	**freedom**	the right to do what you want (without anyone stopping you)		명 1. (사람·동물의) 살, 고기 2. (식물의) 속, 과육
511	**advise**	to tell someone what you think they should do		동 1. 따르다, 붓다 2. (비 등이) 마구 쏟아지다, 퍼붓다
512	**motivate**	to make someone want to do something		동 쏟다, 엎지르다; 엎질러지다 명 유출(물)
513	**rumor**	information or a story that people talk about, but that may not be true		동 작게 썰다, 다지다
514	**obvious**	easy to see or understand		동 1. 눌러 부수다, 찌그러뜨리다 2. 으깨다, 빻다
515	**stick**	to cause something to become fixed with glue, tape, etc.		동 1. (과일 등의) 껍질을 벗기다 2. 벗겨지다
516	**sticky**	sticking to a surface; tending to stick		명 (얇게 썬) 조각 ((of)) 동 얇게 썰다
517	**forward**	toward the direction that is in front of you		동 1. 찌다 2. 김을 내뿜다 명 김, (수)증기
518	**lean**	to bend or move from a straight position		동 젓다, 휘젓다
519	**stick to**	to continue doing something despite difficulties		외식하다
520	**look forward to**	to expect something with pleasure		~을 물려주다, ~을 전해 주다

DAY 08

No.	Word	Definition		Meaning
141	**hunger**	the feeling caused by a need to eat; lack of food	colleague	명 (직장) 동료
142	**thirst**	the feeling of needing or wanting a drink	______	명 1. (비격식) 녀석, 친구 2. 동료, 동년배 형 동료의
143	**supper**	the evening meal	______	명 1. 조직, 단체, 기구 2. 구조
144	**flavor**	how food tastes	______	명 1. (조직의 한) 부서, 부처 2. (백화점 등의) 매장
145	**swallow**	to make food go down your throat and into your stomach	______	명 1. 잘못, 과실 2. 결점, 결함
146	**digest**	to break down food	______	명 위기, 고비
147	**tender**	easy to cut and chew; not tough	______	명 1. 곤란, 어려움 2. 병, 통증
148	**tough**	difficult to cut or chew; not tender	______	명 도전, 시험대 동 1. 도전하다 2. 이의를 제기하다
149	**raw**	not cooked	______	명 노예
150	**flesh**	the soft part between the skin and bones of animal or human bodies	______	명 자유
151	**pour**	to make a liquid flow from a container	______	동 충고하다, 조언하다 ((to))
152	**spill**	to cause (something) to fall or flow from a container, often accidentally	______	동 동기를 부여하다, 자극하다 ((to))
153	**chop**	to cut something into smaller pieces	______	명 소문, 풍문
154	**crush**	to press something so hard that it is made flat or broken into pieces	______	형 1. (누가 봐도) 분명한, 명백한 2. 너무 뻔한
155	**peel**	to remove skin from fruit or vegetables	______	동 1. 붙이다; 붙다 2. (~에 끼여) 꼼짝하지 않다 ((in)) 명 나무 막대기, 채
156	**slice**	a thin, flat piece of food cut from something	______	형 1. 끈적거리는, 달라붙는 2. 난처한, 곤란한
157	**steam**	to cook or heat something with steam	______	부 1. (위치가) 앞으로 2. (시간상) 앞으로 동 전달하다 ((to))
158	**stir**	to mix food or liquid	______	동 1. (몸을) 기울이다, 숙이다 2. 기대다, 의지하다 ((on))
159	**eat out**	to have a meal at a restaurant	______	~을 고수하다, ~을 지키다
160	**pass down**	to hand down	______	~을 고대하다[기대하다]

DAY 27

521	**occasion**	an important event; a time when something happens	household	명 가정, 가구 형 가정의, 가사의
522	**occur**	to happen or take place		명 (일상에서 하는) 허드렛일, 집안일
523	**anniversary**	a date on which an event happened in the past		명 (해야 하는) 일, 과제, 과업
524	**celebration**	an occasion or party that celebrates a special event		명 잔디밭
525	**guest**	a person who is invited to an event		명 수도꼭지 동 (가볍게) 톡톡 치다 ((on/at))
526	**host**	a person who invites guests to an event		동 (문 등을) 두드리다, 노크하다 명 노크 소리 ((on/at))
527	**constant**	happening all the time or repeatedly		동 (액체·기체가) 새다; 새게 하다
528	**constantly**	all the time or very often		동 1. (꽉) 잠그다, 고정시키다 2. 채우다, 매다
529	**crazy**	not sensible; very foolish		동 (문 등을) 닫다; 닫히다 형 닫힌
530	**careless**	not giving enough attention to (what you are doing)		부 1. 단단히 2. 단호히, 확고히
531	**beyond**	on the other side of something		동 (위로) 들다, 들어 올리다
532	**beneath**	under something; in a lower position than something		동 1. 깨다; 깨어지다 2. 고장 내다; 고장 나다 명 (짧은) 휴식
533	**within**	during a particular period of time		명 사다리
534	**without**	not having, using, or doing something		동 수리하다, 보수하다 명 수리, 보수
535	**previous**	existing or happening before the present time		동 1. 잠시 멈추다 2. (정지 버튼을 눌러) 정지시키다 명 멈춤
536	**former**	having a particular position in the past		부 1. 잠시 2. 간단히, 짧게
537	**else**	in addition to something already mentioned		형 완전한, 완벽한 동 1. 완료하다 2. (빠짐없이) 기입하다
538	**instead**	in place of someone or something		부 완전히, 전적으로
539	**can't wait to V / can't wait for N**	to look forward to doing something		1. (기계 등이) 고장 나다 2. 분해하다, 나누다
540	**instead of**	in place of		~하느라 바쁘다

DAY 07

121	**household**	all the people living together in a house	occasion	명 1. (특별한) 행사, 경사 2. (특정한) 경우, 때
122	**chore**	a small job that you do regularly		동 일어나다, 발생하다
123	**task**	a piece of work (that someone has to do)		명 (~주년) 기념일
124	**lawn**	an area of grass in a garden or park		명 기념 행사, 축하 행사
125	**tap**	a device that controls the flow of water from a pipe		명 손님, 하객, 내빈
126	**knock**	to hit a door or window repeatedly		명 1. (손님을 초대한) 주인, 주최자 2. 진행자
127	**leak**	to allow liquid or gas to pass through a small hole		형 1. 끊임없는, 반복되는 2. 일정한, 변함없는
128	**fasten**	to close or fix something together		부 끊임없이, 거듭, 계속
129	**shut**	to close something; to become closed		형 1. 제정신이 아닌, 미친 2. 열광하는, 광적으로 좋아하는 ((about))
130	**firmly**	strongly and tightly		형 1. 부주의한, 조심성 없는 2. 경솔한
131	**lift**	to raise something to a higher position		전 1. [장소] ~ 저편에, ~ 너머 2. [시간] ~을 지나서 3. [한계] ~을 넘어서
132	**break**	to separate or become separated into pieces		전 ~ 아래에, ~ 밑에
133	**ladder**	a device that is used to reach high places		전 1. [기간] ~ 이내에, ~ 안에 2. [거리·범위] ~ 내에
134	**repair**	to fix something that is damaged or broken		전 1. ~ 없이 2. (V-ing) ~하지 않고
135	**pause**	to stop talking or doing something for a short time		형 앞서의, 이전의, 바로 앞의
136	**briefly**	for a short time		형 (이)전의, 전임의 명 (the former) 전자
137	**complete**	to the greatest degree possible; having all parts		부 그 밖에, 달리, 다른
138	**completely**	in every way possible		부 대신에 ((of))
139	**break down**	to stop working properly		빨리 ~을 하고 싶다, ~이 너무 기다려진다
140	**be busy V-ing**	to fill your time doing an activity or task		~ 대신에, ~이 아니라

DAY 28

541	**stuff**	a group of different things, activities, or matters	simple	형 1. 간단한, 쉬운 2. 단순한, 소박한
542	**purchase**	the act of buying something		명 (매일 똑같이 하는) 일, 일상, 루틴
543	**stock**	a supply of goods that is available for sale (in a store)		형 잠이 든, 잠자고 있는
544	**available**	able to be used or can be bought		형 잠들지 않은, 깨어 있는 동 (잠에서) 깨다; 깨우다
545	**afford**	to have enough money to buy or time to do something		동 면도하다 명 면도
546	**affordable**	cheap enough for most people to afford		부 조심스럽게, 주의 깊게
547	**reasonable**	fair, practical, and sensible; not too expensive		동 1. (일을) 거르다, 빼먹다 2. (어떤 부분을) 건너뛰다, 생략하다
548	**inexpensive**	not expensive; reasonable in price		동 급히 움직이다, 서두르다 명 1. 돌진 2. 혼잡
549	**insurance**	a deal where a company promises to pay you money if something bad happens		명 결핍, 부족 ((of)) 동 ~이 없다, ~이 부족하다
550	**loan**	the act of borrowing money		대 충분한 양(의 ~), 풍부한 양(의 ~) ((of))
551	**rate**	how often something happens		형 추가의, 여분의 부 추가로
552	**per**	for each		형 보통이 아닌, 비범한, 특별한
553	**property**	the thing or things that someone owns		명 사례, 경우 ((of))
554	**possess**	to have or own something		명 1. (특정한 상황의) 경우 ((of)) 2. 사건 3. 용기, 통
555	**reduce**	to make something less		형 지쳐 버린, 기진맥진한
556	**replace**	to be used instead of something		동 1. (힘들여) 끌다 2. (몸을) 힘들게 움직이다
557	**supply**	an amount of something that is available for use		형 1. 이상한, 묘한 2. 홀수의
558	**demand**	a strong request; the need for goods or services		형 1. 평평한 2. 고른, 일정한 3. 짝수의 부 (심지어) ~조차도
559	**use up**	to use all of something		(늦게까지) 깨어 있다, 잠을 안 자다
560	**run out of**	to use up; to be used up		~할 경우에 대비하여, 혹시 모르니까

DAY 06

	Word	Definition		뜻
101	**simple**	not difficult or complicated	stuff	명 1. 것[것들], 물건 2. (해야 할) 일[것]
102	**routine**	a regular way of doing things in a particular order		명 구입, 구매 동 구입하다, 구매하다
103	**asleep**	sleeping		명 1. 재고품, 재고 2. 주식
104	**awake**	not sleeping; not asleep		형 1. 이용할 수 있는, 구할 수 있는 2. (사람이) 시간이 있는
105	**shave**	to cut hair from the skin, especially the face		동 (금전적·시간적으로) ~할 여유가 있다, ~할 형편이 되다 ((to))
106	**carefully**	in a careful way		형 (가격이) 알맞은, 부담 없는, 감당할 수 있는
107	**skip**	to not do something that you usually do		형 1. 합리적인, 타당한 2. (가격이) 적정한, 비싸지 않은
108	**rush**	to move very quickly		형 비싸지 않은
109	**lack**	not having (enough of) something		명 1. 보험 2. 보험료
110	**plenty**	a large amount of something		명 대출, 대출금
111	**extra**	more, or more than usual		명 1. 비율 2. 요금 동 평가하다; 등급을 매기다
112	**extraordinary**	not ordinary; very special or unusual		전 ~당, ~마다
113	**instance**	a particular example or case of something		명 1. 재산, 자산 2. 부동산
114	**case**	a particular situation or example of something		동 소유하다, 소지하다
115	**exhausted**	very tired		동 1. 줄이다, 축소하다 2. (가격 등을) 낮추다
116	**drag**	to pull something along the ground, usually with difficulty		동 1. 대체하다, 대신하다 2. 바꾸다, 교체하다 ((with))
117	**odd**	strange or unusual		명 1. 공급(량) 2. (-s) 공급품, 용품 동 공급하다
118	**even**	flat, level, or smooth		명 1. 요구 ((for)) 2. 수요(량) 동 요구하다
119	**stay up (late)**	to stay awake (until a late hour)		다 쓰다, 소진하다
120	**just in case**	as a way of being safe		~을 다 써버리다, ~이 다 되다[다 떨어지다]

DAY 29

561	**government**	the group of people who officially control a country
562	**policy**	a principle of action adopted by a government or business
563	**economy**	the overall economic system of a country or region
564	**economic**	relating to the economy
565	**current**	happening or existing now
566	**announce**	to tell people something officially
567	**factor**	one of several things that cause a situation
568	**element**	a part of something
569	**domestic**	relating to a person's own country
570	**trade**	the activity of buying, selling, or exchanging goods
571	**profit**	the money that you make in business
572	**benefit**	a good or helpful result or effect
573	**continuous**	continuing to happen; not stopping
574	**manage**	to succeed in doing something, especially something difficult
575	**calculate**	to find out an amount or cost by using numbers
576	**estimate**	to guess or calculate the cost, size, etc. of something
577	**productive**	producing a large amount of goods
578	**guarantee**	to promise that something is true or will happen
579	**continue V-ing / continue to V**	to keep doing something
580	**keep (on) V-ing**	to continue doing something

Answer	Meaning
detect	동 감지하다, 탐지하다, 발견하다
	명 탐지기, 감지기
	형 1. (눈에) 보이는 2. 뚜렷한, 가시적인
	형 보이지 않는, 볼 수 없는
	명 비상사태, 응급 상황
	동 1. 탈출하다 ((from)) 2. 피하다, 모면하다 명 탈출, 도망
	동 1. 남다 2. 계속[여전히] ~이다 명 (-s) 남은 것, 유물
	동 지속하다, 계속하다, 유지하다
	동 1. (미리) 계획하다, 준비하다 2. 정리하다, 배열하다
	동 1. (어떤 일을) 준비하다, 조직하다 2. 정리하다, 체계화하다
	명 1. 먼지, 때 2. 흙
	명 얼룩 동 더럽히다, 얼룩을 남기다
	동 응시하다, 빤히 쳐다보다 ((at))
	동 1. 흘끗 보다 2. 대충 훑어보다 명 흘끗 봄 ((at))
	명 역겨움, 넌더리 동 역겹게 하다
	형 역겨운, 구역질 나는
	동 1. 깨닫다, 인식하다 2. (목표 등을) 실현하다
	동 1. 알아보다 2. 인정하다, 인식하다
	~을 응시하다, ~을 빤히 쳐다보다
	~을 지켜보다, ~을 주시하다, ~을 눈여겨보다

DAY 05

081	**detect**	to notice or discover something (that is hidden or not clear)
082	**detector**	a device that detects something
083	**visible**	able to be seen
084	**invisible**	not visible; impossible to see
085	**emergency**	a serious or dangerous situation (that needs immediate action)
086	**escape**	to get away from a dangerous or bad situation
087	**remain**	to continue to exist; to be left
088	**maintain**	to make something continue in the same way
089	**arrange**	to plan something in advance
090	**organize**	to arrange and plan something
091	**dirt**	mud or dust that makes things unclean
092	**stain**	a dirty mark that is difficult to remove
093	**stare**	to look at someone or something for a long time
094	**glance**	to look at someone or something quickly
095	**disgust**	a strong feeling of dislike for something
096	**disgusting**	extremely unpleasant
097	**realize**	to begin to understand something
098	**recognize**	to know who someone is (or what something is)
099	**stare at**	to gaze at
100	**keep an eye on**	to watch over

government	명 정부, 정권
________	명 정책, 방침
________	명 1. 경제, 경기 2. 절약, 아끼기
________	형 경제의, 경제상의
________	형 현재의, 지금의 명 (물·공기의) 흐름, 기류, 해류
________	동 발표하다, 알리다
________	명 요인, 요소, 원인
________	명 요소, 성분
________	형 1. 국내의 2. 가정의, 가사의
________	명 무역, 교역 동 무역하다, 거래하다, 교환하다 ((with/for))
________	명 (금전적인) 이익, 수익
________	명 혜택, 이득 동 득이 되다; 득을 보다
________	형 1. 계속되는, 지속적인 2. 끊임없는
________	동 1. (어떻게든) 해내다 2. 경영하다, 관리하다
________	동 1. 계산하다 2. 추산하다
________	동 추정하다, 어림잡다 ((at)) 명 추정(치)
________	형 (대량으로) 생산하는, 생산적인
________	동 1. 보장하다 2. 품질 보증을 하다 명 보증, 보증서
________	계속해서 ~하다, ~하기를 계속하다
________	계속해서 ~하다, 줄곧 ~하다

DAY 30

581	**manual**	using your hands or physical strength
582	**labor**	work, especially physical work
583	**shift**	to move or change something
584	**strategy**	a plan that you use to achieve something
585	**mission**	a specific task or duty assigned to a person or group
586	**accomplish**	to succeed in doing or completing something
587	**formal**	made or done officially; suitable for official occasions
588	**informal**	relaxed and friendly
589	**quit**	to leave your job, school, etc.
590	**abandon**	to leave someone, especially someone you are responsible for
591	**fortune**	a very large amount of money or property
592	**fortunately**	by good luck; luckily
593	**several**	more than two but not very many
594	**dozen**	a group of twelve of the same thing
595	**expand**	to make something larger or greater; to become larger or greater
596	**extend**	to make something longer or bigger
597	**industry**	a group of businesses that provide a particular product
598	**manufacture**	to produce goods in large numbers
599	**get some rest**	to take a break or relax
600	**wrap up**	to finish or complete

positive	형 1. 긍정적인, 낙관적인 2. (검사 결과가) 양성의
______	형 1. 부정적인, 비관적인; 나쁜 2. (검사 결과가) 음성의
______	형 1. 후한 ((with)) 2. 관대한, 너그러운 ((to))
______	형 엄한, 엄격한
______	형 부지런한, 성실한
______	형 진실된, 진심 어린
______	형 1. 폭력적인, 난폭한 2. 격렬한, 맹렬한
______	명 극심한 공포, 공황 동 겁을 먹다, 공황 상태에 빠지다
______	동 1. 다르다 ((from)) 2. 의견이 다르다 ((with))
______	명 차이(점), 다름
______	동 1. (서로) 다르다 2. (상황에 따라) 달라지다, 변하다
______	명 1. 여러 가지, 갖가지 2. 다양성
______	형 1. 동일한, 같은 2. 동등한, 평등한 동 같다, ~이다
______	형 동일한, 똑같은 ((to))
______	형 뛰어난, 걸출한, 두드러진
______	부 정말, 참으로, 실로
______	형 1. 총명한, 똑똑한 2. 지능이 있는[높은]
______	명 지능, 이해력
______	~와 다르다
______	~와 비슷하다

DAY 04

	Word	Definition
061	**positive**	hopeful and confident (about life or a situation)
062	**negative**	not hopeful; bad or harmful
063	**generous**	often giving people money or presents
064	**strict**	not loose; following the rules
065	**diligent**	working hard with care and effort
066	**sincere**	honest and true; having or showing true feelings
067	**violent**	using physical force
068	**panic**	a sudden strong feeling of fear (that cannot be controlled)
069	**differ**	to be different from someone or something
070	**difference**	the quality or state of being different
071	**vary**	to be different from each other
072	**variety**	many different types of things or people
073	**equal**	the same in amount, number, or size
074	**identical**	exactly the same or very similar
075	**outstanding**	extremely good or excellent
076	**indeed**	really; truly
077	**intelligent**	able to learn and understand things easily
078	**intelligence**	the ability to learn or understand things
079	**be different from**	to differ from
080	**be similar to**	to be alike; to look alike

Answer	Meaning
manual	형 1. 손으로 하는, 육체 노동의 2. 수동의 명 (제품) 설명서
	명 (육체적인) 노동, 작업
	동 옮기다, 이동하다, 바꾸다 ((to)) 명 1. (입장 등의) 변화 ((in)) 2. 교대 (근무)
	명 전략, 계획
	명 1. 임무 2. 사명, 목적 3. 사절단
	동 이루다, 성취하다, 완수하다
	형 1. 공식적인, 정식의 2. 격식을 차린
	형 1. 격식에 얽매이지 않는, 비공식적인 2. 평상복의
	동 1. (직장 등을) 그만두다 2. (하던 일을) 그만하다
	동 1. 버리다, 버리고 떠나다 2. 포기하다, 단념하다
	명 1. 부, 재산, 거금 2. 운
	부 운 좋게, 다행히도
	형 몇몇의, 서넛의, 대여섯의
	명 12개짜리 한 묶음, 다스
	동 (범위·한도를) 확대하다, 확장시키다; 커지다, 확장되다
	동 1. 더 길게[크게] 만들다 2. (기한 등을) 연장하다
	명 1. 산업, 공업 2. (특정 분야의) ~업
	동 (대량으로) 제조하다, 생산하다 명 제조, (대량) 생산
	좀 쉬다, 휴식을 취하다
	1. 마무리하다 2. 싸다, 포장하다

DAY 31

No.	Word	Definition	Answer	Meaning
601	**employ**	to give someone a job to do for payment	feature	명 특징, 특색, 기능 동 ~을 특징으로 하다, ~을 특색으로 삼다
602	**apply**	to make a formal request, usually in writing		명 (특유의) 특징, 특성 형 특유의, 독특한
603	**boss**	the person who is in charge of you at work		형 대머리의, 머리가 벗겨진
604	**secretary**	a person who works in an office and assists another person		형 1. 대담한, 용감한 2. 굵은, 선명한
605	**expert**	a person who is very knowledgeable or skilled in a particular area		형 1. 독특한, 특별한 2. 유일한, 고유의
606	**profession**	a job that needs a high level of education and training		형 전형적인, 일반적인
607	**command**	to order someone (officially) to do something		형 ~을 할 수 있는, 능력 있는 ((of))
608	**order**	to tell someone to do something		형 장애를 가진
609	**advertise**	to tell the public about a product or service		명 진실, 사실
610	**promote**	to help sell a product, service, etc.		동 감히 ~하다, ~할 용기가 있다
611	**commerce**	the activity of buying and selling, especially on a large scale		동 주저하다, 망설이다 ((to))
612	**commercial**	relating to buying and selling things		형 주저하는, 망설이는
613	**magazine**	a thin book published every week or month		형 1. 자신감 있는 2. 확신하는 ((of))
614	**article**	a piece of writing in a newspaper or magazine		명 1. 자신감 2. 신뢰, 신임 ((in))
615	**publish**	to produce (a book, magazine, etc.) for sale		명 용기, 담력 ((to))
616	**release**	to let (someone or something) go free		동 1. 격려하다, 용기를 북돋우다 2. 장려하다 ((to))
617	**boom**	a sudden increase in trade and economic activity		동 시도하다 명 시도 ((to))
618	**boost**	to increase or improve something		동 ~하는 경향이 있다, ~하기 쉽다 ((to))
619	**in order to**	for the purpose of doing something		포기하다, 그만두다
620	**out of order**	not working; broken		~에 성공하다

DAY 03

041	**feature**	a special or important part of something
042	**characteristic**	a quality or feature of something or someone
043	**bald**	having little or no hair on the head
044	**bold**	brave and fearless
045	**unique**	very special or unusual; being the only one of its kind
046	**typical**	having the usual features
047	**capable**	able to do something
048	**disabled**	having a disability
049	**truth**	the real facts about something
050	**dare**	to be brave enough to do something
051	**hesitate**	to be slow to speak or act (because you feel uncertain)
052	**hesitant**	slow to speak or act (because you feel uncertain)
053	**confident**	feeling sure about your own ability
054	**confidence**	a feeling or belief that you can do something well
055	**courage**	the quality of being brave when you are facing a difficult or dangerous situation
056	**encourage**	to give someone support or courage
057	**attempt**	to try to do something
058	**tend**	to be likely to do something
059	**give up**	to stop doing something
060	**succeed in V-ing**	to achieve a goal successfully

employ	동 고용하다
	동 1. 지원하다, 신청하다 ((for)) 2. 적용되다 ((to)) 3. 바르다
	명 1. (직장의) 상사 2. (큰 조직의) 장, 사장
	명 비서
	명 전문가 ((in/on)) 형 전문가의, 전문적인
	명 (전문적인) 직업, 전문직
	동 명령하다, 지휘하다 ((to)) 명 명령, 지휘
	동 1. 명령하다 ((to)) 2. 주문하다 명 1. 명령 2. 주문 3. 순서
	동 (신문 등에) 광고하다, 알리다
	동 1. (제품 등을) 홍보[판촉]하다 2. 촉진하다 3. 승진시키다 ((to))
	명 상업, 무역
	형 상업의, 상업적인 명 (TV·라디오의) 광고 (방송)
	명 잡지
	명 (신문·잡지 등의) 글, 기사
	동 1. 출판하다, 발행하다 2. 공표하다, 발표하다
	동 1. 풀어 주다, 석방하다 ((from)) 2. 공개[발표]하다 명 석방; 발표, 개봉, 출시
	명 1. (사업·경제의) 붐, 호황 ((in)) 2. (갑작스런) 인기, 붐
	동 1. 밀어 올리다 2. 북돋우다 명 격려, 부양책
	~하기 위하여
	고장이 난

DAY 32

621	**exhibit**	to show something in a public place
622	**precious**	worth a lot of money; having great value
623	**worth**	having a particular value, especially in money
624	**value**	how much something is worth in money
625	**talented**	having a natural ability to do something well
626	**genius**	a person who is unusually intelligent or artistic
627	**decade**	a period of 10 years
628	**century**	a period of 100 years
629	**general**	not detailed, but including the most basic information
630	**concept**	an idea or a principle
631	**steal**	to take something that belongs to someone else
632	**thief**	a person who steals things
633	**commit**	to do something wrong or illegal
634	**crime**	activities that involve breaking the law
635	**investigate**	to try to find out the truth about something, such as a crime
636	**inspect**	to look at something carefully to find out more about it
637	**appropriate**	suitable or proper for a particular time, situation, or purpose
638	**moral**	relating to principles of right and wrong in behavior
639	**go through**	to experience a difficult or unpleasant situation
640	**can't help V-ing**	to be unable to control or stop

appearance	명 1. 외모, 겉모습 2. 등장, 출현
	명 1. (사람의) 모습, 형체 2. (중요한) 인물 3. 수치, 숫자
	동 깊은 인상을 주다, 감명을 주다
	동 1. (주의·흥미를) 끌다 2. (관광객 등을) 끌어들이다
	동 1. 흥미를 끌다, 매력적이다 2. 간청[호소]하다 명 1. 매력 2. 간청, 호소 ((to/for))
	동 1. 간청하다, 애원하다 2. 구걸하다 ((for/to))
	동 1. 행동하다, 처신하다 2. 예의 바르게 행동하다
	명 행동, 처신
	형 1. 적절한, 제대로 된 2. (사회적·도덕적으로) 올바른
	부 1. 제대로, 적절히 2. 올바르게
	형 빠른, 급속한
	부 빨리, 급속히
	형 점진적인, 서서히 일어나는
	부 차츰, 서서히
	동 1. 영향을 주다 2. (정서적) 충격을 주다
	동 영향을 미치다 명 영향(력) ((on))
	형 1. 극도의, 극심한 2. 지나친, 과도한
	형 1. 심한, 심각한 2. (처벌이) 가혹한
	알아내다, 이해하다, 계산하다
	~에 영향을 미치다

DAY 02

021	**appearance**	the way a person or thing looks
022	**figure**	the shape of a person's body, or a body seen not clearly or from a distance
023	**impress**	to make a strong impact or effect on someone
024	**attract**	to cause people to pay attention (or to be interested)
025	**appeal**	to attract or interest someone
026	**beg**	to ask for something in a strong and emotional way
027	**behave**	to act in a particular way; to act properly
028	**behavior**	the way a person acts or behaves
029	**proper**	right, correct, or suitable
030	**properly**	in a way that is suitable or acceptable
031	**rapid**	happening or moving quickly
032	**rapidly**	quickly; fast
033	**gradual**	happening slowly; not sudden
034	**gradually**	slowly; over a long period of time
035	**affect**	to produce a change in someone or something
036	**influence**	to have an effect; to affect
037	**extreme**	very great in degree; serious or severe
038	**severe**	extremely bad or serious
039	**figure out**	to understand or solve a problem
040	**have an effect on**	to affect; to influence

exhibit	동 전시하다 명 전시, 전시회
______	형 귀중한, 값비싼, 소중한
______	형 ~의 가치가 있는, ~할 가치가 있는 명 가치, 값어치
______	명 1. (금전적) 가치, 가격 2. 가치, 유용성 ((of))
______	형 (타고난) 재능이 있는 ((in/at))
______	명 1. 천재, 천재성 2. 특별한 재능 ((for))
______	명 10년
______	명 100년, 세기
______	형 1. 전반적인 2. 일반적인, 일반의
______	명 개념 ((of))
______	동 훔치다, 도둑질하다
______	명 도둑, 절도범
______	동 (죄·과실 등을) 범하다, 저지르다
______	명 범죄
______	동 조사하다, 수사하다
______	동 점검하다, 검사하다
______	형 적절한, 적합한, 알맞은 ((for))
______	형 1. 도덕상의, 윤리의 2. 도덕적인
______	1. (어려운 일을) 겪다, 통과하다 2. (꼼꼼히) 검토하다
______	~하지 않을 수 없다

MEMO

personal	형 1. 개인의 2. 개인적인, 사적인
	명 1. 성격, 인격 2. 특성, 개성
	형 1. 정신의, 마음의 2. (건강상의) 정신적인
	형 1. 신체의, 육체의 2. 물질의, 물질[물리]적인
	형 대단한, 굉장한 부 특별히, 대단히
	형 가능성이 있는, 잠재적인 명 가능성, 잠재력
	형 1. 어른스러운, 성숙한 2. 성인이 된, 다 자란
	명 1. (영) 친구 2. [합성어에서] 짝 3. (한 쌍의) 짝 동 짝짓기를 하다
	형 실제의, 사실의
	부 1. 실제로, 정말로 2. 사실은, 실은
	형 1. 사적인, 개인의 2. 사립의, 개인 소유의
	명 사생활(을 누리는 상태), 프라이버시
	명 군중, 사람들 동 가득 메우다; 붐비다
	동 1. (사람들이) 모이다; 모으다 2. (정보 등을) 모으다, 수집하다
	부 아마(도)
	부 아마, 어쩌면
	부 1. 솔직히 2. 솔직히 말하면
	형 1. (~에 대해) 책임이 있는 2. (~을) 책임지고 있는 ((for))
	본인이 직접, 몸소, 실물로
	사실, 사실은

DAY 01

001	**personal**	belonging or relating to one particular person
002	**personality**	the way you are as a person; someone's character
003	**mental**	relating to the mind
004	**physical**	relating to the body
005	**super**	very good; excellent
006	**potential**	likely to develop into something
007	**mature**	behaving like an adult; fully grown or developed
008	**mate**	a friend or partner; someone you work with or share with
009	**actual**	real; true
010	**actually**	really; in fact
011	**private**	personal; not open to or shared with the public
012	**privacy**	the state of being alone and not seen or heard by others
013	**crowd**	a large group of people
014	**gather**	to come together
015	**probably**	very likely; maybe
016	**perhaps**	maybe
017	**frankly**	honestly; to be honest
018	**responsible**	having caused something to happen, especially something bad
019	**in person**	personally; face to face
020	**as a matter of fact**	in fact; actually; to tell the truth

MEMO

MEMO

A*List VOCA

어휘 암기장

중학 필수

연관어로 익히는 중학 만점 필수 영단어

A*List VOCA

어휘 암기장

무료 온라인학습

A*List

중학 필수